SPANISH

MEANS

BUSINESS

A multi-media language course in business Spanish

MARIA DEL ROSARIO WIMPORY

Visiting Lecturer, University of Teesside

with additional articles by

Tom Burns

of the

Financial Times

BBC BOOKS

This book is based on material specially recorded in Spain and on material filmed for the
BBC Continuing Education television series *Spain Means Business*, first broadcast from
September 1993.
Three 75-minute cassettes are available for sale from booksellers: ISBN 0 563 36989 2.
A business pack containing the course book and three cassettes is also available from
booksellers: ISBN 0 563 36990 6

A video language pack containing the TV programmes, an additional tutor video and a
video handbook, together with the course book and three cassettes is available to
businesses and educational institutions from
BBC Training Videos, BBC Enterprises Ltd, 80 Wood Lane, London W12 0TT
UK Sales Office and world sales: 081 576 2361
Canada: 416 469 1505   Australia: 02 331 7744

For information on the full range of
BBC language books and cassettes write to
BBC Books
Language Enquiry Service
Room A3116
Woodlands
80 Wood Lane
London W12 0TT

DEVELOPED BY BBC LANGUAGE UNIT
COURSE CONSULTANT: DEREK UTLEY
DESIGNED BY em ASSOCIATES
ILLUSTRATED BY: KATE SIMUNEK and TECHNICAL ART SERVICES
COVER ILLUSTRATION BY PAUL DAVIS
PRODUCER, BBC TV SERIES SPAIN MEANS BUSINESS: TERRY DOYLE

ISBN 0 563 36724 5

Published by BBC Books
a division of BBC Enterprises Ltd
Woodlands
80 Wood Lane
London W12 0TT
First published 1994

Typeset in 10/12 pt Adobe Bembo and Helvetica

Printed and bound in Great Britain by Butler & Tanner Ltd
Frome and London

Cover printed by Clays Ltd
St Ives plc

CONTENTS

INTRODUCTION

Spanish Means Business is a course for business people who have never used Spanish before, but it can equally well be used by those who have a general knowledge of the language and now wish to use it specifically for business.

Based on recordings and printed material collected in Spain, the course aims to develop active, effective communication in a variety of situations, from simple, everyday practicalities to specific business transactions. A number of dialogues have been taken from interviews recorded as part of the BBC television series *Spain means Business*. Other interviews were recorded specially for this book. The programmes provide invaluable background information, while this book and the accompanying recordings provide the complete business language course.

Spanish means Business will help you to operate successfully in a variety of situations connected with business. You will be able to talk about your job and responsibilities, as well as your company and its products. You will learn how to make effective contact by phone with Spanish companies, and make, change, postpone or bring forward appointments. You will learn about transport in Spain, especially in the two largest cities, Madrid and Barcelona. In addition, you will learn how to give and understand directions and hire a car. You will learn something about Spanish regional cookery and will be able to hold a basic conversation at the dinner table. There will be opportunities for you to learn and practise the basic vocabulary of industrial visits and production processes, as well as company accounts, essential figures and terms of payment and delivery. You will also become acquainted with the language of trade fairs through interviews carried out at IFEMA, the largest trade fair centre in Madrid. You will also learn how to write simple, straightforward business letters.

THE STRUCTURE OF THE BOOK

There are ten units covering ten different areas of business life. Within each unit there are three or four sections, each made up of the following elements: **Frases, Dialogues, Infraestructura, Práctica, Reading material, Inventario** and **Punto de control.** At the end of each unit there is a special article providing an insight into the world of business Spain.

At the end of the book is a guide to Pronunciation and a Grammar summary which provides a fuller explanation of points arising in the units. There is a Helpfile with useful vocabulary (like names of foreign currencies in Spanish, numbers, days of the week) as well as some advice on practical matters. The Mini Phrasebook offers a summary of some of the key practical phrases the business visitor will need. Then there are Answers to all the exercises within the book, together with transcripts for those dialogues not printed in the main units. Finally, there is a Glossary providing a translation of all the important words in the book.

HOW TO USE THE COURSE

Dialogues: Each unit begins with authentic listening and reading material. The listening symbol [🎧] indicates a recording and gives the track number. Some dialogues are not printed in the units. These are strictly for listening and although a transcript is given at the back of the book, you should practise understanding spoken language without written support.

The **Frases** list provides key phrases so you can check you've understood the main points. Go over each item until you feel you have understood it.

The **Infraestructura** box explains relevant grammar points as briefly as possible and includes examples for practise. It also cross-refers to the Grammar summary at the back of the book, where a fuller explanation can be found.

The **Práctica** section includes a number of exercises which practise the key points of each unit. The exercises have been designed to develop effective communication skills.

The **Inventario** contains the main expressions introduced in the unit according to the functions they serve.

The **Punto do control** provides a checklist to monitor learning and progress before moving on to the next unit.

At the end of each unit, there is a specially commissioned article by Tom Burns of the Financial Times providing a cultural briefing and insight into business practices in Spain.

The **cassettes** contain all the conversations and interviews included in the book, together with pronunciation practice and some additional information. They have been designed so they can be used either on their own or in conjunction with the book. It is possible to listen to the cassettes and work through material without having the book to hand - although it will always be useful to review everything later with the book.

As you work through **Spanish means Business**, we hope you will become a more effective business communicator as well as coming to appreciate and enjoy Spanish language and culture. **Spanish means Business** has been designed to make your learning a pleasant experience

1

PREPARATIVOS

◆ Greetings ◆ Introductions ◆ Spelling your name
◆ Describing your job and company

¡Hola!

Adrián Piera

Jesús Bahillo

el apoderado/la apoderada de
  extranjero *person in charge
  of overseas affairs*
la Cámara de Comercio e
  Industria *Chamber of
  Commerce and Industry*
la compañía *company*
el director/la directora *director*
Inglaterra *England*
el/la presidente *president*
Sr/señor *Mr, sir*
Sra/señora *Mrs, madam*
dígame *Can I help you?*
(yo) soy *I'm*
bien *well*
de *of, from*
en *in*

In this section you will practise greeting people and introducing yourself in Spanish.

Listen to these business people introducing themselves.

Adrián Piera   Yo soy Adrián Piera. Soy el presidente de la Cámara de Comercio e Industria de Madrid.

Jesús Bahillo   Bien, soy Jesús Bahillo, Director de Mercedes en Vigo.

Listen for greetings as well as introductions.

Maite García   Buenos días. Mi nombre es Maite García y yo soy la apoderada de extranjero.

Francisco Martínez   Buenas tardes. Soy Francisco Martínez.
Pablo Suárez   Encantado.

Louise Taylor Buenos días, señora.
Maite García Hola, buenos días, dígame.
Louise Taylor Me llamo Louise Taylor de la compañía Traditional Furniture de Inglaterra.
Maite García   Mi nombre es Maite García. Mucho gusto.

Listen once more to the recordings and answer the following questions:
Who is a director and who is a president?
Where is Louise Taylor's company based?

Listen to these dialogues. Who does Pablo Suárez work for? What is the name of the businesswoman he is visiting?

Recepcionista	Buenas tardes.
Pablo Suárez	Buenas tardes. Soy Pablo Suárez, de Porcelanas Denia S.A.
Recepcionista	¿En qué puedo servirle?
Pablo Suárez	Quisiera hablar con la señora Elvira Sánchez, por favor.
Recepcionista	Sí. Un momento, por favor.

The receptionist rings her number.

Pablo Suárez	Gracias.

He passes the Director's secretary on his way out afterwards.

Pablo Suárez	Muchas gracias. Adiós. Buenas noches.
Secretaria	De nada. Adiós.

FRASES ➤

¡Hola!   *Hello!*
Buenos días   *Good morning*
Buenas tardes   *Good afternoon, Good evening*
Buenas noches   *Good night, Good evening*
Me llamo...   *I'm called...*
Mi nombre es...   *My name is...*
Mucho gusto   *Pleased to meet you*
Encantado/a   *Pleased to meet you*
¿En qué puedo servirle?   *How can I help you?*
Quisiera hablar con...   *I would like to speak to...*
Un momento   *One moment*
Por favor   *Please*
(Muchas) gracias   *Thank you (very much)*
De nada   *Not at all/You're welcome*
Adiós   *Goodbye*

Did you know?
The greeting **Buenos días** is generally used in the morning; you can start using **Buenas tardes** after about 1 pm. You can use **Buenas noches** not only to say *Good night* to someone before leaving but also when you meet someone after about 8 pm. **Adiós** is a final goodbye, while **Hasta luego** means *See you later.*

 Pronunciation
The Spanish alphabet:
a b c ch d e f g h i j k l ll m n ñ o p q r rr s t u v w x y z

Listen to how these letters are pronounced. Notice the four extra ones **ch**, **ll**, **ñ** and **rr**.

Pay particular attention to the pronunciation of **c** before **e** and **i**, **ch**, **c** before all other letters, **g** before **e** and **i**, **g** before all other letters, **h**, **j**, **ll**, **ñ**, **q**, **r**, **rr**, **v**, **y** and **z**.

7

C   Before **a**, **o** and **u** or any consonant it is pronounced like the 'c' in *cost*, eg **encantado** but before **e** and **i** it is like the 'th' in *thin*, eg **García**, **porcelana**.

Practise saying the following words: **calle** (*street*), **cero** (*zero*), **cinco** (*five*), **ciudad** (*city*), **costa** (*coast*), **Cuenca** (Spanish town).

CH is pronounced like the 'ch' in *chair*, eg **muchas**.

D at the beginning of a word is pronounced like the 'd' in *day*, eg **días**, **Denia**, but between vowels or after **r** it is like 'th' in *them*, pronounced very lightly, eg **adiós**, **buenas tardes**.

G   Before **a**, **o** and **u** or any consonant it is pronounced like the 'g' in *go*, eg **gusto**, **García** but before **e** and **i** it is like a strong 'h' (as in *loch*), eg **gerente**. Practise saying the following words: **García**, **gente** (*people*), **Gijón** (Spanish town), **amigo** (*friend*), **gusto**.

The combination **qu** in **que** and **qui** is pronounced like the 'c' in *cake* (in this particular combination the **u** is silent), eg **¿qué?**, **quisiera**.

For a complete pronunciation guide see page 146.

INFRAESTRUCTURA ➤

El/la
Both words mean *the*: **el** is masculine and **la** is feminine. You use **el** or **la** depending on whether the word that follows is masculine, eg **el presidente**, or feminine, eg **la apoderada**. In Spanish, **el** and **la** are used before titles when you refer to people, eg **el señor Muñoz**, **la señora Hernández**. You would not use them when speaking to people though, eg **Buenos días, Señor Muñoz.**

Un/una
You have come across the expression **un momento, por favor** (*one moment, please*). **Un** means *a*, *an* or *one*. **Un** is used with masculine words, eg **un director**, and **una** with feminine words, eg **una mañana**.

Saying who you are
(Yo) soy means *I am*; **es** means *it is*. **Es** can also mean *he is* or *she is* – **(él) es**, **(ella) es**. In Spanish you often miss out the word for *I*, *you*, *he*, *she*, etc. (**yo**, **tú/usted**, **él**, **ella**), as the ending of the verb usually shows exactly who is being referred to. **Soy** could only mean *I am*, so the **yo** is not usually used. (See Grammar file on page 151.)

Punctuation
In written Spanish you must always include an inverted question mark at the beginning of a question, eg **¿En qué puedo servirle?** and an inverted exclamation mark at the beginning of an exclamation, eg **¡Sí!**

Agreement
When a female person is speaking **encantado** becomes **encantada**.

1 What greeting would you use in each of these scenes?

2 Make up dialogues between these pairs of business executives as in the example. Use different greetings for different times of the day. If possible, practise with a colleague, eg

Sr Suárez	Buenos días. Soy Pablo Suárez.
Sra Sánchez	Mucho gusto. Yo soy Elvira Sánchez.
Sr Suárez	Encantado.

César Gil → Castor Cañedo
Miguel Muñoz Alonso → José Antonio Más
Marta Medina López → Russell Willmoth

3*a* Practise introducing yourself and saying which company you represent and who you want to speak to, eg
Louise Taylor Buenos días. Soy Louise Taylor, de Traditional Furniture de Inglaterra. Quisiera hablar con el señor César Gil, por favor.
b You arrive at a Spanish company in the afternoon. Greet the receptionist, introduce yourself and say which company you represent. Ask to speak to Señora Elvira Sánchez.

4 Raúl, a salesman, arrives at the office of his friend Pablo, a buyer.
a How many different greetings can you hear?
b Listen to the dialogue again. This time listen for the questions given on the left.

Starting now, make a habit of noting down any words you think will be particularly useful to you. Keep them in a notebook under separate headings.

¿Qué tal? *How are things?*
¿Cómo estás? *How are you? (informal)*
Muy bien ¿y tú? *Very well, and you? (informal)*

1 ¿Cuál es su nombre?

In this section you will practise spelling your name in Spanish and asking people who they are.

FRASES

¿Me dice su nombre, por favor?   *Could you tell me your name, please?*
¿Cómo?   *Pardon?*
¿Me lo puede repetir?   *Could you repeat it for me?*
¿Cuál es su nombre?   *What's your name?*
¿Cómo se llama usted?   *What are you called?/What's your name?*
¿Cómo se escribe su apellido?   *How do you spell your surname?*

 Louise Taylor arrives at a Spanish company.

Recepcionista	¿Me dice su nombre por favor?
Louise Taylor	Sí. Louise Taylor.
Recepcionista	¿Cómo? ¿Me lo puede repetir?
Louise Taylor	Louise Taylor. L-o-u-i-s-e.
Recepcionista	¿Y el apellido?
Louise Taylor	T-a-y-l-o-r.

The receptionist asked Louise Taylor to repeat her name. What did she say? Spell your own name out in Spanish.

Identify three different ways of asking people their name.

Recepcionista	¿Cuál es su nombre, por favor?
Francisco Martínez	Mi nombre es Francisco Martínez.
Recepcionista	¿Cómo se llama usted?
Pablo Suárez	Me llamo Pablo Suárez.
Recepcionista	¿Su nombre, por favor?
Jane Wilson	Jane Wilson.
Recepcionista	¿Cómo se escribe su apellido?
Jane Wilson	W-i-l-s-o-n

escribirse   *to be written/spelt*
llamarse   *to be called*
mi   *my*
su   *your (formal)/his/her/its*

Pronunciation

Listen to how these letters are pronounced. In Spanish the consonant **H** is silent, eg **Hernández**, **Héctor**. Practise pronouncing these names: **la señora Julia Hernández**, **el señor Hugo Muñoz**, **¡Hola Héctor!**, **¡Hombre!**

The consonant **J** should be pronounced like the 'ch' in *loch*, eg **Julia**, **José**. Practise with these words: **Jarama** (Spanish river), **jerez** (*sherry*).

LL should be pronounced like the 'll' in *million*, eg **Me llamo…**, **¿Cómo se llama?**

Ñ is pronounced like 'ni' in *onion*, eg **Cañedo**, **Muñoz**.

Usted/tú

Usted (*you*) is used when addressing somebody you don't know, in a fairly formal situation. **Tú** also means *you*, but is generally used between friends and family.

Me/se

You will find these in expressions such as: **¿Cómo se llama?**, **Me llamo...** (*What's your name?*, *I am called...*). Don't try to translate these expressions word for word. (See Reflexive pronouns on page 151.)

Mi/su

These words mean *my* and *your*, eg **mi nombre** and **su nombre**. (See Possessive adjectives on page 149.)

Did you know?

Most Spaniards use two surnames – first, the father's first surname, then the mother's first surname, in that order, eg Sra Marta Medina López, Sr Miguel Muñoz Alonso. Both surnames should be used in all transactions. If you just use one, use the first of the two.

1 Answer the questions below, using the names on the cards. Practise with a colleague if possible.

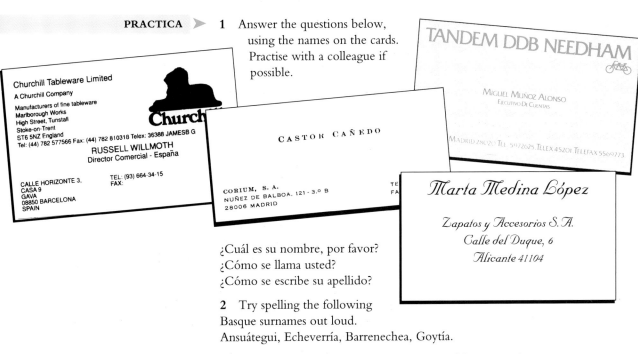

¿Cuál es su nombre, por favor?
¿Cómo se llama usted?
¿Cómo se escribe su apellido?

2 Try spelling the following Basque surnames out loud.
Ansuátegui, Echeverría, Barrenechea, Goytía.

3 Spell out your own name and the name of the town where your company is based.

11

4 Match each of the questions or statements on the left with the appropriate response.

1 ¿Cómo se llama usted?	a Adiós. Hasta luego.
2 ¿Cuál es su nombre, por favor?	b Me llamo Pablo Suárez.
3 ¡Hola! soy José Martínez.	c Encantado.
4 Hasta luego.	d De nada.
5 Muchas gracias.	e Mucho gusto.
6 Mi nombre es Ramón Pérez	f Soy Elvira Sánchez.

Le presento a mi socio

This section is about introducing yourself and your colleagues and being introduced to other people.

FRASES ▶

Te presento a...   *May I introduce...?* (informal)
Le presento a...   *May I introduce...?* (formal)

Maite García is introducing her colleague. What's his name?

Maite García   Aurelio, te presento a la señorita...
Louise Taylor   Louise Taylor.
Maite García   Louise Taylor de la compañía...
Louise Taylor   Traditional Furniture.
Aurelio Cuadrado   Hola, buenos días. Soy Aurelio Cuadrado, el apoderado de la oficina.

el banco   *bank*
el director gerente/la directora
   gerente   *managing director*
el socio   *colleague, business
   partner*
presentar   *to introduce*

These business executives are introducing each other. What's the name of Francisco Martínez's business partner? Who does Elvira Sánchez introduce?

Sr Martínez   Buenos días. Mi nombre es Francisco Martínez. Le presento a mi socio, el señor Pérez Cuenca.

Sra Sánchez   Le presento a la Directora de Marketing de Arte Iberia.

Sr Martínez   Encantado. Le presento al Director Gerente del Banco del Mediterráneo.

Pronunciation
R in Spanish is slightly rolled, eg **señora**, **señorita**, **nombre**.
    R at the beginning of a word and **RR** are strongly rolled, eg **restaurante**, **Mediterráneo**.
    V and **B** are both pronounced like the 'b' in *bar*, eg **Elvira**, **buenos días**.

Nouns and gender
Nouns in Spanish are either masculine or feminine. As a general rule, words ending in **o** are masculine and words ending in **a** are feminine. But there are exceptions; see page 147.

a, de
A means *to* or *at* and **de** means *of* or *from*. When **a** or **de** go before **el**, **a+el** becomes **al** and **de+el** becomes **del**, eg **Le presento al Director del Banco del Mediterráneo**.

PRACTICA ➤

MAITE GARCIA

APODERADA DE
EXTRANJERO

Alfredo Pastor

Director

Castor Cañedo

Corium S.A.

Miguel Muñoz Alonso

Ejecutivo de Cuentas

1a Introduce yourself and introduce Sr Pastor to Sra Maite García.
b Greet Sr Muñoz Alonso and introduce Sr Cañedo.
c Greet Sr Cañedo and say who you are.
d Say who you are and that you wish to speak to...(your choice).

 2 Listen to the speaker and answer the following questions:
a What is his full name?
b What surname would you address him by?
c What's the name of his company?

 3 Listen to David Horta Segarra introducing himself.
a Is he a president, councillor or managing director?
b He works in the Town Hall. Which three areas is he in charge of?

el ayuntamiento *Town Hall*
el comercio *business, commerce*
el/la concejal *councillor*
la industria *industry*
el turismo *tourism*

David Horta

13

1 ¿Cuál es su ocupación?

This section deals with talking about your job and company.

FRASES ➤

¿Cuál es su ocupación? *What do you do for a living?*
Trabajo en... *I work for...*
Soy representante de... *I'm a salesperson for...*
¿Qué cargo tiene usted en la compañía? *What's your position in the company?*
¿Qué tipo de compañía es? *What type of company is it?*
El tema que llevo/mi tema es... *My area of responsibility is...*
Me dedico a... *My occupation is...*

Listen to two people talking about their work. What's the name of Francisco's company? What's Elvira's job?

Mariá Saenz Me llamo Mariá Saenz.
Francisco Martínez ¿Cuál es su ocupación?
Mariá Saenz Trabajo en Creaciones Roma. ¿Y usted?
Francisco Martínez Soy representante de Estudios Madrid. ¿Qué cargo tiene usted en la compañía?
Mariá Saenz Yo también soy representante.
Francisco Martínez ¿Qué tipo de compañía es Creaciones Roma?
Mariá Saenz Es una compañía textil.

These three sisters work in the same firm. What are their full names?

Reme Hola, mi nombre es Reme Sánchez Bocanegra y el tema que llevo yo en la gestoría es el de permiso de trabajo de residencia.

Ana Hola, soy Ana Sánchez Bocanegra, trabajo en la gestoría Bocanegra, y mi tema es la renovación de placas de matrícula turística española.

Fátima Hola, buenos días, soy Fátima Sánchez Bocanegra, trabajo en la gestoría Bocanegra, y me dedico a tramitar permisos de trabajo de residencia para extranjeros que vienen a vivir en España.

Listen again. Which two sisters have more or less the same job?

Las hermanas Bocanegra

el extranjero/la extranjera
   foreigner
la gestoría *agency dealing with governmental departments*
el permiso de trabajo de residencia *resident's work permit*
la placa de matrícula *car number plate*
la renovación *renewal*
trabajar *to work*
tramitar *to process*
venir *to come*
vivir *to live*
español/española *Spanish*

More jobs and job titles

el camarero/la camarera *waiter/waitress*
el cocinero/la cocinera *cook*
el/la contable *accountant*
el diseñador/la diseñadora *designer*
el empleado/la empleada *employee, clerk*
el/la fabricante *manufacturer*
el/la gerente *manager*
el/la gerente de marketing *marketing manager*
el importador/la importadora *importer*
el jefe/la jefa de ventas *sales manager*
el jefe/la jefa de compras *purchasing manager*
el jefe/la jefa de personal *personnel manager*
el/la recepcionista *receptionist*
el secretario/la secretaria *secretary*
el vigilante jurado *security guard*

INFRAESTRUCTURA ▶

Soy representante/soy gerente

In Spanish **un** and **una** are not used before job titles, eg *I am a designer* but **soy diseñador**, *I am a manufacturer* but **soy fabricante**. (See Grammar file on page 147.)

Adjectives

An adjective is the word you use when you want to describe something. Adjectives are normally placed after the noun and must agree with the gender of the noun, eg **es *una* empresa vasca** (*it's a Basque enterprise*), **es *un* nombre vasco** (*it's a Basque name*).

   Buenas noches, **buenas tardes** and **buenos días** are exceptions in that the adjective comes before the noun – but it must still agree and in this case an **s** is added because **noches**, **tardes** and **días** are plural. (See Adjectives on page 147.)

Se llama

You have seen **¿Cómo se llama usted?** (*What's your name?*). **Se llama** also means *he/she/it is called*, eg **¿Cómo se llama su socio?** (*What's your business partner called?*), **Mi socio se llama Jane Wilson**; **¿cómo se llama la compañía?** (*What's the name of the company?*), **La compañía se llama Modern Kitchens Ltd.**

0	cero	6	seis
1	uno/	7	siete
	una	8	ocho
2	dos	9	nueve
3	tres	10	diez
4	cuatro	11	once
5	cinco	12	doce

Numbers

primero/a	*first*	**cuarto/a**	*fourth*
segundo/a	*second*	**el promedio**	*average*
tercero/a	*third*	**por ciento**	*per cent*

Primero and **tercero** become **primer** and **tercer** before a masculine noun, eg **el primer año** (*the first year*) but **la tercera planta** (*the third floor*).

PRACTICA ▶

1 Look at this example: Soy Julia Hernández. Soy representante de Creaciones Roma. Le presento a mi socio, el señor Héctor Cañedo. Now say similar things about the following people:

a Pablo Suárez - Gerente de Marketing - Porcelanas Denia S.A. - socio Señora Carmen Tenorio.

b Ana López Martínez - Contable - Arte Iberia - socio Señor José Gómez Ruiz

2 What questions would produce the following answers?

a Mi nombre es Alejandro Muñoz.

b Soy vigilante jurado.

c Soy Directora de Marketing.

d Es una compañía de publicidad.

15

3 You are telling someone the name of your business partner (who is not present in the room) and your company, eg

Mi socio se llama Héctor Cañedo. La compañía se llama Creaciones Roma.

Give similar information using these cards:

ANTONIO MALDONADO

ARTE IBERIA

JOSEFINA RIOS ESTRADA

Porcelanas Denia S.A.

Peter Webb

Modern Kitchens Ltd

4 The speaker works for a tourist agency called Bidón 5.

a What's his name and surname? Choose from Alfonso/Alfredo and Castor/Santor/Pastor.

b Listen once more and this time listen especially for the following expressions: **turismo alternativo**; **turismo verde**; **turismo ecológico**; **turismo de aventura**. What do you think these expressions mean?

5 Find out what your job title is in Spanish. Practise introducing yourself, saying who you work for and what you do.

6 Match the answers to the questions.

a ¿Cuál es su nombre?
b ¿Cómo se escribe su apellido?
c ¿Cuál es su ocupación?
d ¿Cómo se llama la empresa?
e ¿Qué tipo de compañía es?
f ¿Qué cargo tiene usted en la compañía?

1 La empresa se llama Arte Iberia.
2 M-a-r-t-í-n-e-z
3 Es una compañía de Publicidad.
4 Soy Jefe de Compras.
5 Mi nombre es Juan García.
6 Soy secretaria.

Vicente Roca Montesinos
DISEÑADOR

María Angeles Ballester
CONTABLE

7 Look at these business cards and practise introducing these people to somebody else, eg

Le presento a la señora Ballester. La señora Ballester es contable.

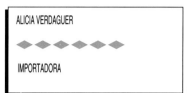

ALICIA VERDAGUER

◆ ◆ ◆ ◆ ◆

IMPORTADORA

Enrique López Miralles
Fabricante

Intergift

Study the entries in the Intergift trade fair catalogue. You should be able to answer the following questions with the help of the Glossary and some guesswork.

a Is Vilo Sainz C.B. a designer or a manufacturer?
b What does Ramón Faus Santaeularia S.A. Europa import?
c What does Vicente Fornes do for a living?
d Who sells glasses, handkerchieves/headscarves and buttons?

	ACTIVIDAD / *ACTIVITY*	NOTAS/*NOTES*
STAND N.º **D-404** PABELLON N.º 6	FABRICANTE DE VENTA AL DETA-LLISTA - MAYORISTA - IM-PORTADOR.	
EXPOSITOR/*EXHIBITOR*		
	SECTORES / *SECTORS*	
RS	BISUTERIA - GAFAS - ADORNOS DEL CABELLO - PAÑUELOS - BOLSOS - CINTURONES -BOTONES.	
	MARCAS / *TRADE MARKS*	
RAMON FAUS SANTAEULARIA, S.A. *EUROPA RAMBLA CATALUÑA, 40 08007 BARCELONA TEL.: (93) 487 87 20 TELEX: 93141 RAMN FAX: (93) 487 87 85	ALEXANDRE DE PARIS (FRANCIA) - E.P. (DINAMARCA) - L'OFFICIEL (ITALIA) RAMON SANTAEULALIA (ESPAÑA).	

	ACTIVIDAD / *ACTIVITY*	NOTAS/*NOTES*
STAND N.º **G-727** PABELLON N.º 6	FABRICANTE DE VENTA AL DETA-LLISTA - DISEÑADOR.	
EXPOSITOR/*EXHIBITOR*		
	SECTORES / *SECTORS*	
	BISUTERIA.	
	MARCAS / *TRADE MARKS*	
VICENTE FORNES PARTIDA PINELLA, 25 03700 LA JARA-DENIA ALICANTE TEL.: (96) 578 18 99	VICENTE FORNES (ESPAÑA).	

	ACTIVIDAD / *ACTIVITY*	NOTAS/*NOTES*
STAND N.º **E-512** PABELLON N.º 6	FABRICANTE DE VENTA AL DETA-LLISTA - DISEÑADOR.	
EXPOSITOR/*EXHIBITOR*		
	SECTORES / *SECTORS*	
VILO SAINZ	BOLSOS - CINTURONES - MARRO-QUINERIA.	
	MARCAS / *TRADE MARKS*	
VILO SAINZ C.B. LAVIANA, 17 BAJOS 33209 GIJON ASTURIAS TEL.: (98) 516 06 89 FAX: (98) 538 94 79	VILO SAINZ. (ESPAÑA).	

1

Inventario means 'inventory' or 'stocktaking'. In this section you will find a comprehensive list of the expressions introduced throughout this unit. Use it in conjunction with Punto de control to practise the language, if possible with a fellow student or colleague, or by recording yourself on cassette, and review the progress you have made so far.

Inventario

Greetings and goodbyes
¡Hola!   *Hello!*
Buenos días   *Good morning.*
Buenas tardes   *Good afternoon,
    Good evening*
Buenas noches   *Good evening,
    Good night*
Hasta luego   *See you later*
Adiós   *Goodbye*

Introducing yourself
(Yo) soy...   *I am...*
Me llamo...   *I'm called...*
Mi nombre es...   *My name is...*

Asking someone their name
¿Cuál es su nombre?   *What's your
    name?*
¿Cómo se llama usted?   *What are
    you called?*
¿Su nombre?   *Your name...?*
¿Me dice su nombre?   *Could you
    tell me your name?*

Asking someone to spell a word
¿Cómo se escribe?   *How is it
    written/spelt?*

Introducing someone
Le presento a...   *May I introduce...?*

Asking to speak to someone
Quisiera hablar con...   *I would like
    to speak to...*

Talking about jobs and companies
(Yo) soy...   *I'm (your occupation)*
Trabajo en...   *I work for...*
Me dedico a...   *My occupation is...*
¿Cuál es su ocupación?   *What's
    your job?*
¿Qué cargo tiene usted en la
    compañía?   *What's your
    position in the company?*
¿Qué tipo de compañía es?   *What
    type of company is it?*
El tema que llevo/Mi tema es...   *My
    area of responsibility is...*

Punto de control

Check you can do each of the following in Spanish:
◆ Greet people and say goodbye to them: in the morning, in the afternoon, in the evening, at night.
◆ Say 'thank you', 'not at all', 'please' and 'how are you?'.
◆ Introduce yourself.
◆ Introduce someone else.
◆ Reply when someone is introduced to you.
◆ Ask someone their name and job.
◆ Say what your job is and who you work for.
◆ Spell out your name.
◆ Tell someone about your job.

Preparativos

Why Spain? Those who have successfully done business in Spain will sooner or later refer to the often told story of the two shoe exporters who arrive in a country where all are barefoot. One exporter leaves straightaway, convinced that such a society is not worth the time of day. The other stays and sells, rejoicing that such a market has landed in his lap. Time and again the key to business success in Spain has been based on the approach of the second shoe exporter.

The knack is to view a relatively under-developed market as a challenge, not as a disincentive. Spain is big and youthful by European standards, fascinated by modernity, by innovation and by change, and determined to close the gap that separates it from Europe's richer economies. Success in Spain belongs to those who have seized the opportunity of an environment that, with all its warts, has developed fast, is continuing to develop and will develop further.

The usual impression of first-time visitors to Spain is that they have arrived in a society that is already highly developed. Madrid and Barcelona are very sophisticated cities and they exude an impressive pace and vitality. But this first impression of the country is deceptive. There is a wide gap between Spain's two largest cities and its more backward areas and Spain's overall per capita income is around 75 per cent of the average in the European Community.

Employment, or rather the lack of it, represents, the greatest divergence between Spain and its European Community partners. Over 3 million Spaniards, representing more than 22 per cent of the active labour population, are statistically jobless. This appalling figure should be adjusted for anything up to 1.5m of those officially unemployed who are in fact working in what is called the submerged economy – a flourishing area of economic activity that hides itself from the tax authorities.

The disparity between an official and a real economy, and specifically the widespread fraud that is inherent to such a situation, highlights how much "catching up" Spain has still to do. On a general level, the visitor will be perplexed at the manner in which the ultra-modern and the obsolete co-exist in Spain.

The financial sector, for example, is over-staffed and often resorts to arcane auditing methods. But, at the same time, it is a global leader in its use of telephone banking and in the scope of its cash dispenser network. Spain boasts huge hypermarkets and flashy shopping malls as well as a host of small, and increasingly uncompetitive, family-run stores.

As they come to terms with what Spain is about and with the potential it has to offer, visiting business executives will learn of the open-door policy for foreign investment, of the generous start-up and employee-training subsidies that are made available by the European Community as well as by the domestic authorities, and also of the profit margins that can be created by simply importing business skills into a demand-led economy.

Spain's large auto sector is wholly foreign owned and foreign companies own 75 per cent of the components business that has been built up around it. Foreign interests control eight of the top ten companies in the chemical sector, an industry that accounts for 12 per cent of Spain's gross domestic product. Nearly 20 per cent of the food producing business is controlled by non-Spaniards.

The foreign invasion of Spain has been mostly in the form of acquisitions but new businesses have also been lured in by grants that, in the more backward areas, can represent well over half the initial investment. An experience common to most who take up the Spanish challenge is that income can increase dramatically by analysing management, production and distribution systems. Such investors take Spain's rapidly growing consumer society for granted.

LLEGADA

◆ Taking a taxi ◆ Checking into a hotel ◆ Booking a room
◆ Buying a train ticket

¡Taxi!

FRASES ▶

This section will help you when travelling by taxi in Spain.

Quisiera ir a...   *I'd like to go to...*
¿(Me dice) cuánto es, por favor?   *How much is it please?*
Son ... pesetas   *It's ... pesetas*
¿Me podría dar una factura por favor?   *Could you give me a receipt please?*
(No) faltaría más   *Of course*
Aquí tiene   *Here you are*
Muchísimas gracias   *Thank you very much*
A usted   *Thank **you***

Pilar Alvarez is catching a taxi. Where is she going?

Pilar Alvarez   Buenos días.
Taxista   Buenos días.
Pilar Alvarez   Quisiera ir al Hotel Hilton por favor.
Taxista   Muy bien.

Pilar Alvarez   ¿Me dice cuánto es, por favor?
Taxista   Pues, son dos mil cuatrocientas veinticinco.
Pilar Alvarez   Muchas gracias. ¿Me podría dar una factura por favor?
Taxista   Faltaría más... aquí tiene.
Pilar Alvarez   Muchísimas gracias.
Taxista   A usted.
Pilar Alvarez   Adiós.
Taxista   Adiós, buenos días.

el hotel   *hotel*
una factura   *a receipt*
el/la taxista   *taxi driver*
dar   *to give*
muy bien   *very well*
pues   *well...*

1 uno/un/una	40 cuarenta
2 dos	50 cincuenta
3 tres	60 sesenta
4 cuatro	70 setenta
5 cinco	80 ochenta
6 seis	90 noventa
7 siete	100 cien
8 ocho	200
9 nueve	doscientos/as
10 diez	300
11 once	trescientos/as
12 doce	400
13 trece	cuatrocientos/as
14 catorce	500
15 quince	quinientos/as
16 dieciséis	600
17 diecisiete	seiscientos/as
18 dieciocho	700
19 diecinueve	setecientos/as
20 veinte	800
21 veintiuno/a	ochocientos/as
22 veintidós	900
23 veintitrés	novecientos/as
24 veinticuatro	1000 mil
25 veinticinco	2000 dos mil
26 veintiséis	3000 tres mil
27 veintisiete	4000 cuatro mil
28 veintiocho	
29 veintinueve	
30 treinta	
31 treinta y uno	
32 treinta y dos,	
etc	

es/son

Es means *he/she/it is…* as well as *is he/she/it…?* **Son** means *they are…* and *are they…?* You have seen **es** in **¿Cuánto es?**, **Mi nombre es…** and **Son 2.425 pesetas**. **Es** and **son** are also used with **usted** and **ustedes**, eg **¿Es usted el señor López?** (*Are you Mr López?*), **¿Ustedes son de Madrid?** (*Are you from Madrid?*)

Numbers
More numbers

From **doscientos** to **novecientos** numbers must be read in the masculine or in the feminine depending on the gender of the word that follows, eg £200 = **doscientas libras esterlinas** (fem.), $200 = **doscientos dólares** (masc.), 200 ptas = **doscientas pesetas** (fem.). For more currencies see page 159

Cien/ciento

Cien is used on its own for a round hundred, eg **cien pesetas**; otherwise **ciento** is used, without **y**, eg **ciento diez pesetas**.

In numerals, a full point is used in Spanish to indicate thousands (**2.400 ptas = dos mil cuatrocientas**); a comma is used for decimals (**2,25 = $2^{1/4}$**).

PRACTICA ➤

1 You're catching a taxi at Barcelona airport.

a Complete this conversation.

Taxista Buenas tardes.

Usted (You'd like to go to Plaza de España.)

Taxista Muy bien.

Usted (You want to know how much it is.)

Taxista Son 1.450 pesetas.

Usted (You want a receipt.)

b Using this fare chart, repeat the dialogue, putting in different destinations and the appropriate fares. Practise with a colleague if possible.

2 You're on a business trip in Spain. Say the following things in Spanish: you want to go to the Chamber of Commerce; you want a receipt; you want to go to the airport.

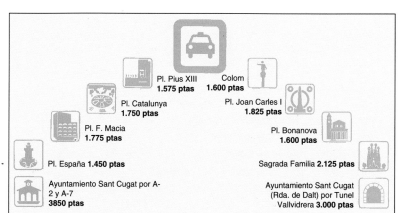

Pl. Pius XIII **1.575 ptas**
Colom **1.600 ptas**
Pl. Catalunya **1.750 ptas**
Pl. Joan Carles I **1.825 ptas**
Pl. F. Macia **1.775 ptas**
Pl. Bonanova **1.600 ptas**
Pl. España **1.450 ptas**
Sagrada Familia **2.125 ptas**
Ayuntamiento Sant Cugat por A-2 y A-7 **3850 ptas**
Ayuntamiento Sant Cugat (Rda. de Dalt) por Tunel Vallvidrera **3.000 ptas**

Un momentito. Lo voy a comprobar.

In the next two sections you'll practise booking into a hotel.

FRASES ▶

Tengo una habitación reservada   *I've got a room reserved*
Para esta noche   *For tonight*
¿A qué nombre por favor?   *What name is it in?*
A nombre de...   *In the name of...*
¿Me lo puede deletrear?   *Could you spell it for me?*
Lo voy a comprobar   *I'm going to check*
¿Era para dos personas o para una?   *Was it for two people or one?*
Está conforme   *That's fine*
No hay de qué   *You're welcome*
¿Hay ducha?   *Is there a shower?*
Tiene baño   *It's got a bathroom*
De ocho a once   *From eight to eleven o'clock*
Un momento/un momentito   *Just a minute*
¿Me deja el pasaporte?   *Could you leave me your passport?*
Tenga   *Here it is/Here you are*
¿Qué habitación es?   *Which room is it?*

When you listen to spoken Spanish, don't expect to understand every word. You often only need to catch the 'gist', or one or two pieces of key information. So, anticipate what you are likely to hear and concentrate on picking out the key words. This will help you build up a mental jigsaw.

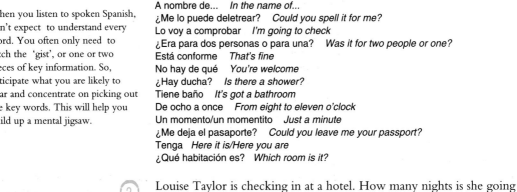

Louise Taylor is checking in at a hotel. How many nights is she going to stay?

Louise Taylor   Buenos días, señor. Tengo una habitación reservada para esta noche.
Recepcionista   ¿A qué nombre por favor?
Louise Taylor   A nombre de Taylor.
Recepcionista   Taylor. ¿Me lo puede deletrear?
Louise Taylor   T-a-y-l-o-r.
Recepcionista   Sí, un momento que lo voy a comprobar.
Louise Taylor   Gracias.
Recepcionista   ¿Era para dos personas o para una?
Louise Taylor   Para una.
Recepcionista   Sí, está conforme.

la agencia   *agency*
el almuerzo   *lunch*
la cena   *dinner*
el comedor   *dining room*
la comida   *lunch, meal*
el desayuno   *breakfast*
la habitación   *room*
la hora   *hour*
el IVA (impuesto al valor añadido)   *VAT*
el turno   *shift, sitting*
comprobar   *to check*
dejar   *to leave*
de la mañana   *in the morning*
de la tarde   *in the afternoon/ early evening*
para   *for*

Listen to the rest of the dialogue. Are these statements true or false?
a   There is an extra 6% VAT on the price of the room per night.
b   They serve breakfast between seven and ten.

Louise Taylor   ¿Cuánto es la... noche?
Recepcionista   Son 7.600 más el... el seis por ciento de IVA.
Louise Taylor   Gracias.
Recepcionista   De nada. No hay de qué.
Louise Taylor   ¿Y hay ducha?
Recepcionista   Sí, tiene baño.
Louise Taylor   Y... ¿las horas del comedor?
Recepcionista   Sí, son de ocho a once. De ocho de la mañana a once

de la mañana son los desayunos y de una a tres de la tarde son las comidas en dos turnos.

Louise Taylor   Muchísimas gracias.

Another guest arrives at the same time. Listen for the expression: **¿me deja el pasaporte?**

Recepcionista   Buenos días.
Margarita Fernández   Buenos días. Soy Margarita Fernández y tengo reservada una habitación aquí a través de esta agencia.
Recepcionista   Sí, un momentito. Lo voy a comprobar. Sí, está conforme. ¿Me deja el pasaporte?
Margarita Fernández   Sí, tenga.
Recepcionista   Gracias.
Margarita Fernández   ¿Qué habitación es?
Recepcionista   314.

INFRAESTRUCTURA

Useful time expressions
¿Cuándo?   *When?*
¿A qué hora...?   *At what time...?*
¿Qué hora es?   *What's the time?*
Desde las... hasta las...   *From... until...*
Las once de la mañana   *11 a.m.*
Las cuatro de la tarde   *4 p.m.*
Las once de la noche   *11 p.m.*
A mediodía   *At midday*
A medianoche   *At midnight*

Time

To ask when something happens you use **¿A qué hora?**, eg **¿A qué hora se sirve el desayuno?** (*What time is breakfast served?*) **De siete a nueve** or **Desde las siete hasta las nueve** (*From seven to nine*).

Telling the time is very simple in Spanish: **¿Qué hora es?** – **Es la una** (*It's one o' clock*), **son las cuatro** (*It's four o' clock*).

son las siete y diez (*It's ten past seven*), **son las diez y cuarto** (*It's quarter past ten*), **son las ocho y media** (*It's half past eight*).

son las doce menos veinticinco (*It's twenty-five to twelve*), **son las dos menos cuarto** (*It's quarter to two*).

De/por la mañana

Notice the difference: **a las siete de la mañana** (*at seven in the morning*), but **por la mañana temprano** (*early in the morning*).

The 24-hour clock

Look at these examples: 0.30: **las cero treinta**; 1.30: **la una treinta**; 15.25: **las quince veinticinco**; 19.15: **las diecinueve quince**; 22.00: **las veintidós** or **las veintidós cero-cero**.

¿Me deja...?

Apart from asking you to leave your passport, a hotel receptionist might ask you **¿Me rellena esta hoja con sus datos, por favor?** (*Could you fill in this form with your details for me, please?*) **¿Me firma aquí, por favor?** (*Could you sign here for me, please?*).

The following expressions follow the same pattern: **¿Me dice...?** (*Could you tell me...?*), **¿Me da...?** (*Could you give me...?*), **¿Me llama?** (*Could you call me?*). The word **me** means *me* or *for me*. See page 151.

Hay, ¿Hay?
Hay means *there is* or *there are* and **¿Hay...?** means *is there?* or *are there?* It can be used to ask if something is available, eg **¿Hay ducha?** (*Is there a shower?*). When something isn't available you use **No hay...**, eg **No hay baño** (*There isn't a bathroom*).

Did you know?
The Spanish working day starts at about 9 a.m. and goes on until 1 or 1.30 p.m.; lunch follows at about 2.30 until 3.30 or 4 p.m. Work in the afternoon goes on until 7 or 8 p.m. and dinner is served at about 10 or 10.30 p.m. More companies are now operating a timetable called **la jornada intensiva** which starts at 8 or 9 a.m. and finishes at 3 or 5 p.m. with only one hour for lunch.

PRACTICA ➤

1 Read this dialogue out loud; practise with a colleague if possible.

Recepcionista   Buenos días.
John Cartwright Buenos días. Soy John Cartwright de JC Builders de Inglaterra. Tengo una habitación reservada.
Recepcionista   Un momentito. Lo voy a comprobar. Sí, está conforme. ¿Cómo se escribe su apellido?
John Cartwright C-a-r-t-w-r-i-g-h-t.
Recepcionista   ¿Me deja su pasaporte, por favor?
John Cartwright Sí, tenga. ¿A qué hora se sirve el desayuno?
Recepcionista   De 7 a 9 de la mañana.
John Cartwright Muy bien. ¿Me llama a las 6, por favor?

Now re-enact the dialogue using the following information.
afternoon/Jane Parker/EC Travel/England/
breakfast from 7 to 10/morning call at 7

Listen again to the pronunciation of the letters of the Spanish alphabet (Unit 1, track 3) as you will probably often have to spell out names in Spanish.

2 Say the following times, eg **Son las tres de la tarde**.
3 p.m.   4 p.m.   1 a.m.   11.30 p.m.   8.20 a.m.   21.00   3.45 p.m.
12.05 p.m.   14.25   6.15 a.m   5.40 p.m.   11.50 a.m.   9.10 p.m.

3 Complete these sentences using **llama**, **rellena**, **firma** or **deja**.
a   ¿Me....................aquí, por favor?
b   ¿Me....................su pasaporte, por favor?
c   ¿Me....................esta hoja, por favor?
d   ¿Me....................a las seis y media, por favor?

4 The hotel receptionist asks you the following questions. What do you have to do in each case?
a   ¿Me rellena esta hoja? – bring your luggage/fill in a form/show your passport

El tiempo es oro — Time is money

¡Cómo corre el tiempo! — How time flies!

b ¿Me firma aquí? – confirm the booking/give the name of the company you work for/sign something

5 What do these Spanish timetables refer to: **el desayuno**, **el almuerzo** or **la cena**?

a desde las dos de la tarde hasta las tres y media

b desde las seis de la mañana hasta las nueve y media

c desde las diez de la noche hasta la medianoche

¿Tienen habitación para esta noche?

FRASES

No tenemos a este nombre nada reservado   *We don't have anything reserved in that name*

¿(Ustedes) tienen habitación para esta noche?   *Have you got a room for tonight?*

Estamos completos   *We're full*

¿Qué puedo hacer entonces?   *What can I do, then?*

Si quiere, le puedo facilitar algún hotel   *If you like I can contact another hotel for you*

Por aquí cercano   *Near here*

Si puede ser   *If that's possible*

Louise Taylor is checking into a hotel. What is the problem?

Louise Taylor	Buenas noches, señor.
Recepcionista	Buenas noches, señorita.
Louise Taylor	Tengo reservada una habitación para esta noche.
Recepcionista	¿A qué nombre?
Louise Taylor	A nombre de Taylor.
Recepcionista	Un momento que lo voy a comprobar. No, no tenemos a este nombre nada reservado, ¿eh?
Louise Taylor	Bueno, ¿ustedes tienen habitación para esta noche?
Recepcionista	Pues estamos completos.
Louise Taylor	¿Qué puedo hacer entonces?
Recepcionista	Si quiere, le puedo facilitar algún hotel por aquí cercano.
Louise Taylor	Pues si puede ser, gracias.
Recepcionista	Sí, un momento que lo voy a comprobar. (*Al teléfono*) Hola, buenas noches. Te llamo del hotel Casón del Tormes. ¿Tienes una habitación simple para esta noche...?

What does the receptionist offer to do? Is there any alternative accommodation?

una habitación simple   *single room*

el teléfono   *telephone*

25

2 INFRAESTRUCTURA

(yo) soy   *I am*
(tú) eres   *you are*
(usted/él/ella) es   *you are, he/she/it is*
(nosotros) somos   *we are*
(vosotros) sois   *you are*
(ustedes/ellos/ellas) son   *you/they are*

(yo) tengo   *I have*
(tú) tienes   *you have*
(usted/él/ella) tiene   *you have, he/she/it has*
(nosotros) tenemos   *we have*
(vosotros) tenéis   *you have*
(ustedes/ellos/ellas) tienen   *you/they have*

Ser and estar – to be

In Spanish there are two verbs – **ser** and **estar** – which translate *to be*. They are not interchangeable.

Ser is used to refer to a permanent or inherent quality. It is also used when referring to nationality, profession, price, time, date, size and possession.

Study these examples: **Soy Elvira Sánchez** (who somebody is); **Soy apoderada** (profession); **¿Qué hora es?** (time); **¿Cuánto es?** (price); **Es una compañía española** (nationality); **Mi nombre es..** (possession).

Estar is used to express a temporary state or quality. It is also used when indicating location, position, moods and state of health. You have only come across two expressions which use part of this verb: **Estamos completos** (temporary situation) and **¿Cómo estás, Pablo?** (present state of health)

Tener – to have

You have seen a variety of expressions which use parts of **tener**: **¿Qué cargo tiene usted en la compañía?**; **Aquí tiene**; **Tenga**; **Tengo una habitación reservada**; **¿Tienen habitación para esta noche?**

Use **tener** to talk about your age – not **ser** or **estar**, eg **Tengo 25 años** (*I'm 25 years old*; literally 'I have 25 years'). The corresponding question is: **¿Cuántos años tiene?** (*How old are you?*).

PRACTICA

1 Complete these sentences using: **son/soy/es/estamos/estás/tengo/tiene**

a .... Francisco Martínez.
b .... completos.
c ¿Cómo .... , Pablo?
d ¿Cuánto ....?
e Este .... mi socio.
f .... las nueve de la mañana.
g ¿Cuántos años................ ?
h .... una habitación reservada.
i .... 37 años.

2 Pilar Alvarez arrives at a hotel, in Madrid. She hasn't got a reservation. What type of room does she want? For how many nights?

Pilar Alvarez   Buenas tardes.
Recepcionista   Buenas tardes.
Pilar Alvarez   ¿Tienen una habitación individual?
Recepcionista   ¿Para cuántas noches?

26

More hotel vocabulary
una habitación individual/doble
 a single/double room
con baño/ducha/lavabo *with bathroom/shower/washbasin*
para una/dos/tres noche(s) *for 1,2,3 nights*
¿qué precio tiene? *how much is it?*

Pilar Alvarez Para tres noches.
Recepcionista ¿Con baño o con lavabo?
Pilar Alvarez Con baño, por favor.
Recepcionista Muy bien. Una habitación individual, con baño para tres noches.
Pilar Alvarez ¿Qué precio tiene, por favor?
Recepcionista Un momento, por favor.

3 You arrive at the Hotel Las Torres. You don't have a room booked in your name. Practise asking for the type of room you want.

a

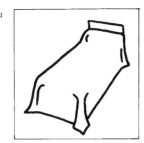   

b

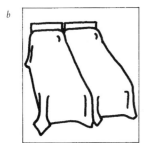   

marzo *March*
libre *free, available*
buscar *to look for*

4 Pilar is checking in at a hotel. She also has problems with the room reservation.
a For which days had the reservation been made?
b Is there a room available at the hotel or will they have to find alternative accommodation?

5a At a hotel you want to ask if there is a room available. You say...
¿Hay un bar en el hotel?/¿Tiene una habitación disponible?/¿A qué hora se sirve el desayuno?
b You want to book a single room for two nights. You say...
Una habitación doble para tres noches/Una habitación individual para cuatro noches/Una habitación individual para dos noches.

27

2

FRASES

In this section you will practise buying a train ticket.

Vamos a ver...   *Let's see...*
Sale a...   *Leaves at...*
Llega a...   *Arrives at...*
¿Me podría dar el precio?   *Could you give me the price?/How much is it?*
En segunda (clase)   *Second class*
En primera (clase)   *First class*
Quisiera comprar un billete   *I would like to buy a ticket*
¿Para qué día?   *For which day?*
¿Paga con metálico/con tarjeta de crédito   *Are you paying cash/by credit card?*
¿Puedo...?   *Can I...?*
Por supuesto   *Of course*

Pilar Alvarez is getting information about trains at the RENFE (Spain's national railway) office in Madrid. Where does she want to go? What time does the Talgo leave Chamartín station? What else does the clerk tell her?

Oficial   Vamos a ver, para Vigo tiene usted dos trenes: un tren Talgo que sale a las 13.30 desde la estación de Chamartín y llega a Vigo a las 21.30 y un tren expreso que sale de Príncipe Pío a las 22.25 y llega a Vigo a las 8.45.
Pilar Alvarez   ¿Me podría dar el precio del Talgo, por favor?
Oficial   El precio del Talgo...un momento...son 6.605 en segunda y 9.140 en primera.

The clerk explains what **Días Azules** (blue days) means. How much is the discount on **Días Azules**?

Oficial   Los días azules es un descuento que se hace por ida y vuelta y es un doce por ciento de la tarifa general de Renfe.

Pilar is buying her train ticket. Which train does she choose to catch? When is she travelling?

Pilar Alvarez   Buenas tardes.
Oficial   Buenas tardes.
Pilar Alvarez   Quisiera comprar un billete para el tren Talgo de Madrid a Vigo.
Oficial   ¿Para qué día sería el viaje?
Pilar Alvarez   Para el domingo.
Oficial   ¿Para este domingo?
Pilar Alvarez   Sí.
Oficial   Muy bien. ¿El viaje lo efectuaría en primera o en segunda clase?
Pilar Alvarez   En primera, por favor.

el billete de ida y vuelta   *return ticket*
el descuento   *discount*
el domingo   *Sunday*
la estación   *station*
el fumador   *smoking (carriage)*
el no fumador   *non-smoking (carriage)*
la tarifa   *fare*
el (tren) expreso   *express train*
el (tren) Talgo   *intercity train*
el viaje   *journey*
llegar   *to arrive*
pagar   *to pay*
salir   *to leave*
que   *which, that*
desde   *from*
o   *or*

Listen to the rest of the dialogue. Does Pilar smoke? Is she paying in cash?

Oficial En primera clase. ¿Fumador o no?
Pilar Alvarez No fumador.
Oficial Vamos a ver... ¿Paga con métalico o con tarjeta de crédito?
Pilar Alvarez Con tarjeta de crédito. ¿Puedo pagar con Visa?
Oficial Sí, sí, por supuesto. Déjemela.

INFRAESTRUCTURA ➤

Days of the week
Listen to the recording and practise saying the days of the week.
el/los lunes *Monday(s)* el/los martes *Tuesday(s)*
el/los miércoles *Wednesday(s)* el/los jueves *Thursday(s)*
el/los viernes *Friday(s)* el sábado/los sábados *Saturday(s)*
el domingo/los domingos *Sunday(s)*
In Spanish the words for Monday to Friday do not change in the plural. The plural is indicated by the use of **los** before them.

Months of the year
Practise saying the months of the year.
enero *January* febrero *February* marzo *March* abril *April* mayo *May* junio *June* julio *July* agosto *August* septiembre *or* setiembre *September* octubre *October* noviembre *November* diciembre *December*

The days of the week and the months of the year do not start with a capital letter in written Spanish.

Dates
The first of January is **el primero de enero.** But all other dates use ordinary numbers: *2nd January* – **el dos de enero**; *3rd January* – **el tres de enero**; *21st January* – **el veintiuno de enero**; *22nd January* – **el veintidós de enero**, etc.

Listen to the tape and practise saying dates.

PRACTICA ➤

1 Name the following in Spanish:
a the last day of the normal working week
b two dates of historical importance in your country
c the second day of your own working week
d the day and month you joined the company you work for
e the day of the week you don't normally work
f the month you normally take your holidays
g the month(s) of the year which is/are on average more profitable for your company
h the dates Christmas Day and New Year's Day fall on

El Talgo

2 You're at Chamartín station in Madrid, buying a ticket for Bilbao.

Oficial Buenos días.

Usted (Greet clerk and say you'd like to buy a ticket for Bilbao.)

Oficial ¿Ida o ida y vuelta?

Usted (You want a return ticket.)

Oficial ¿Para qué día es el viaje?

Usted (You want to travel on Friday.)

Oficial ¿En primera o en segunda?

Usted (You want to travel first class. Ask how much it is.)

Oficial Son 9.560 pesetas. ¿Paga con tarjeta de crédito o con metálico?

Usted (You'd like to pay by cash.)

3 Intergift and Fitur are exhibitions at the Madrid Fair. The dates and times you have don't coincide with those in the brochure. Correct the statements in Spanish practising with a colleague if possible, eg **Intergift exhibe desde el 27 de enero. – No, Intergift exhibe desde el 17 de enero**.

SEMANA INTERNACIONAL DE LA DECORACION Y EL REGALO

INTERGIFT

Salón Internacional del Regalo

Fechas 17-21 de enero y 19-23 de septiembre

Horario De 10 a 20 h.

FITUR

Ferial Internacional de Turismo

Fechas 29 de enero-2 de febrero

Horario 29, 30 y 31 de enero: de 10 a 19 h.

1 y 2 de febrero: de 10 a 20 h.

Sectores Agencia de Viajes • Tour Operadores • Compañias de Transportes • Hostelería • Organismos Oficiales • Medios de Comunicación • Varios

Entrada 2.000 ptas

A Intergift exhibe desde el 27 de enero hasta el 31 de enero

B Fitur exhibe desde el 14 hasta el 22 de marzo

el premio   *prize*

4   Listen to the recording of the Madrid Lottery and repeat each number as it is called out. How much is the first prize announced? How much is the next prize?

5*a* You want to buy a train ticket. You say...
¿Qué trenes hay?/Quisiera el precio del billete/Quisiera un billete
b How do you ask if something is available?
¿hay?/¿cuántos?/¿tiene?/¿podría?/¿cómo?/¿qué?

¿Qué hotel?

el aire acondicionado   *air conditioning*
la lavandería   *laundry*
la piscina   *swimming pool*
la pista   *court*
la sala de reuniones   *meeting room*
el salón   *room, hall*
las vistas al mar   *sea views*
tranquilo/a   *peaceful*

These two hotels situated several kilometres outside Barcelona could be an ideal choice for any company planning to hold an international business conference in Spain. Study the list of facilities and name in English three advantages and three possible disadvantages that could influence your choice.

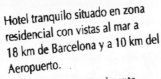

GRAN HOTEL REY DON JAIME

Hotel tranquilo situado en zona residencial con vistas al mar a 18 km de Barcelona y a 10 km del Aeropuerto.

240 habitaciones totalmente equipadas y climatizadas : piscina climatizada y exterior, fitness center, pistas de squash, sauna, gimnasio,...

Salas de reuniones con capacidad de 25 a 500 personas.

Restaurante Internacional.

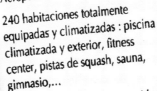

Avda. del Hotel, 22 - 08860 CASTELLDEFELS (Barcelona)
Telefax (93) 665 18 01 - Telex 50151 - RDJH - E - Teléf. (93) 665 13 00

HOTEL CIUTAT DE VIC***

• **Dirección:**
Jaume I el Conqueridor, s/n
08500 VIC (Barcelona)
Tel. (93) 889 25 51 - Fax (93) 889 14 47

• **Situación y Características:**
Edificio de nueva planta, en el corazón de la ciudad, a 2 minutos andando de la Plaza Mayor, entre las Rondas.

• **Servicios:**
• 36 habitaciones alto confort
• TV con mando a distancia
• Antena parabólica
• Teléfono directo
• Mini bar
• Aire acondicionado
• Cafetería-Restaurante
• Desayuno-buffet
• Salones privados para reuniones
• Salones para banquetes
• Servicio de lavandería
• Parking propio

• **Información y Reservas:**
• Centrales de Reservas NH
• Barcelona
Tel. (93) 418 63 32 - Fax (93) 418 61 54
• Madrid
Tel. (91) 578 16 00 / 14 75 - Fax (91) 578 13 29

• **Representantes internacionales:**
• KEYTEL • HOTEL REP • UTELL INTERNATIONAL

2

Inventario

Catching a taxi

Quisiera ir a/al/a la... *I would like to go to...*

¿(Me dice) Cuánto es, por favor? *How much is it, please?*

¿Me podría dar un recibo/una factura, por favor? *Could you give me a receipt please?*

Checking into a hotel

Tengo una habitación reservada a nombre de... *I have a room reserved in the name of...*

¿Me deja el pasaporte? *Could you leave me your passport?*

Booking a room

¿Tiene/tienen una habitación individual/doble? *Have you got a single/double room?*

¿Tienen habitación para esta noche? *Is there a room available for tonight?*

Con baño/ducha/lavabo *With bathroom/shower/washbasin*

Para dos/tres noches *For 2/3 nights*

¿Qué precio tiene? *How much is it?*

¿Hay ducha? *Is there a shower?*

¿Me llama a las siete y media? *Could you call me at half past seven?*

¿Me da...? *Could you give me...?*

¿A qué hora se sirve el desayuno? *What time is breakfast served?*

Time

¿Qué hora es? *What time is it?*

Es la una/son las cinco *It's one o'clock/five o'clock*

De... a... *From... to*

Desde las... hasta las... *From... until...*

¿Cuándo? *When?*

Booking a train ticket

Quisiera un billete para... *I would like a ticket for...*

En primera/Segunda clase *First/Second class*

Fumador/No fumador *Smoking/non-smoking*

Un billete de ida *A single ticket*

Un billete de ida y vuelta *A return ticket*

Punto de Control

Check you can do each of the following in Spanish:

➤ Say where you'd like to go.

➤ Buy a train ticket.

➤ Ask how much something is.

➤ Ask for a receipt.

➤ Book a room.

➤ Check into a hotel.

➤ Ask what time breakfast is served.

➤ Ask for a morning call.

➤ Tell the time.

Llegada

Visitors to the Basque Country's industrial capital will soon realise that the town they thought was called Bilbao is known in the local language as Bilbo. Travellers arriving in Barcelona will discover they are entering Catalunya, not Cataluña as Castilian Spanish would have it, and that taxis for hire at the city's El Prat airport display cards saying "Lliure", not "Libre".

In the Basque Country, in Catalonia, and also in the north-western area of Galicia, the visitor comes face to face with the pluri-national reality of Spain. Each of these regions has its own language that is co-official with Spanish (or Castilian Spanish as purists would have it) - Basque or Euskerra in the Basque Country, Catalan in Catalonia and Gallego in Galicia.

Spain is divided up into 17 autonomous communities but it is in the Basque Country, in Catalonia and in Galicia, which each have their own language, an ethnic pride and a strong cultural tradition of separateness, that home rule has struck firm and, seemingly, deepening roots. A visitor is not just in Spain but in a specific autonomous community in Spain. Business visitors seeking official contacts will, accordingly, have to place contact in the autonomous government of any given area high on their agenda.

Decentralisation has meant that the autonomous communities, which each have their own executive, legislature and judiciary, wield a considerable degree of power, much like that of the Lander in Germany or the states in the US, although there are variations from one area to another. The *Comunidades Autónomas* have a say

in their local savings banks, run their own development agencies and have jurisdiction over investment incentives, building permits, local communications and trading hours. Several of the autonomous governments have responsibility for internal security, health and education in their areas and the executives in the Basque Country and in the adjoining community of Navarre run their own fiscal systems.

Madrid is the centre of its own autonomous community in addition to being the Spanish capital. It is the seat of the national government and parliament, of the civil service and of the supreme court, the headquarters of the banking system and of nearly all the large domestic and foreign companies, and the home of Spain's main stock exchange.

Sooner rather than later, visitors doing business in one or other of the autonomous communities will have to pass through Madrid whether they have appointments in the capital or not. This is because although Spain might be administratively decentralised, the national transportation is heavily concentrated on its capital.

Barcelona, Bilbao, La Coruña in Galicia are all served by international flights as

are Valencia and Seville, respectively Spain's third and fourth largest cities and the capitals of the Comunidad Valenciana and Andalucia. Madrid, through Barajas airport, is however by far the best of all Spain's cities for international connections, and is consequently the main entry point to the country.

Located in the very middle of the country, Madrid is in addition the main domestic communications centre. National highways start from Madrid like spokes from a hub and every guide book will inform the visitor that all Spanish roads lead to Madrid. The city is linked to Seville by a high speed train, to Barcelona by an air-shuttle and to every other important urban centre in the country by fast inter-city trains, by domestic flights and, of course, by the long established radial road system - a network that has in recent years been upgraded into motorways and dual carriageways.

3

CITAS

◆ Using the phone ◆ Making and changing appointments

¡Dígame!

This section will help you get through to the right person on the phone.

FRASES

Correcto   *That's right*
Quisiera hablar con...   *I'd like to speak to...*
Lo siento muchísimo   *I'm terribly sorry*
No está   *He/she isn't in*
No va a volver en todo el día   *He/she won't be back all day*
Si quiere hablar conmigo...   *If you'd like to talk to me...*
¡Dígame!   *Hello* (when answering phone) (literally *Tell me*)
¿De parte de quién?   *Who's calling?/Who shall I say?*
Está comunicando   *The line's/It's engaged*
No cuelgue, por favor   *Hold on, please*
Antonio Pérez al habla   *Antonio Pérez speaking*
Llamaré más tarde   *I'll call later*
... está en reunión   *... is in a meeting*
¿Cuándo puedo llamarle?   *When can I call him/her back?*

An assistant from the Banco de Sabadell rings a company called Tixa to talk to Sr Sivil. What time of day is it? Is Sr Sivil available?

Secretaria   Hola, buenas tardes.
Auxiliar   Hola, buenas tardes. ¿Es la empresa Tixa?
Secretaria   Correcto.
Auxiliar   Mire. Quisiera hablar con el señor Sivil, por favor.
Secretaria   Bueno, lo siento muchísimo, pero no está, y no va a volver en todo el día. Yo soy la secretaria. Si quiere hablar conmigo...

Ben Smith phones Castellana S.A. The telephonist wants to know who's calling. What does she say? How does she ask him to hang on?

Telefonista   Buenos días. ¡Dígame!

34

el despacho	*office*
la empresa	*enterprise, company*
pero	*but*

Ben Smith	¿Es la empresa Castellana S.A.?
Telefonista	Correcto.
Ben Smith	Quisiera hablar con el Sr Pérez, por favor.
Telefonista	¿De parte de quién?
Ben Smith	Soy Ben Smith de Modern Kitchens Ltd., de Inglaterra.
Telefonista	Un momento, por favor. Está comunicando. No cuelgue por favor.
Ben Smith	Gracias.
Sr Pérez	Antonio Pérez al habla. ¡Dígame!

Mr Smith is ringing Castellana S.A. again. Why is Sr Pérez unable to come to the phone?

Telefonista	Lo siento. El Sr Pérez no está en su despacho.
Ben Smith	Bueno. Llamaré más tarde.

This time when Mr Smith rings, where is Sr Pérez?

Telefonista	Lo siento. El Sr Pérez está en reunión.
Ben Smith	¿Cuándo puedo llamarle?

Say in Spanish 'I'll call later' and 'When can I call him/her back?'

The word lists give you useful vocabulary to learn. Most of the words appear in the recordings, but occasionally, related words are added to give you flexibility.

More useful expressions

La señora García está ocupada   *Sra García is busy*
La señora García está de vacaciones   *Sra García is on holiday*
La señorita Alvarez está en viaje de negocios   *Srta Alvarez is away on business*
Llamaré esta tarde   *I'll ring this afternoon*
Llamaré mañana por la mañana   *I'll ring tomorrow morning*
Llamaré mañana por la tarde   *I'll ring tomorrow afternoon*
Llamaré el jueves   *I'll ring on Thursday*
Es urgente   *It's urgent*
Quisiera dejar un recado, por favor   *I'd like to leave a message please*
¿Me puede llamar a... (time)?   *Could he/she ring me at...(time)?*
Estoy en el hotel Hilton   *I'm at the Hilton Hotel*
El (número de) teléfono es...   *The (phone) number is...*

INFRAESTRUCTURA ▶

Estar – to be
You first met this verb on p26. Refresh your memory by checking back.

This unit introduces more expressions using **estar**. Most of them refer to location and temporary states. **No está en su despacho; Está en reunión; Está comunicando; Está ocupado; Está de vacaciones**.

To indicate where you are or why you're unavailable, you use **estoy**, eg **Estoy en el hotel Hilton; Estoy ocupado/a**.

You can easily turn a statement into a question without changing the order of the words, eg **¿Está en el hotel Hilton?**

3

Mi/su

If you want someone's phone number, you ask: **¿Cuál es su (número de) teléfono?** As you have seen, **su** means *your*; it also means *his/her*, so you use the same question for both *What's your (phone) number?* and *What's his/her (phone) number?*

If you are giving your phone number, you would say: **Mi (número de) teléfono es el...**

Did you know?

Phone and fax numbers are normally read out in Spanish as follows: 597 16 25: **cinco, noventa y siete, dieciséis, veinticinco**. 88, 00, etc. they will not be read out as double eight or double O, but as **ochenta y ocho and cero-cero.**

PRACTICA ➤

1 Match the secretary's statements with the most appropriate answers. In one case more than one answer is suitable.

The secretary says...
a   Está comunicando.
b   No cuelgue por favor.
c   Está de vacaciones.
d   ¿De parte de quién, por favor?

You answer...
1   Quisiera dejarle un recado, por favor.
2   ¿Cuándo puedo llamarle?
3   Soy la señora Pelayo.
4   Llamaré más tarde.
5   Gracias.

2 Turn these statements into questions and then answer them in the negative, eg **¿Está en su despacho? – No, no está en su despacho.**
a   Está de vacaciones.
b   Está en reunión.
c   Está en viaje de negocios.

3 How do you say the following in Spanish?
a   I'll ring on Tuesday.
b   I'll ring on Wednesday.
c   I'll ring this afternoon.
d   I'll ring tomorrow morning.

4 In a phone call, what would be your response to the following?
a   ¿De parte de quién?
b   ¿Cómo se escribe su apellido?

5 Complete the sentences with words from the list provided.

¿Cuándo puedo ....?	llamaré
El Sr García está	llamarle
Quisiera dejar un	ocupado
Le .... mañana por la tarde.	recado

El alfabeto telefónico (when spelling words over the phone...)

A	Antonio	Ñ	Ñoño
B	Barcelona	O	Oviedo
C	Carmen	P	París
Ch	Chocolate	Q	Querido
D	Dolores	R	Ramón
E	Enrique	S	Sábado
F	Francia	T	Tarragona
G	Gerona	U	Ulises
H	Historia	V	Valencia
I	Inés	W	Washington
J	José	X	Xiquena
K	Kilo	Y	Yegua
L	Lorenzo	Z	Zaragoza
LL	Llobregat		
M	Madrid		
N	Navarra		

6 Listen and write down the phone number. Listen also for the following expression: **Le voy a dar mi tarjeta.**

7 Answer these questions for each of the cards. Practise with a colleague if possible, eg **Mi número de teléfono es el 597 16 25. Mi número de fax es el 538 36 79.**

¿Cuál es su número de teléfono?

¿Cuál es su número de fax?

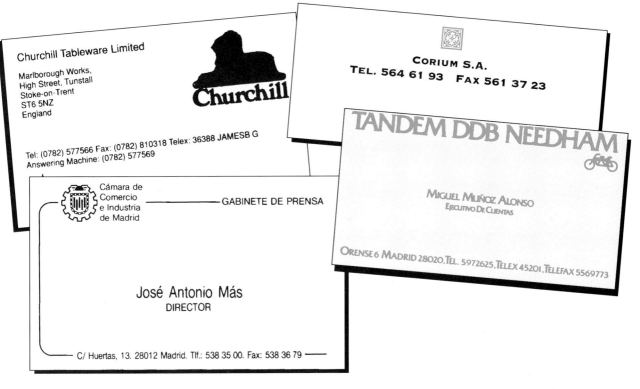

Churchill Tableware Limited

Marlborough Works,
High Street, Tunstall
Stoke-on-Trent
ST6 5NZ
England

Tel: (0782) 577566 Fax: (0782) 810318 Telex: 36388 JAMESB G
Answering Machine: (0782) 577569

Churchill

CORIUM S.A.
TEL. 564 61 93   FAX 561 37 23

Cámara de
Comercio
e Industria
de Madrid ———— GABINETE DE PRENSA

José Antonio Más
DIRECTOR

C/ Huertas, 13. 28012 Madrid. Tlf.: 538 35 00. Fax: 538 36 79

TANDEM DDB NEEDHAM

MIGUEL MUÑOZ ALONSO
Ejecutivo De Cuentas

ORENSE 6 MADRID 28020, TEL. 5972625, TELEX 45201, TELEFAX 5569773

una entrevista   *meeting*

8 Jaime Melgarejo of Treserra has an appointment with Josep Rojas and Susana Paz.

a Why can he not see them straight away?

b Will he have long to wait?

9 The telephonist asks you to stay on the line. Which two expressions might she/he use? **Lo siento./Un momento, por favor./Llamaré más tarde./No cuelgue./¿Su nombre, por favor?**

3

El departamento de exportación, por favor.

This section is about getting through to the right department.

FRASES ▶

¿Me pone con...?   *Could you put me through to...?*
En este momento no podemos atenderle   *We can't take your call at the moment*
Rogamos deje...   *Please leave...* (name and telephone number)
Nos pondremos en contacto con usted...   *We'll be in touch with you...*

Ben Smith is phoning two different companies, Arte Iberia and Creaciones Roma. Which departments is he trying to get through to?

Telefonista	Arte Iberia. Buenos días. ¡Dígame!
Ben Smith	El departamento de marketing, por favor.
Telefonista	Creaciones Roma. Buenas tardes.
Ben Smith	El departamento de exportación, por favor.
Telefonista	No cuelgue, por favor...
Secretaria	Departamento de exportación, dígame.
Ben Smith	¿Me pone con la señora Sáenz, por favor?
Secretaria	Un momentito.

Now you... Say who you are and ask to be put through to Sra Garzón in the export department.

Listen to the recorded message on an answering machine.

«Le habla el contestador automático de la firma Comercial Suiza. En este momento no podemos atenderle. Rogamos deje el nombre y el número de teléfono después de la señal. Nos pondremos en contacto con usted lo antes posible. Gracias.»

Now listen especially for the following words and phrases: **contestador automático**; **rogamos deje**; **después; en contacto; lo antes posible**.

Now you... Listen once more to the recorded message on the answering machine and when you hear the beeps be ready to leave your message. Record yourself on cassette. Speak slowly and clearly.

Say who you are, your job title, the name of your company and the country where the company is based. Say that you are at the Savoy Hotel and your phone number is 37 62 18 89.

Departments
el departamento de importación
import department
... de exportación   *export*
... de compras/ventas
purchasing/sales
... de marketing   *marketing*
... de personal   *personnel*
... de producción   *production*
... de publicidad   *publicity*
... técnico   *technical*

---

el contestador automático
answering machine
la firma   *firm*
la señal   *beep*
después   *after*
lo antes posible   *as soon as possible*

Prepare a standard message to read out in case you get an answering machine. That message should include your name, job title, name of the company you work for and where you are based, who you would like to talk to, when, etc.

Countries and nationalities

You will soon be talking about countries, origin and nationalities in a variety of contexts: about yourself, eg **Soy británico/a** (*I'm British*); about your company, eg **Es una compañía inglesa** (*It's an English company*); about your product, eg **Es de los Estados Unidos** (*It comes from the USA*). For a fuller list see page 159.

Remember: use **soy**, **es** and **son** when you talk about origin or nationality.

Plural of nouns and adjectives

Words ending in **a**, **e** or **o** (without an accent) add **s** to the singular form. The plural of **el** and **la** is **los** and **las** (*the*), eg **el día/los días, la tarjeta/las tarjetas, moderno/modernos**.

For words ending in a consonant, add **es** to the singular form, eg **la estación/las estaciones, azul/azules**. See page 159.

Agreement of adjectives

An adjective must agree with the word it describes in gender as well as number. Look at these examples: **el contestador automático, los contestadores automáticos; la empresa es moderna; el director es español; las empleadas son inglesas**.

Expressing possession

If you have one business partner you say **mi socio/a**; if you have two or more you say **mis socios/as**. The word **mi** also becomes plural in Spanish.

With singular masculine nouns, use **mi** (*my*), **tu** (*your* – informal), **su** (*his/her/its/your* – formal), **nuestro** (*our*), **vuestro** (*your* – informal), **su** (*their*); eg **mi teléfono, su despacho**.

With singular feminine nouns, **nuestro** and **vuestro** become **nuestra** and **vuestra**, eg **nuestro director, nuestra directora, vuestro diseñador, vuestra diseñadora**.

With plural nouns, use **mis, tus, sus, nuestros/(as), vuestros/(as), sus**; eg **mis apellidos, sus empleados, vuestras vacaciones**.

1 Many hotels, restaurants and large firms employ staff from various countries. Say in Spanish:

a Our cook (male) is Spanish.

b The secretary (female) is English and the secretary (male) is Spanish.

c Our designers (female) are French.

d I am (your nationality).

e The manager (female) is Italian.

3

2 Study this example dialogue.

1a. Telefonista   Porcelanas Denia. Buenos días.
Persona que llama   El departamento de exportación, por favor.
2a Telefonista   Exportación, buenos días.
Persona que llama   ¿Me pone con el Sr Pablo Suárez, por favor?

Now try to get through to these people. Practise the dialogue with a
fellow student if possible.

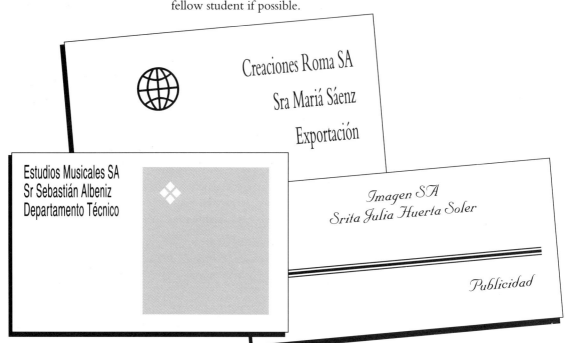

3 Change these phrases into the plural,. eg **mi** tarjeta – **mis** tarjetas, el
producto británico – los producto**s** británico**s**.

el producto europeo   el mercado internacional   la feria industrial
la compañía británica   el apellido español   la empresa moderna
su socio   tu oficina   vuestra recepcionista   nuestro apoderado.

4 Describe these employees in Spanish, eg my secretary (female), your
(formal) telephonist and our employees (male) – mi secretaria, su
telefonista y nuestros empleados

a   my secretary (male), your (formal) receptionist and our employees
(female)
b   our cook (male), our waiters and our waitresses
c   my designers (female) and your (informal) designers (male)

5 Which two of these departments are involved in selling?
compras/ventas/importación/exportación/publicidad/personal

Estoy libre el martes.

In this section you will practise making and changing appointments.

FRASES

Quisiera concertar una cita con... *I'd like to make an appointment with...*
La semana que viene *Next week/The coming week*
Estoy libre *I'm free*
Quisiera cambiar la fecha de la cita *I'd like to change the date of the appointment*
Vale *Right/OK*

Ben Smith phones to make an appointment to see don Antonio Farías Griñán. When does he want to see Sr Farías Griñán? What's the secretary's answer? When do they arrange the meeting for?

la fecha *the date*
la semana *week*
este/esta *this*
imposible *impossible*
posible *possible*
entonces *then*

Ben Smith   Buenos días. Quisiera concertar una cita con don Antonio Farías Griñán para esta semana.
Secretaria   ¿De parte de quién?
Ben Smith   Ben Smith de Modern Kitchens Ltd., de Inglaterra.
Secretaria   Un momentito, Sr Smith. (*Consults diary*) Esta semana es imposible.
Ben Smith   Para la semana que viene, entonces. Estoy libre el martes por la mañana.
Secretaria   Sí, el martes es posible. ¿A las diez y media?
Ben Smith   A las diez y media. Muchas gracias.

More meeting vocabulary
la reunión *meeting*
adelantar *to bring forward*
aplazar *to postpone*
cancelar *to cancel*
confirmar *to confirm*
necesito cambiar la fecha
 I need to change the date

Ben Smith is going to be busier than he thought and will not be able to keep the appointment on Tuesday... Which day of the week does he suggest this time?

Before making a phone call, think about what you want to say in Spanish first, make sure you know the name of the person you want to speak to, then start your call.

Ben Smith   Quisiera cambiar la fecha de la cita, por favor. Estoy libre el miércoles.
Secretaria   Vale. El miércoles a las diez y media.
Ben Smith   Muchas gracias.

Now you... Say you would like to change an appointment. You are free on Thursday.

INFRAESTRUCTURA

Getting clarification or repetition
If you're unsure what a person has said or a particular word has thrown you, just say **¿Perdón?** (*Pardon?*) or **¿Cómo?** (*What?*) or **¿Me lo puede repetir, por favor?** (*Could you repeat that for me, please?*) or **¿Puede hablar más despacio, por favor?** (*Could you speak more slowly, please?*).

 If you don't know the meaning of a word, ask: **¿Qué quiere decir...?** (*What does ... mean?*) or if you need something spelt out: **¿Cómo se escribe?** (*How do you spell it?*)

3

Do not forget to make a note of any expressions particularly useful to you. Keep your notes in a special notebook under separate headings. Also, make a note (in your diary, for instance) of the expressions **Quisiera aplazar**, **cancelar**, etc. next to your prepared answerphone message.

Comparing times

The following expressions are very useful when you want to make, change or postpone appointments. Look at these examples.
el 23 de junio...
...es más conveniente (que...)   ...*is/will be more convenient (than...)*
...es menos conveniente (que...)   ...*is/will be less convenient (than...)*
...es mejor/peor (que...)   ...*is/will be better/worse (than...)*
...es demasiado temprano/tarde   ...*is/will be too early/late*
See Comparisons on page 148.

Expressing possession

To say something belongs to a particular person, use, **de** (*of*), eg **el pasaporte de John** (*John's passport*) **el diario de la recepcionista** (*the receptionist's diary*).

Did you know?

Don and **Doña** are polite forms of address. They are used with the Christian name or with this and the first surname, eg **Don Antonio**, **Doña Maite** or **Don Antonio Farías**, **Doña Maite García**.

PRACTICA

estaba prevista   *was planned*
en vez de   *instead of*

1   Paloma is ringing to change the time of an appointment.
a   Does this phone call take place in the morning or in the afternoon?
b   Do you think that Paloma and Begoña are friends?
c   What time was the original meeting for?
d   In whose office is the meeting going to take place?

2   You have an appointment for Wednesday. Consider each of the following situations and say whether you wish to confirm, cancel, postpone, etc. the appointment.
a   You've just been told that you are flying back to head office in England on Tuesday.
b   You will not be free until Thursday.
c   There is no need now for a meeting with this company executive.
d   You cannot risk not having this meeting. You must confirm it.

3   Listen to the assistant from the Banco de Sabadell ringing to confirm an appointment with the secretary from Tixa. ¿Verdad o mentira? (True or false)
a   The talks will be about the United States.
b   The meeting has been planned for two o'clock.

la calle   *street*
una ronda de consultas   *round of talks*
próximo/a   *next*

4   What would you say in these situations?
a There is one word you can't understand.
b You don't understand at all.
c The speaker is talking too quckly.

5 Listen again to the recorded message on the answering machine. After the beeps, say who you are, give the name and location of your company, the phone and fax number and leave one of these messages.

Message: I would like to confirm the appointment with Sra Maite García for Friday.

Message: I would like to make an appointment to see Sr Martínez on Wednesday at 2 p.m.

6 Say who these things belong to, eg **el teléfono de la sra García.**

3

Did you know?

Días puente (literally *bridge days*) refer to the days between a public holiday and a weekend. **Puentes** should always be taken into account when making appointments in Spain. If a public holiday falls on a Thursday, for instance, Friday also becomes part of the holiday by making a 'bridge' between the holiday and the weekend.

When in Spain

Castilian is the official language of Spain. There are also several regional languages: Catalan (**el catalán**) in Catalonia; Galician (**el gallego**) in Galicia; and Basque (**el vasco** or **el vascuence**) in the Basque country.

If you are in Catalonia and someone answers the phone in Catalan the word you are likely to hear is **Digui?** (*May I help you?*).

If you do not speak Catalan, you can ask: **Parla espanyol?** (*Do you speak Spanish?*), **Parla anglés?** (*Do you speak English?*).

If you want to ask for someone, say **El senyor/La senyora X, sisplau** or **si us plau**. **Gràcies** means *thank you*.

When in Catalonia... What would you answer?

Telefonista Digui?
Usted   (Do you speak Spanish?)

Telefonista Digui?
Usted   (Sr Carreras, please.)

D I A R I O — J U N I O

Domingo 15

Lunes 16 *Conferencia de Marketing (todo el día)*

Martes 17 *10-11 reunión Ordenadores Data S.A.*

Miércoles 18 *reunión con el Sr Pérez 10.30 am*

Jueves 19 *Renfe talgo 13-30 estación Chamartín*

Viernes 20 *Vigo*

Sábado 21

You have a number of entries in your diary for the week of 15 June. On 12 June your secretary give you two messages. Consult your diary and change your appointments as necessary.

Practise the conversations with a fellow student or a colleague if possible.

los ordenadores *word processors/computers*

Recados:
Urgente. Llamaré el miércoles a las diez y media de la mañana.
Antonio Romero. Director de Marketing.
Arte España.

Reunión con el Sr. Javier López y el Director de Ventas de Almacenes Estrella.
Martes 17 de Junio - 11am - 1pm
almuerzo en el restaurante Terraza.

45

3

Inventario

Talking on the phone

¡Dígame!... *Hello!*

Antonio Pérez al habla *Antonio Pérez speaking*

Quisiera hablar con... *I'd like to talk to...*

¿Me pone con...? *Could you put me through to...?*

¿De parte de quién? *Who's calling?*

No cuelgue, por favor *Hold on, please*

¿Cuál es su número de teléfono? *What's your phone number?*

Mi número de teléfono es... *My phone number is...*

When who you want is unavailable

Está comunicando *The line's engaged*

Lo siento. El Sr X no está en su oficina *I'm sorry. Sr X is not in his office*

¿Cuándo puedo llamarle? *When can I call him/her back?*

Llamaré más tarde *I'll call back later*

Es urgente. Quisiera dejar un recado. *It's urgent. I'd like to leave a message*

¿Me puede llamar a las dos? *Can he/she ring back at two?*

Making or changing appointments

Quisiera concertar una cita con... *I'd like to make an appointment with...*

Para esta semana *For this week*

Para la semana que viene *For next week*

Estoy libre el jueves *I'm free on Thursday*

Quisiera cambiar la cita *I'd like to change the appointment*

El 23 de junio es más conveniente *23 June is more convenient*

Language problems

If you don't understand: ¿Me lo puede repetir, por favor?

If someone is speaking too fast: ¿Puede hablar más despacio por favor?

If you don't know the meaning of a word: ¿Qué quiere decir...?

Punto de Control

Check you can do the following in Spanish:

- Ask to be put through to someone.
- Ask when you can call back.
- Say that you will phone again tomorrow morning, etc.
- Say that you wish to leave a message.
- Ask if X can call you back.
- Leave a short message on an answering machine.
- Ask someone to repeat something
- Make an appointment – for this week/next week/next month.
- Change an appointment.
- Confirm an appointment.
- Cancel an appointment.
- Say that next Tuesday is more convenient than Monday.
- Say that nine o'clock is too early.

46

Citas

Spain can be a confusing mix of the formal and the informal. Business meetings are a case in point. They invariably entail a lot of etiquette but arranging them is frequently an exasperating exercise. The stereotype has it that Spaniards are unpunctual and that their second cardinal sin is that they do not answer letters. Both generalisations, as usually occurs with such sweeping statements, carry elements of truth.

Spain often comes across to first-time visitors as a society that is laid back to the point of frivolity. Its easy going pace suggests extensive informality and the truth of the matter is that it is difficult to pin people down to serious talk. Paradoxically, when a meeting does take place, and business is done face to face, the visitor will, in the main, encounter personalities who are skilled negotiators and, above all, sticklers for formality.

Setting up a meeting is certainly the most difficult part. Letters that are posted well in advance suggesting dates for a rendezvous well in the future may be of only limited value. Experienced business-in-Spain hands tend to rely more on a direct approach that borders the foot-in-the-door method. They will seek a meeting at short notice using the momentum of an urgent telephone call to carry them through to the desired encounter.

The success of the 'battering ram' tactic, naturally, depends on reaching the right person in that last minute 'phone call, and this, all-important, 'right' person is inevitably the chief executive. Spanish company management, especially when foreign visitors are involved, is utterly hierarchical. This can be true of large corporations but it is especially the case among mainline Spanish businesses which are medium and, most often, small concerns almost exclusively controlled by one family and run by a patriarch-type figure.

If the visitor starts with the patriarch at the top of the pyramid and, from there, works down the executive ladder, this will offer a short cut to a possible deal. Initial negotiations with low-ranking executives can be a total waste of time, for in Spain there is little real delegation of power or decision-making responsibility by the patriarch at the top of the pyramid. The initial focus should, therefore, be exclusively trained on the top person.

Access to the top in Spanish companies, be they large, medium or small, usually requires the sort of contacts and introductions that only a well-placed middleman can provide. Networking is important throughout the global business world. But in Spain, an inward-looking country that has a long protectionist history behind it and is burdened with red tape, the use of networks is little short of essential.

Visitors seeking serious business in Spain should equip themselves with good professional advice from the very beginning. They will require analysts and lawyers but, if newly arrived, they will, in particular, need the services of a good consultant who will help them reach the people at the top of the corporate ladder. The system can be as Byzantine as that.

Once the desired meeting is agreed, formality is order of the day. The visitor should approach it punctually, despite the stereotype, soberly dressed and with business card at the ready. The Briton, as indeed the American or any North European, starts with an advantage once the initial civilities have been dispensed with. As a rule Spanish business executives are receptive to such foreign visitors. They will nevertheless drive the hardest bargain they are capable of.

4

DESPLAZAMIENTOS

Getting and giving directions ◆ Hiring a car

¿Está lejos?

In this section you will learn how to ask and give directions when walking about.

FRASES ➤

Perdone   *Excuse me*
¿Dónde está...?   *Where is...?*
Siga todo recto/derecho   *Keep straight on/straight ahead*
Coja...   *Take...*
Está en la plaza   *It's in the square*
¿Hay un autobús para...?   *Is there a bus to...?*
Gire usted a la derecha   *Turn right*
Tres calles más arriba   *Three streets further up*
Lo encontrará   *You'll find it*

la estación de Metro   *the underground/tube station*
la oficina de Correos   *post office*
la parada de taxis   *the taxi rank/the taxi stand*
cerca (de...)   *near/close (to...)*
a la derecha   *to the right/on the right*
a la izquierda   *to the left/on the left*
allí   *there*
aquí   *here*
enfrente (de)   *in front (of)*
luego   *then; after that; later*
también   *also*

 En Madrid: Can you get to Atocha station by tube?

A   Perdone. ¿Dónde está la estación de metro?
B   Siga todo recto. Luego coja la primera a la izquierda.
A   ¿Dónde está la parada de taxis?
B   Está en la plaza.
A   ¿Hay un autobús para la estación de Atocha?
B   Sí. También hay metro.

Oficina de Correos

48

Louise Taylor is asking directions to the post office. Listen to the directions and mark the route on the map. Is the post office quite near?

More directions vocabulary

la avenida	*avenue*
la carretera	*road*
un mapa de carreteras	*road map*
un plano de la ciudad	*street map*
la primera	*the first (street)*
la segunda	*the second (street)*
al lado de	*next to*
al otro lado de	*on the other side of*
al final de	*at the end of*
en el centro	*in the centre*
en el este	*in the east*
en el norte	*in the north*
en el oeste	*in the west*
en el sur	*in the south*
en la esquina de	*on the corner of*
entre	*between*
hacia	*towards*
bastante cerca/lejos de	*quite near/far from*
por aquí	*around here*
¿Está lejos?	*Is it far?*
Está a dos minutos andando	*It's two minutes' walk away*
¿Para ir a...?	*How do I get to...?*

Louise Taylor ¿Hay una oficina de Correos cerca de aquí?
Transeúnte Gire usted a la derecha, ¿eh?
Louise Taylor A la derecha...
Transeúnte Exactamente. Tres calles más arriba.
Louise Taylor Tres calles arriba...
Transeúnte ...gire hacia la izquierda...
Louise Taylor ...a la izquierda...Sí.
Transeúnte Pues tres calles incluso más arriba...
Louise Taylor Tres calles más arriba...
Transeúnte ...a la derecha...
LouiseTaylor A la derecha.
Transeúnte Y enfrente lo encontrará.
Louise Taylor Entonces
Transeúnte Sí.
Louise Taylor A la derecha
Transeúnte Correcto.
Louise Taylor Tres calles más arriba.
Louise and Transeúnte A la izquierda.
Louise Taylor Entonces, tres calles más arriba.
Louise and Transeúnte A la derecha.
Transeúnte Y allí justo tendrá la oficina de Correos.
Louise Taylor Muchísimas gracias. Adiós.
Transeúnte De nada, adiós.

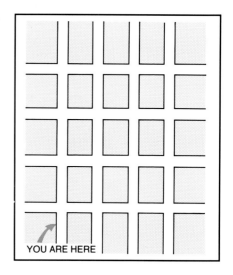

YOU ARE HERE

INFRAESTRUCTURA ▶

¿Dónde?
¿Dónde está...? means *Where is...?*; **¿Dónde están...?**, *Where are...?*, eg **¿Dónde está la estación?** (*Where is the station?*); **¿Dónde están los servicios?** (*Where are the toilets?*)

¡Coja usted...!
The use of **usted** after the words **¡coja!** (*take*), **¡siga!** (*continue*) and **¡gire!** (*turn*) makes these expressions sound more polite.

4

¿Hay...?

You first met **Hay** on page 24. In this unit, it is used in a number of expressions, eg **¿Hay un autobús para la estación de Atocha?**, **¿Hay metro?**, **¿Hay una oficina de Correos cerca de aquí?/por aquí?**

The usual answer is **Sí, hay (uno/una)** (*Yes, there is (one)*) or **No, no hay** (*No, there isn't*).

PRACTICA ➤ **1** Study the town plan and do the exercises which follow.

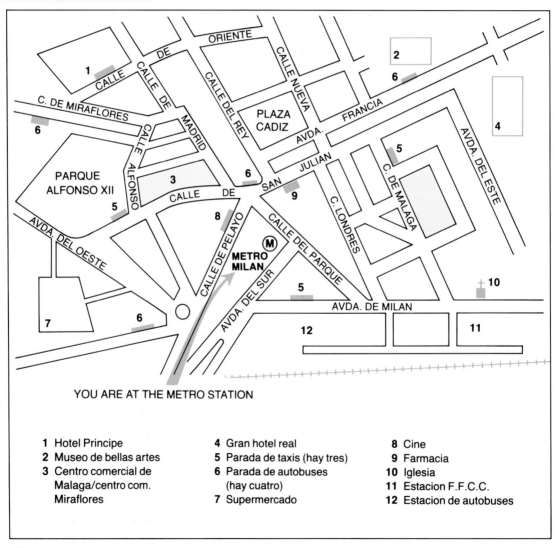

YOU ARE AT THE METRO STATION

1 Hotel Principe	**4** Gran hotel real	**8** Cine
2 Museo de bellas artes	**5** Parada de taxis (hay tres)	**9** Farmacia
3 Centro comercial de Malaga/centro com. Miraflores	**6** Parada de autobuses (hay cuatro)	**10** Iglesia
	7 Supermercado	**11** Estacion F.F.C.C.
		12 Estacion de autobuses

el centro comercial *shopping centre*
el cine *cinema*
la estación del FFCC (ferrocarril) *railway station*
la estación de autobuses *bus/coach station*
la farmacia *chemist's*
la iglesia *church*
el metro *tube/underground*
el museo *museum*
la parada de autobuses *bus-stop*
el supermercado *supermarket*

There are many useful words in this section and it would be a good idea to stop at this point and make a note of those words and expressions you feel will be particularly useful to you.

Which buildings are being referred to? eg **Está en la Avenida del Oeste. – El supermercado**.
a Está en la Calle de Oriente.
b Está entre la Calle Alfonso y la Calle de Madrid.
c Está en la Avenida del Este.

What questions would produce these answers? eg **Está en la Avenida del Sur – ¿Dónde está el metro Milán?**
d Está en el Parque Alfonso XII.
e Está en la Avenida Francia.
f Está en la Calle de Pelayo.

¿Bastante cerca? or **¿Bastante lejos?** eg **la estación del FFCC está bastante lejos del Hotel Príncipe**.
g El cine está...................del metro Milán.
h El Gran Hotel Real está..................del Parque Alfonso XII.

What is being referred to?
i Hay una en la Avenida de Milán enfrente de la estación de autobuses.
j Hay una en la Calle de San Julián entre la Calle Londres y la Calle del Parque.

You're at the metro. Follow the instructions. Where do you end up?
k Gire a la izquierda en la Calle del Parque. Siga todo recto hacia la Calle de San Julián. Gire a la izquierda y allí está, al otro lado de la calle, entre la Calle de Madrid y la Calle Alfonso.

2 Pilar Alvarez asks directions to a post office. Listen and find it on the map.

3 To ask if there is a post office nearby you'd say – ¿Hay una oficina de correos cerca de aquí?/por aquí?

Now ask if there is a bank, a chemist's, a restaurant and a bar nearby.

YOU ARE HERE

4

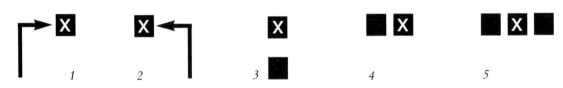

4 Match each symbol with the right set of directions.

1   2   3   4   5

a Aquí, a la derecha.
b Está entre el hotel y la oficina de Correos.
c Está enfrente del cine.
d Está al lado de la estación de Metro.
e Aquí a la izquierda.

5 Put the following items into the correct order to make sentences.

a El Museo Naval...

entre / está / la Calle Juan de Mena y la Calle de Montalbán / Paseo del Prado / en el

b Para ir a...

en la / Alicante / coja / de Atocha / el Talgo de / estación / las 13.30

c La oficina...

en la / está / Calle de Cervantes / de la compañía / a quince minutos andando.

Estación de Metro

6 Ask the appropriate questions.
a You want to take the underground.
b You want to find a taxi rank.
c You want to know where the railway station is.
d You want to know if Calle de Cervantes is far.

Helpline

When in Spain always try and get an up-to-date town plan because street names change quite often. By the way... the word **mapa** (*map*) is not feminine. You have to remember this exception to the rule and say **el mapa** or **un mapa, por favor**.

Public lavatories: the best ones are at hotels, cafeterias, restaurants and museums. Ask for **los servicios** or **los aseos**, eg **¿Los servicios, por favor?**

Voy a ir en coche.

When travelling by car, there are other directions you'll need to know how to ask and understand.

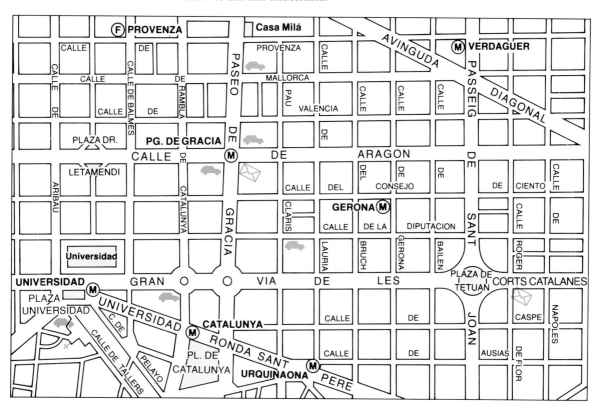

FRASES ➤ Voy a ir en coche   *I'm going to go by car*
Siga las señales de tráfico   *Follow the road signs*
A mano derecha   *On the right hand side*

Jane Carter has a meeting at an office in central Barcelona. She is travelling by car. She phones to ask for directions.

- ☛ What's the day and time of the meeting? Who's the meeting with?
- ☛ Where exactly is the office?
- ☛ Could Ms Carter use public transport to get there?

el aparcamiento   *car park*
la glorieta   *roundabout*
el piso   *floor, flat/apartment*
la señal de tráfico   *traffic sign*
muy cerca (de)   *very near (to)*
después   *after, later*
exactamente   *exactly*
en dirección a   *towards/ in the direction of*

Telefonista   Estudios Gaudí S.A. ¡Dígame!
Jane Carter   Buenas tardes. Mi nombre es Jane Carter, de Star Constructions Ltd., de Inglaterra. Tengo una cita el miércoles a las 10 de la mañana con la señora Berenguer. ¿Dónde está la oficina exactamente?

53

4

More directions vocabulary

el paso de peatones *pedestrian crossing*
la planta baja *ground floor*
el semáforo *traffic light*
la zona peatonal *pedestrian precinct*
alquilar *to rent, hire*
aparcar *to park*
telefonear *to telephone*
viajar *to travel*

Telefonista   Estamos en Gran Vía de les Corts Catalanes entre la Calle de Pau Claris y la Calle de Lauria, en el tercer piso, oficina número 302. Estamos muy cerca del Metro Passeig de Gracia.

Jane Carter   Voy a ir en coche.

Telefonista   ¡Ah, muy bien! Entonces siga las señales de tráfico para Gran Vía. Siga todo recto por Gran Vía en dirección a Plaza de Tetuán. Después de la glorieta de Gran Vía y Paseo de Gracia, la primera a la izquierda es la Calle de Pau Claris. A mano derecha, en la esquina de Pau Claris y Calle de la Diputación hay un aparcamiento.

Jane Carter   Perfecto. Muchas gracias.

Now look at the map of central Barcelona, listen to the dialogue again and follow the route Ms Carter will take.

INFRAESTRUCTURA ▶

(yo) voy   *I go*
(tú) vas   *you go*
(usted/él/ella) va   *you go, he/she/it goes*
(nosotros) vamos   *we go*
(vosotros) vais   *you go*
(ustedes/ellos/ellas/ustedes) van   *they/you go*

Ir a – to go to

Look at these examples:

> **Voy a España todos los años**   *I go to Spain every year*
> **Voy a España**   *I'm going to Spain*
> **Voy a ir a España**   *I'm going to go to Spain*

To talk about things you or your company are doing or are going to do, use: **Voy a…** (*I go/am going to…*) or **Vamos a** (*we go/are going to…*) followed by a verb, eg **Voy a ir en coche** (*I am going to go by car*), **Vamos a alquilar un coche** (*We are going to hire a car*).

Ir en – to go by

To say you are going somewhere *by* a particular means of transport use **ir en**, eg **¿Vamos en tren o en coche?**; **Voy a ir en coche**; **Va a ir a Vigo en Talgo.**

A (to/at), de (of/from), en (in/at/on/by)

Study the different uses of these three prepositions:

A – A las 10 (*at 10 o'clock*), **Voy a Madrid** (*I'm going to Madrid*), **Llego a Barcelona** (*I arrive at Barcelona*).

De – a nombre de… (*in the name of…*), **Salimos de Madrid** (*We leave from Madrid*), **a las 3 de la tarde** (*at 3 in the afternoon*).

En – Hay Correos en el aeropuerto (*There's a post office at the airport*), **El museo está en el centro** (*The museum's in the centre*), **¿Vamos en tren o en coche?** (*Are we going by train or by car?*), **Está en la esquina de la Calle Sol** (*It's on the corner of Calle Sol*).

54

5 **1** The head office of Banco de Sabadell is also in central Barcelona. Listen once more to the dialogue between an assistant from the Bank and a secretary from Tixa.

la sede central *central headquarters*

a On which day and at what time is the appointment?
b Where is the meeting going to take place?
c What's the address given?

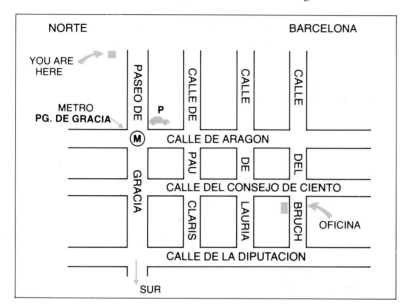

2 Still in Barcelona... You have to give someone directions to come from their office to your hotel. Look at the map and use the following expressions:
coja/coja usted/ siga/hacia (el sur; el norte)/ gire/el hotel está/ el hotel se llama...

3 Use a phrase from each of the three columns to make a complete sentence, eg **La secretaria va a cancelar la cita**.

a Yo	vas a alquilar	Torrevieja
b Mi cliente	va a cancelar	la cita
c Los socios	vais a reservar	un coche
d La secretaria	voy a llegar	una habitación
e Tú	vamos a ir a	tarde
f Marisa y yo	va a dejar	un contrato
g Vosotros	van a firmar	un recado

4 Fill in the blanks using **a**, **de** or **en**. Remember **a+el=al** and **de+el=del**.

a Vamos a salir.......aeropuerto......Teesside......las 8......la mañana, el 7.......junio y luego vamos a salir.......Heathrow el mismo día.......el vuelo BA 373.
b Vamos a llegar......aeropuerto.....Barajas.......las 6......la tarde.
c Vamos a viajar.......centro.....Madrid......taxi.
d El hotel está......Gran Vía. Tenemos reservada la habitación número 115...... el primer piso.

5 Match the symbols at the airport with the right word or expression.

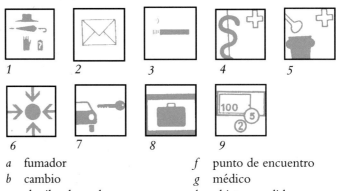

1   *2*   *3*   *4*   *5*

6   *7*   *8*   *9*

a fumador
b cambio
c alquiler de coches
d consigna
e correos

f punto de encuentro
g médico
h objetos perdidos
i farmacia

6 Look at the pictures and answer the questions with **Sí, se puede** or **No, no se puede**.
a ¿Se puede telefonear?
b ¿Se puede fumar?
c ¿Se puede aparcar?

7 Back in London... Some Spanish business people are coming to the UK to visit an exhibition at the National Hall, Olympia. You are on the phone to one of them and must explain, in Spanish, how to get to Olympia, eg **Se puede coger el autobús número 9** or **Coja el tren a...**
By train:
Kensington (Olympia) Station.
By tube:
Earl's Court, then Kensington (Olympia).
By bus: Nos 9, 10, 27, 28, 31, 49, 391
By car: Car park at Kings Mall, Hammersmith.

8 Here is your itinerary for your business trip to Spain. Explain what you'll be doing using **Voy a** + verb (**viajar/aplazar/confirmar/alquilar/salir/llegar/llamar**).

Monday - Madrid. Departure Heathrow 09.00 Arrival Barajas 12.20. Phone Porcelanas Denia S.A. Confirm appointment for Wednesday. Hire a car.
Friday - travel by car to Valencia. Go to trade fair (la feria).
Postpone appointment with Modern·Kitchens Ltd.

Necesito alquilar un coche

In this section you will learn how to hire a car in Spanish.

FRASES ➤

Necesitaría/Necesito alquilar un coche   *I need to hire a car*
¿Qué tipo de...?   *What type of...?*
¿Para cuánto tiempo sería?   *For how long?*
Por día   *Per day*
¿Esto incluye el kilometraje?   *Does this include mileage?*
¿Puedo dejar...?   *Can I leave...?*

Pilar Alvarez is going to hire a car. As you listen to the dialogue, find out what kind of car she hires and for how long. Which two documents does the clerk ask to see.

el aeropuerto   *airport*
el contrato   *contract*
el ocupante   *passenger*
el permiso de circulación/de conducir   *driving licence*
el seguro   *insurance*
la tarifa   *rate*
el vehículo   *vehicle*
cualquier/a   *any whatsoever*
ilimitado/a   *unlimited*
otro/a   *another, other*
pequeño/a   *small*
más   *plus*

Before listening again to the dialogue, check the vocabulary list and make a note of the main expressions used in this conversation.

Pilar Alvarez Buenas tardes.

Empleado   Hola, buenas tardes.

Pilar Alvarez Mire, necesitaría alquilar un coche.

Empleado   Sí. ¿Qué tipo de coche necesitaría?

Pilar Alvarez Pues yo creo que un coche pequeño.

Empleado   Un coche pequeño. ¿Para cuánto tiempo sería?

Pilar Alvarez Una semana.

Empleado   ¿Una semana?

Pilar Alvarez Voy a estar una semana en España.

Empleado   Bueno, tenemos una tarifa para una semana con kilometraje ilimitado ¿eh? Para un coche pequeño serían 6.200 pesetas por día, ¿eh? más los seguros que serían 1.250 pesetas por el seguro de accidentes del vehículo y 425 el seguro de ocupantes.

Pilar Alvarez ¿Esto incluye el kilometraje?

Empleado   Sí, sí, es ilimitado el kilometraje. Si permite, su pasaporte y permiso de circulación.

Pilar Alvarez Sí, yo tengo el permiso de circulación internacional. Aquí tiene mi pasaporte y mi permiso de conducir.

Empleado   Gracias. Muy bien, pues rellenamos un contrato y usted puede disponer del vehículo por una semana, ¿eh?

Listen again and answer these questions:
- How much is the basic rental charge?
- Will Pilar Alvarez have to pay a small charge per mile? If not, why not?

Read the next extract. What does Pilar Alvarez want to know about returning the car?

Pilar Alvarez ¿Puedo dejar el coche en otra ciudad de España?

Empleado   Sí, por supuesto. En cualquier punto de España.

Pilar Alvarez Entonces voy a dejar el coche en el aeropuerto de Alicante.

Empleado   Vale.

More motoring vocabulary
el cinturón (de seguridad)   *safety belt*
el cinturón de Madrid   *the Madrid ring road*
la hora punta   *rush hour*
conducir   *to drive*
¿A qué distancia está...?   *How far away is...?*
¿Cuál es la distancia?   *How far is it?*

4

Otro/otra

Otro/otra (*other, another*), like all adjectives, must agree with the word it refers to, ie singular or plural, masculine or feminine. Note that to say 'another', **otro/otra** are never preceded by the indefinite article, eg **(el) otro coche, (la) otra ciudad, (los) otros socios, (las) otras calles**.

PRACTICA ▶

1a Renting a car. Look at the list of car rental charges, decide which car you are going to rent and for how long. Then work out approximately how much it will cost you with insurance.

b What would you say to hire the car? Work out the dialogue.

2 Pilar Alvarez would like to avoid driving in Madrid during the rush hour. When is the rush hour in Madrid?

La hora punta

la salida *coming out*
el trabajo *work*
evitar *to avoid*

RENT SERVICES, S.L.

RENT A CAR

Luna, 21 - Tels. (972) 61.14.60 - 61.21.50
Cavallers, 17 - Telf. 30.48.00
Fax 61.03.97
17200 PALAFRUGELL (Gerona)

Tarifas

LISTA DE PRECIOS · PRICE LIST · PREIS LISTE · LISTE DES PRIX

Alquiler de Coches - Renting of Cars
Autovermietung - Locations de Voiture

Group	Seats	MODELO	1-2 Días Days per Day	Km	3-6 Días Days per Day	7 Días -Days or more per Day	Seguro Insurance per Day
A	4/5	Fiat Panda 1.0-	2.200	22	4.000	3.600	1.000
B	4/5	Panda Descapotable	2.400	23	4.200	3.800	1.000
C	4/5	Fiat Uno / Ford Fiesta 1.1 3P / Renault Super 5 / Citroën AX	2.500	24	4.500	4.100	1.000
D	4/5	Ford Fiesta 1.1 C 5 Puertas	2.800	26	4.700	4.300	1.200
E	5	Ford Orión 1.4	3.600	28	6.000	5.200	1.200
F	5	Renault 19 TR 5 Puertas	4.000	30	6.200	5.900	1.300
G	5	Renault 21 GTS (aire acondicionado) / Ford Sierra 2.0 CL	5.500	35	10.000	9.000	1.500

MINIBUSES

	9	Ford Kombi (Carnet de 2º)	7.500	35	14.000	10.000	2.000

FURGONETAS DE CARGA

	3	Ford Transit 100 L (sobreelevada) 10 m3	6.500	30	14.000	9.500	1.500

(UNLIMITED MILEAGE)

58

El Bonocity

los días azules   *'blue days'*
el interventor   *inspector*
la plaza   *seat (in train, etc.)*
la tarjeta   *card*
mostrar   *to show*
presentar   *to show, present*
en ruta   *on route*

 Renfe offers different types of discounts to commuters and those who, for business and other reasons, have to cover long distances by train throughout Spain on a regular basis.

The Bonocity is a card which offers passengers a few thousand train miles at a reasonable discount price.

1 Read this information leaflet about the Bonocity card and answer the following questions.
a How much does it cost?
b Which class do you travel by?
c Which route does it apply to?
d Can it be used on 'Blue Days'?
e On which two occasions do you have to show your Bonocity card?

UNO, DOS, TRES Y CUATRO

Por sólo 8.000 Ptas., el Bonocity le permitirá realizar hasta cuatro veces el trayecto Madrid-Valencia, ida ó vuelta, en la fecha que ud. decida -antes del 31 de Diciembre- en cualquiera de los trenes que se determinen y efectúen este recorrido, pudiendo viajar en plazas sentadas de 2ª clase.

AZUL, ROJO Y BLANCO

No hay color.
Utilizando el Bonocity ud. puede viajar en las fechas que quiera, beneficiándose de las ventajas de esta tarjeta, independientemente de los colores del calendario Renfe-Días Azules, Días Rojos, Días Blancos.

LO PRIMERO ES LO PRIMERO

Antes de iniciar el viaje, deberá reservar su plaza, sin cargo alguno, en los puntos de venta de billetes presentando su tarjeta Bonocity.

• Ya en ruta, deberá mostrar al interventor su Bonocity junto con el billete.

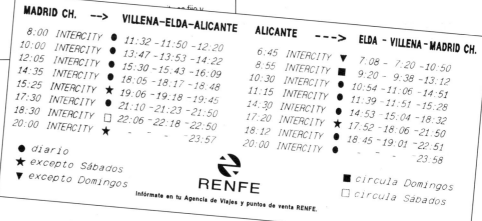

2 Now look at the Intercity and Bonocity timetable and answer the following in Spanish.
a ¿Se puede viajar de Madrid a Alicante todos los días en el tren de las 8.00?
b ¿Qué día no se puede viajar de Alicante a Madrid en el tren de las 6.45?
c ¿Se puede viajar el domingo en el tren de las 18.30 de Madrid a Alicante?

Inventario

Finding your way around
Perdone   *Excuse me*
¿Dónde está la estación del Metro?
   Where is the tube station?
¿Dónde están los taxis?   *Where are the taxis?*
Coja la primera calle a la derecha
   Take the first street on the right
Siga todo recto/derecho   *Continue straight ahead*
Gire a la izquierda   *Turn to the left*
Está aquí/allí   *It's here/there*
Está en la plaza   *It's in the square*
Está en el norte   *It's in the north*
¿Está lejos/cerca?   *Is it far/near?*
¿Para ir a...?   *How do I get to...?*
¿Hay un autobús/metro/tren?   *Is there a bus/tube train/train?*

Talking about your itinerary
Voy a Barcelona   *I'm going to Barcelona*
Voy a ir en coche/tren   *I'm going to go by car/train*
Voy a llegar a las diez   *I'm going to arrive at ten o'clock*

Hiring a car
Necesito/necesitaría alquilar un coche   *I need to rent a car*
¿Qué tipo de coche?   *What type of car?*
¿Para cuánto tiempo?   *For how long?*
¿Es ilimitado el kilometraje?   *Is it unlimited mileage?*

Punto de control

Check you can do these things in Spanish:
- Ask someone how to get to Puerta del Sol.
- Tell someone to turn left, then right, then go straight ahead.
- Ask if it is the second street on the left.
- Ask directions to go to the city centre by car.
- Say something is in the north/south/east/west.
- Say you want to hire a car.
- Say the following in Spanish
  'I am going to Barcelona on Thursday 4 June – I'm going to leave Heathrow at 09.25 on flight BA 231 – I have an appointment with Sra Elvira Sánchez on Friday 5 June at 10.00.'

Desplazamientos

Spain has, since the mid-1980's, invested massively to overhaul its communications and the dramatic improvement of the domestic transport infrastructure, paid for in part by the European Community funds, cannot be overstated. New highways and outer-city ring roads, high-speed train links and revamped airports have utterly transformed the whole business of getting around Spain.

It is now possible to drive without encountering a traffic light from the town of Almonte, which borders Portugal's Algarve, to the French frontier at La Junquera in the foothills of the Pyrenees. Distances can, however, be long and that particular drive which crosses Spain diagonally from the south-west to the north-east, involves some 850 miles. Experienced business travellers in Spain would not dream of driving between these two points: they would combine hired cars with planes and with trains.

The hiring of a car in Spain is as problem-free as it is elsewhere in Western Europe and North America. The main multinational hire firms, along with domestic ones, are stationed at airports and main railway stations as well as in city centres. Just about the only difference is that Spanish hire rates are comparatively higher and that, usually, there are savings to be made by booking cars and paying for them in advance before travelling to Spain.

Experienced travellers who wanted to cross Spain diagonally, and as quickly as possible, from the north-east to the south-west would drive from the French frontier to Barcelona where they would take a shuttle flight, or Puente Aereo, to Madrid. They would then travel from Madrid to Seville on the bullet train which is known as the AVE, and finally hire a second car for the 90-minute drive to Almonte and the Portuguese border.

Despite the good motorway which links Madrid and Barcelona via Zaragoza, the well-established Puente Aereo shuttle is the umbilical cord that links Spain's two main cities. There are flights every hour, every half hour at peak times, and the planes, flying in either direction, are normally packed out in the early mornings and late evenings.

Madrid and Seville are also now well linked by road, as well as by air, but the AVE bullet train, which provides several services a day and covers the distance in little more than two hours, has become the natural choice for those travelling from one city to the other. When check-in times and airport to city centre travel times are accounted for, the AVE is faster than the plane and considerably cheaper.

The success of the Madrid-Seville AVE link has spurred plans to extend the bullet train network from Madrid to Barcelona and to Bilbao, in a move which will further undermine the domestic air travel routes. Business travellers visiting Bilbao from Madrid can at present choose between several regular flights a day, moderately fast inter-city rail services and travelling by car. Links between Madrid and Valencia, Spain's third-ranked city, are similar to those between the capital and Bilbao.

Business travellers who intend to drive around Spain should note the difference between an *autovía*, a dual lane highway, and an *autopista*, a motorway which may, although not always, have three or more lanes. An autovia, such as the one linking Madrid and Seville, is free, while an autopista, such as the Mediterranean coast link between Barcelona and Valencia, charges a toll.

Once in a city, travellers should forget about driving themselves around. Inner-city traffic can be hair-raising and parking is a major problem in every big town. Taxis are cheap, and also plentiful, by European standards; buses are normally efficient and Madrid and Barcelona have good, as well as safe, metro systems. Even in large cities such as Madrid and Barcelona, business appointments are often within reasonable walking distance from each other.

5

¡A COMER!

Ordering food and drink ◆ Spanish cuisine
◆ Inviting people to a meal ◆ Making conversation

¿Qué van a tomar?

In this section you will learn how to order food and drink.

¿Qué va(n) a tomar (usted(es))?   *What are you going to have?*
Para mí...   *For me...*
¿Qué tapas hay?   *What snacks/tapas are there?*
Una ración de...   *A portion of...*
¿Para usted?   *For you?*
¿Cuál es el menú del día?   *What's the fixed menu?*
¿Para beber?   *What are you going to drink?*

Pilar Alvarez and Louise Taylor are in a tapas bar. What's Srta Alvarez going to eat and drink? Does Ms Taylor order the same things?

las aceitunas	*olives*
los calamares	*squid*
los champiñones	*mushrooms*
el chorizo	*spicy sausage*
el fino	*dry sherry*
las gambas	*prawns*
el jamón serrano	*traditional cured ham*
el jamón de York	*cooked ham*
la patata	*potato*
las patatas alioli	*potato salad in garlic mayonnaise*
el queso	*cheese*
la tortilla de patatas	*potato omelette*
el vermú	*vermouth*
frito/a	*fried*

Camarero   Buenas tardes. ¿Qué van a tomar?
Pilar Alvarez   Un fino, por favor.
Louise Taylor   Para mí, un vermú.
Camarero   Muy bien.
Pilar Alvarez   ¿Qué tapas hay?
Camarero   Patatas, chorizo, jamón serrano, jamón de York, queso, gambas, calamares fritos, champiñones, aceitunas...
Pilar Alvarez   ¿Qué patatas hay?
Camarero   Patatas alioli y tortilla de patatas.
Pilar Alvarez   Una ración de tortilla, por favor.
Camarero   ¿Para usted?
Louise Taylor   Unas patatas alioli.

Ben Smith and Elvira Sánchez are at the local restaurant, ready to order lunch. The waitress forgets to mention one item on the

el agua mineral	*mineral water*
el ajo	*garlic*
la botella	*bottle*
la ensalada mixta	*mixed salad*
la fruta	*fruit*
la fruta del tiempo	*fruit in season*
el pescado	*fish*
el pollo	*chicken*
la sopa	*soup*
la sopa juliana	*vegetable soup*
el vino blanco	*white wine*
el vino de la casa	*house wine*
asado/a	*roast*
con gas	*fizzy*

menu. Which one? What do Ben and Elvira decide to have for lunch?

Camarera   Buenas tardes. ¿Qué van a tomar?

Elvira Sánchez ¿Cuál es el menú del día?

Camarera   Sopa juliana o sopa de ajo; ensalada mixta; pescado frito o pollo asado con patatas. Fruta del tiempo.

Elvira Sánchez Vale. Para mí, sopa de ajo y pescado frito.

Camarera   Muy bien.

Ben Smith   ¿Hay tortilla española?

Camarera   Sí, hay.

Ben Smith   Entonces, la tortilla y una ensalada mixta para mí.

Camarera   ¿Para beber?

Ben Smith   (To Elvira) ¿Vino blanco?

Elvira Sánchez Sí, vino blanco. (To Ben) ¿De la casa?

Ben Smith   Sí, vale.

Elvira Sánchez Y una botella de agua mineral con gas.

INFRAESTRUCTURA ➤

Calamares

¿Me pone...? ¿Me da...? ¿Me sirve...?

Use these expressions in bars and restaurants to ask *Can I have...?* or *Could I have...?* **Pone** and **sirve** are the forms used for **usted** (the polite *you*) of the verbs **poner** (*to put*) and **servir** (*to serve*).

These expressions are similar in their construction to those you've already met in Unit 2: **¿Me deja...?, ¿Me llama...?** (See page 151).

You can also say **Quisiera** (*I'd like...*), eg **Quisiera un vino blanco, por favor** (*I'd like a white wine, please*).

Unos/unas

The plural of **un/una** (*a, an, one*) is **unos/unas**, meaning *some*, eg **unas gambas** (*some prawns*), **Unas aceitunas por favor** (*Some olives, please*).

¿Cómo lo quiere?

You will sometimes be asked how you'd like your food cooked: **¿Cómo lo quiere? ¿Cómo la quiere? ¿Cómo los quiere? ¿Cómo las quiere? Lo** replaces a masculine noun; **la** replaces a feminine noun; **los/las** replace masculine and feminine nouns in the plural. These are called object pronouns (see page 151). They are used when you and the person you are talking to already know the object you are talking about. These pronouns usually come in front of the verb, eg

    – **Para mí, el pescado, por favor.**

    – **¿Cómo lo quiere?** (**lo** refers to **el pescado**).

    – **Lo quiero frito.**

5

The diminutive – -ito/-ita

You have already met **Un momentit**o (*Just a minute!*) in Unit 3. To form the diminutive, add **-ito/-ita** to a noun or adjective, eg **el plato – el platito, la botella – la botellita**.

In Spanish, as in English, the diminutive is to show the smallness of something or to emphasize its goodness, quality or particularly pleasing characteristics, eg **una manzanita** (*a nice little apple*).

PRACTICA ➤

1 How would these customers order at the tapas bar ? eg **¿Me pone una ración de calamares**?

Main Courses

los mariscos *shellfish*
las almejas *clams*
los boquerones *kind of anchovy*
los calamares *squid*
el camarón *shrimp*
las cigalas *larger type of prawn*
las gambas *prawns*
la langosta *lobster*
los langostinos *crayfish*
los mejillones *mussels*

los pescados *fish*
el atún *tuna*
el bacalao *cod*
el besugo *sea bream*
el dorado *dorado*
el lenguado *sole*
la merluza *hake*
el mero *grouper*
la pescadilla *whiting*
el rape *angler*
el rodaballo *turbot*
las sardinas *sardines*
el salmón *salmon*

los espetitos *small kebabs*
lo típico de aquí *the local speciality*
de primero *for first course*
de segundo *for second course*
para la espalda *boned*
a la plancha *grilled*
aliñadito/a *nicely dressed*
grande *big*
el perejil *parsley*

a José likes traditional Spanish ham. *b* Juanita likes seafood.
c Elena is a vegetarian. *d* Ramón loves spicy sausage and mushrooms.

2 You're in the same tapas bar with three non-Spanish speakers.
a Order some tapas for them. Use: **para el señor/para la señora/para la señorita**. *b* Now decide what you are going to have. *c* Order drinks for the four of you.

3 These customers are ready to order their meal.
a Listen for the question: **¿Qué nos recomienda**? What do you think it means?
b The waiter mentions three types of fish: **dorado, rodaballo, lenguado**. Check the vocabulary list and find out what they are.
c What kinds of seafood does the waiter suggest?

La sirena del mar
Restaurante

Servicio e IVA incluído

SOPAS Y ENTREMESES

ESPARRAGOS
asparagus
ENSALADA MIXTA
mixed salad
ENSALADA DE MARISCOS
seafood salad
ENTREMESES VARIADOS
mixed cold meats
SOPA DE PESCADO
fish soup
SOPA DE AJO
garlic soup
SOPA JULIANA
vegetable soup
GAZPACHO
gazpacho
TORTILLA ESPAÑOLA
Spanish omelette

PLATOS PRINCIPALES

PAELLA VALENCIANA
paella
COCIDO
stew
MERLUZA A LA ROMANA
fried hake
POLLO FRITO
fried chicken
BISTEC A LA PLANCHA
grilled steak
RIÑONES AL JEREZ
kidneys braised in sherry
CHULETAS DE CORDERO
lamb chops

LEGUMBRES Y VERDURAS

PATATAS FRITAS
chips
PURÉ DE PATATAS
mashed potato
JUDIAS VERDES
green beans

POSTRES

FRUTA DEL TIEMPO
fruit of the season
MACEDONIA DE FRUTAS
fruit salad
HELADO
ice cream
FLAN
crème caramel

* * * * * * *

BEBIDAS

VINO BLANCO
white wine
VINO TINTO
red wine
VINO ROSADO
rosé wine
CERVEZA
beer
AGUA MINERAL CON GAS/SIN GAS
mineral water fizzy/still
CAFÉ SOLO
black coffee
CAFÉ CON LECHE
white coffee

4 Order your meal at this restaurant. Study the menu and then complete the dialogue.

Camarero Buenas tardes. ¿Qué va a tomar?
Usted (Say good evening, then choose a starter.)
Camarero Sí. ¿Y de segundo?
Usted (Tell him what you're going to have as a main course.)
Camarero ¿Para beber?
Usted (Choose something to drink.)
Camarero Vale. ¿Agua mineral?
Usted (Yes, order water too, and specify either still or carbonated.)

5 A group of friends are eating out: José, Julia, Manolo, Francisco and Teresa. Everyone wants their food prepared differently. Choose from **el bistec**; **las gambas**; **el pescado**; **las chuletas de cordero**, and then complete each dialogue with **lo/la/los/las**.

a José Para mí ....
Camarero ¿Cómo .... quiere?
José .... quiero a la plancha.

b Julia Para mí ....
Camarero ¿Cómo .... quiere?
Julia .... quiero al ajillo.

c Make up similar dialogues between Manolo, Francisco, Teresa and the waiter. Practise with a fellow student if possible.

¿Cómo lo quiere?

a la parrilla/plancha *grilled*	bien hecho/a *well done*
asado/a *roast*	poco hecho/a *rare*
frito/a *fried*	en su punto *medium*
guisado/a *stewed*	al ajillo *in garlic*
hervido/a *boiled*	en salsa *with a sauce*
rebozado/a *in batter*	

5

¿Qué nos recomienda?

This section is about food from the different regions of Spain.

FRASES ▶

¿Qué nos recomienda?   *What do you recommend?*
Para mí también   *For me too*
Yo prefiero...   *I prefer...*

el arroz   *rice*
el bacalao a la vizcaína
    cod Biscay style
el cliente   *client*
un plato típico   *a local dish*
un plato vegetariano   *a
    vegetarian dish*
un plato de vigilia   *a meatless
    dish*
el potaje   *stew*
la selección   *selection*
verde   *green*

Special needs
sin sal, por favor   *no salt, please*
sin ajo/cebolla, por favor   *no
    garlic/onion, please*
Estoy a dieta   *I am on a diet*
Soy vegetariano/a   *I am a
    vegetarian*
Lo siento, no me gusta el/la....
    sorry, I don't like....
¿Tiene algún plato sin carne?
    *Are there any dishes without
    meat?*

Other essential ingredients:
el aceite de oliva   *olive oil*
la pimienta   *pepper*
el pimiento   *capiscum*
el tomate   *tomato*
el vinagre   *vinegar*

Four business people are at the Restaurante Savoy, in Bilbao. Listen to their conversation with the waiter.

➡ What does merluza en salsa verde consist of?
➡ How does the second client like his steak?

Camarero   ¿Qué les puedo servir?
Cliente 1   ¿Qué nos recomienda?
Camarero   Les puedo recomendar el bacalao a la vizcaína, o un plato típico del País Vasco: la merluza en salsa verde.
Cliente 1   ¿Qué es eso?
Camarero   Merluza con ajo en salsa de perejil.
Cliente 1   Muy bien. Para mí, la merluza.
Cliente 2   ¿Hay bistec?
Camarero   Sí, señora.
Cliente 2   Entonces, para mí, el bistec. En su punto.
Cliente 3   Para mí también. Yo prefiero el bistec poco hecho, por favor.
Camarero   La señora, ¿qué va a tomar?
Cliente 4   ¿Tiene algún plato vegetariano o de vigilia?
Camarero   Sí. Tenemos arroz, potaje de vigilia con o sin pescado y una selección de verduras.
Cliente 4   Perfecto. Voy a tomar el arroz y las verduras.

Did you know?
If you want a non-meat dish, you can ask for **un plato de vigilia**. These dishes (which may include fish) are traditionally served at times of religious fasting such as Lent. Even outside these times, the expression **vigilia** will help make it clear that you want a non-meat dish.

INFRAESTRUCTURA ▶

Con/sin
Con and **sin** mean *with* and *without*, eg **con patatas**; **sin gas**.

Me/nos, le/les
To ask the waiter or waitress for their recommendation say: **¿Qué me/nos recomienda?** (*What do you recommend [to me/us]?*). The waiter or waitress will reply: **Le recomiendo...** if you are alone or **Les recomiendo...** if there is a group of you. **Me**, **nos**, **le**, and **les** are object pronouns; see page 151.

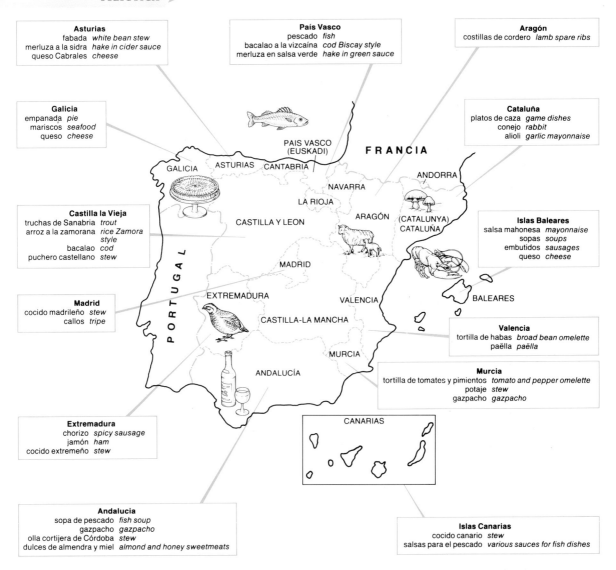

Asturias
fabada *white bean stew*
merluza a la sidra *hake in cider sauce*
queso Cabrales *cheese*

País Vasco
pescado *fish*
bacalao a la vizcaína *cod Biscay style*
merluza en salsa verde *hake in green sauce*

Aragón
costillas de cordero *lamb spare ribs*

Galicia
empanada *pie*
mariscos *seafood*
queso *cheese*

Cataluña
platos de caza *game dishes*
conejo *rabbit*
alioli *garlic mayonnaise*

Castilla la Vieja
truchas de Sanabria *trout*
arroz a la zamorana *rice Zamora style*
bacalao *cod*
puchero castellano *stew*

Islas Baleares
salsa mahonesa *mayonnaise*
sopas *soups*
embutidos *sausages*
queso *cheese*

Madrid
cocido madrileño *stew*
callos *tripe*

Valencia
tortilla de habas *broad bean omelette*
paëlla *paëlla*

Murcia
tortilla de tomates y pimientos *tomato and pepper omelette*
potaje *stew*
gazpacho *gazpacho*

Extremadura
chorizo *spicy sausage*
jamón *ham*
cocido extremeño *stew*

Andalucia
sopa de pescado *fish soup*
gazpacho *gazpacho*
olla cortijera de Córdoba *stew*
dulces de almendra y miel *almond and honey sweetmeats*

Islas Canarias
cocido canario *stew*
salsas para el pescado *various sauces for fish dishes*

GALICIA ASTURIAS CANTABRIA PAIS VASCO (EUSKADI) FRANCIA ANDORRA NAVARRA LA RIOJA CASTILLA Y LEON ARAGÓN (CATALUNYA) CATALUÑA PORTUGAL MADRID EXTREMADURA CASTILLA-LA MANCHA VALENCIA BALEARES MURCIA ANDALUCÍA CANARIAS

A sales rep is visiting different regions in Spain. She'd like to try the local specialities. What would she ask the waiter in each case, and how would he reply?

a   In Asturias she'd like some fish.
b   In Valencia she'd like something typical other than paella.
c   In Extremadura she'd like a local stew.
d   In Andalucia she'd like a soup, but not gazpacho.

67

5   Sí, gracias.

This section is about invitations, booking a table, and paying the bill.

FRASES ▶

¿Quiere(n) tomar una copa con nosotros?   *Would you like to have a drink with us?*
No, gracias/Sí, gracias   *No, thank you/Yes, please*
¿Quiere(n) cenar con nosotros?   *Would you like to have dinner with us?*
Muy amable   *Very kind of you*
Voy a buscarle   *I'll pick you up*
De acuerdo   *OK*
Quisiera reservar una mesa   *I'd like to book a table*
Para el próximo jueves   *For next Thursday*
La cuenta, por favor   *The bill, please*
¿Me la pone en la cuenta del hotel?   *Would you put it on my hotel bill?*

Louise Taylor can't go for a drink with Pilar Alvarez. Why not?

Pilar Alvarez   ¿Quiere tomar una copa con nosotros?
Louise Taylor   No, gracias. Lo siento. Tengo una reunión.

Pablo Suárez invites Louise Taylor to dinner. Where are they going to eat? What time are they going to meet?

Pablo Suárez   ¿Quiere cenar con nosotros?
Louise Taylor   Sí, gracias. Muy amable.

Pablo Suárez   Tenemos una mesa reservada en el restaurante Cádiz. Voy a buscarle a las nueve.
Louise Taylor   De acuerdo.

Listen to Ben Smith booking a table at his hotel restaurant.

Ben Smith   Buenas tardes. Quisiera reservar una mesa, por favor.
Camarero   ¿Para qué día?
Ben Smith   Para el próximo jueves.
Camarero   ¿Para cuántas personas?
Ben Smith   Para tres personas, por favor.
Camarero   ¿Para qué hora?
Ben Smith   Para las nueve y media.
Camarero   ¿A nombre de quién?
Ben Smith   Ben Smith.
Camarero   ¿Habitación número...?
Ben Smith   Trescientos ventiuno.
Camarero   Muy bien. Muchas gracias.
Ben Smith   Gracias. Adiós.

¿Verdad o mentira?
Ben Smith wants a table for five.
His room number is 231.

Towards the end of the meal... How does Ben pay?

Ben Smith La cuenta, por favor.
Camarero Sí señor. Un momento.
Ben Smith ¿Me la pone en la cuenta del hotel, por favor?
Camarero Muy bien.

INFRAESTRUCTURA ➤

Para

One of the meanings of **para** is *for* and it is used in expressions such as: **Para mí, una copa de vino**; **Para mí también**.

When you want to book a table (**una mesa**) at a restaurant and you are asked **¿Para cuántas personas?** (*For how many people?*) you can say **Para dos/tres/cuatro,** etc. **personas.**

PRACTICA ➤

1 You wish to invite your Spanish partners to a bar or restaurant. Ask the following in Spanish:

a Would you like to have a drink with us?

b Would you like to have dinner with us?

2 Book a table at your hotel restaurant. Make up the dialogue between you and the waiter, choosing from the following information:

a table for four; for next Tuesday; for nine o'clock; name; room 167.

b table for five; for next Saturday; for half past nine; name; room 203.

3 Listen to Sr Arango talking about the success of VIPS restaurants.

a When are the restaurants open?

b Explain in English the menu they offer at VIPS.

c What else do they offer apart from a good menu?

el aire acondicionado *air conditioning*
el ambiente *atmosphere*
la limpieza *cleanliness*
la madrugada *early morning*
incluir *to include*
muy poco dinero *very little money*

5

¿Conoce España?

Practising the art of mealtime conversation!

FRASES ➤

¿De dónde es?   *Where are you from?*
¿Conoce España?   *Have you been to Spain before?*
¿Qué tal el arroz?   *How's the rice?*
¿Qué le gusta más?   *What do you like best?*
¿Un poco más?   *Would you like some more?*
He comido bien   *I've had plenty*
¿Viaja mucho?   *Do you travel a lot?*
Por toda Europa   *All over Europe*
¿Qué tal los negocios?   *How's business?*

¡Salud y Pesetas!

Health and wealth!
[traditional toast]

Ben Smith and Louise Taylor are having dinner
with their Spanish business associate, José Moreno.

José Moreno   ¿Conoce España?
Louise Taylor   No, no conozco España. Esta es mi primera visita.
José Moreno   ¿Y usted, Sr Smith?
Ben Smith   Sí. Conozco Madrid, Barcelona, Valencia y Vigo.
José Moreno   ¿De dónde es usted?
Ben Smith   Soy de Sheffield pero vivo y trabajo en Londres.
José Moreno   ¿Y usted?
Louise Taylor   Yo soy de Londres. ¿Conoce Londres?

¿Verdad o mentira?
➤ This is not Ben Smith's first visit to Spain.
➤ Ben Smith is from London.
➤ Louise Taylor has been to Valencia and Vigo.

¡Buen provecho!

Enjoy your meal!

What's Ms Taylor eating? What's Mr Smith's favourite Spanish dish?

Louise Taylor   Las verduras están muy buenas.
José Moreno   ¿Qué tal el arroz a la zamorana?
Louise Taylor   Muy bueno, también.
José Moreno   ¿Le gusta la cocina española, Señor Smith?
Ben Smith   Sí, me gusta bastante.
José Moreno   ¿Qué le gusta más?
Ben Smith   Me gusta la paella; me gustan los mariscos...
José Moreno   ¿Un poco más?
Ben Smith   No, gracias. He comido bien.
José Moreno   ¿Un postre, entonces?

el postre   *dessert*
el tiempo   *weather*
conocer   *to know, to have visited*
me gusta(n)...   *I like...*
le gusta(n)...?   *do you like...?*
bastante   *quite a lot*

70

A little later... Where is Ben Smith going the following Monday?

José Moreno ¿Viaja mucho?

Ben Smith Sí, viajo bastante.

José Moreno ¿Por España?

Ben Smith Sí. Por toda Europa. Viajo bastante a Francia y a Alemania. El viernes próximo voy a ir a París y el lunes voy a ir a Francfort.

José Moreno ¿Qué tal los negocios?

Ben Smith Bastante bien.

Did you know?

The Spanish prefer to do business with people they get on well with personally. The best place to establish a good social and business relationship is at the dinner table, where general conversation about topics such as family, sports and interests is very important. The Spanish do not think of this as being just small talk. Instead, it gives them a profile of the visiting businessman or woman which can, in the long run, be just as important as a good cv.

Remember that heavy smoking in bars and restaurants is quite normal in most Mediterranean countries.

Remember also that a business lunch in Spain can take most of the afternoon. If you're using a parking meter, make sure that you put enough money in it for several hours!

INFRAESTRUCTURA ➤ **Me/le/te gusta(n)...**

To express likes and dislikes, use **Me gusta** (*I like it*) or **No me gusta** (*I don't like it*) and **Me gustan** (*I like them*) or **No me gustan** (*I don't like them*). These expressions translate literally as *It/they please(s) me* and *It/they do(es) not please me*, **Me gusta el arroz**, **No me gusta la merluza**; **Me gustan las gambas**, **No me gustan los pimientos**.

Me gusta can also be followed by a verb to say what you like doing, eg **Me gusta jugar al fútbol** (*I like playing football*).

If someone wants to know if you like something you'll be asked: **¿Le gusta...?** (one thing); **¿Le gustan...?** (two or more things), eg **¿Le gusta beber vino? ¿Le gustan los mariscos?** When using the familiar from **tú**, **le** becomes **te**, eg **¿Te gusta...?**; **¿Te gustan...?**

5

Question words
¿Qué...? (*What/How...?*), eg **¿A qué hora?** (*At what time?*); **¿Dónde...?** (*Where...?*); **¿De dónde...?** (*Where... from?*); **¿Cuál...?** (*What...?*), eg **¿Cuál es su nombre?**; **¿Cómo?...** (*How/What...?*), eg **¿Cómo se escribe?**, **¿Cómo se llama?**

Trabajar, comer, vivir
These and all verbs in Spanish end in one of three ways: **-ar**, **-er** or **-ir**

Verbs can be regular or irregular. Regular verbs in the present tense follow the pattern shown below. In each case, **–ar/–er/–ir** is removed and replaced by an individual ending. See page 152 for more on verbs.

-ar trabajar		-er comer		-ir vivir	
trabaj**o**	*I work*	com**o**	*I eat*	viv**o**	*I live*
trabaj**as**	*you work*	com**es**	*you eat*	viv**es**	*you live*
trabaj**a**	*you/he/she works*	com**e**	*you/he/she eats*	viv**e**	*you/he/she lives*
trabaj**amos**	*we work*	com**emos**	*we eat*	viv**imos**	*we live*
trabaj**áis**	*you work*	com**éis**	*you eat*	viv**ís**	*you live*
trabaj**an**	*you/they work*	com**en**	*you/they eat*	viv**en**	*you/they live*

PRACTICA ➤

1 Talk about yourself. Use these phrases:
– Me llamo (name)
– Soy (nationality)
– Soy de (place of origin)
– Tengo (age)
– Trabajo en (name of the company)
– Soy (job title)
– Vivo en (town and country)
– Me gusta(n) (name your favourite dish(es))
– Me gusta beber (name your favourite drinks)
– Viajo (a lot/a little, in Europe, elsewhere – see Countries, page 159)

2 Now describe a colleague in the same way:
– El/Ella se llama (name)
– Es de (place of origin)
– Vive en (town and country)
– Trabaja en (name of the company)
– Viaja a (Spain or elsewhere)
– Le gusta(n) (sports, interests, Spanish food, etc.)

Los platos Placer de Campofrío

A good dictionary will be an invaluable companion. But don't look up *every* word you don't know, just select words you think are crucial or ones that you keep coming across – and so probably are important.

In this advert, Campofrío present their new range of ready-made meals. Read the advert and find:

a   Three (or more) of the dishes mentioned.
b   Three (or more) features listed to attract the buyer.
c   The cooking method used by Campofrío.
d   Two ways of preparing the dishes for eating.

el buen gusto   *good taste*
los calamares en su tinta
    squid cooked in their ink
la cazuela de pollo   *chicken casserole*
los colorantes   *colourings*
los conservantes
    preservatives
el estofado de perdiz
    partridge hot pot, stew
el frigorífico   *refrigerator*
la guarnición   *garnish*
el microondas   *microwave oven*
los pimientos (de piquillo)
    rellenos   *small stuffed peppers*
aderezar   *to prepare, garnish*
congelar   *to freeze*
elaborar   *to prepare*
a la jardinera   *with vegetables*
al baño María   *steamed*
cocinado al vacío   *vacuum cooked*
destacado   *distinguished*
innovador   *innovative*
al lado de   *at the side of*

No tienes nada que hacer means two things: *You have nothing to do* and also *You can't compete.* The last line of the article means *You needn't lift a finger because Ramón Roteta has done all the work for you.*

AL LADO DE RAMON ROTETA NO TIENES NADA QUE HACER.

Ramón Roteta.
Premio Nacional de la Crítica Gastronómica al Cocinero más Creativo.

Ramón Roteta es uno de los más destacados Chefs de la Nueva Cocina Vasca. Tiene, además del Premio de la Crítica Gastronómica, otros reconocimientos internacionales de gran prestigio. Y es quien ha elaborado los nuevos platos de la Cocina Placer de Campofrío. Calamares en su tinta. Estofado de perdiz al aroma de Jerez. Osso-Buco a la Jardinera. Lomos de salmón al vino blanco. Pimientos de piquillo rellenos de bacalao. Cazuela de pollo a la campesina. Seis especialidades aderezadas con el buen gusto y la imaginación propias de un gran Chef. Son naturales. Sin conservantes ni colorantes. En raciones individuales. Con ingredientes de primera calidad. Y con la guarnición más adecuada.

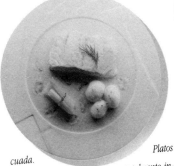

Platos cocinados siguiendo un proceso totalmente innovador. Al vacío. Para mantener todas sus vitaminas y minerales. Para poder conservarlos en el frigorífico. Sin congelar. Y por supuesto, fáciles y rápidos de preparar. Unos minutos en el microondas o al baño maría, y ya están listos para servir. Por eso, permítenos una sugerencia. Si hoy quieres disfrutar del sabor de la cocina más exquisita, no tienes nada que hacer, Ramón Roteta te lo da hecho.

Cocina Placer

73

5

Ordering food and drink

¿Qué tapas hay?   *What tapas are there?*

Para mí (también)...   *For me (too)...*

Yo prefiero...   *I prefer...*

¿Qué van a tomar?   *What are you going to have?*

¿Cuál es el menú del día?   *What's the fixed menu?*

¿Qué nos recomienda?   *What do you recommend?*

¿Cómo lo quiere?   *How would you like it?*

Offering, accepting and refusing an invitation

¿Quiere(n) tomar una copa con nosotros?   *Would you like to have a drink with us?*

¿Quiere(n) cenar con nosotros?   *Would you like to have dinner with us?*

Sí, gracias/No, gracias   *Yes, thank you/No, thank you*

Booking a table

Quisiera reservar una mesa   *I'd like to book a table*

Para el jueves   *For Thursday*

Para tres personas   *For three people*

Para las nueve   *For nine o'clock*

Paying the bill

La cuenta, por favor   *The bill, please*

¿Me lo pone en la cuenta, por favor?   *Can you put it on my bill, please?*

Making conversation

¿Conoce España?   *Have you been to Spain before?*

Conozco Madrid   *I've been to Madrid*

¿De dónde es?   *Where are you from?*

Soy de...   *I'm from...*

¿Dónde vive?   *Where do you live?*

Vivo en...   *I live in...*

¿Tiene hijos?   *Have you got any children?*

¿Viaja mucho?   *Do you travel a lot?*

Sí, viajo bastante   *Yes, I travel quite a lot/a fair amount*

¿Qué tal los negocios?   *How's business?*

¿Le gusta(n)...?   *Do you like...?*

Me gusta(n)...   *I like...*

No me gusta(n)...   *I don't like...*

Me gusta jugar al fútbol   *I like playing football*

¿Qué tal la merluza?   *How's the hake?*

He comido bien.   *I've had plenty. That was fine*

Punto de Control

Make sure you can do the following in Spanish:
- Ask the waiter or waitress what he/she recommends.
- Say that you don't want any salt/garlic/onion..
- Ask for a vegetarian dish.
- Offer, accept or refuse an invitation to a drink or a meal.
- Book a table and ask for the bill.
- Say: your name; where you come from; where you live; how frequently you travel abroad and what your interests are.
- Name a few Spanish dishes and give a favourite of yours.

A comer

The visitor seeking to do business in Spain will need a strong stomach and a stronger head. Business lunches and dinners are misnomers in Spain, for meals right across the country acquire banquet-type proportions. Efficient, low-calorie food, washed down with mineral water, will not impress potential Spanish clients or partners. Food is a serious celebration that should be appreciated and enjoyed.

The sheer volume of food in Spain will be the visitor's first surprise. Its variety and novelty will be the second. The visitor is likely to find the drinking customs - from aperitifs through to liqueurs by way of different wines - demanding and will certainly be disconcerted by the timing of Spain's eating rituals. British visitors will find themselves halfway through a Spanish lunch when at home they would be having afternoon tea and they will be sitting down to dinner in Spain when in England they would normally expect to go to bed.

The uninitiated will certainly be daunted by the lunches and dinners. Large platters of vegetables, elaborate salads and rich lentil- or bean-based stews which are meals in themselves are served as starters. The entrée will be either fish, which is abundant in Spain and very good, or meat and it will be normally served without an accompaniment. The whole ritual usually starts off with tapas served at the table - cheese, ham, olives and other snacks - and it always winds up with the dessert trolley.

Spanish food has travelled less than French and Italian cuisine although it is none the less excellent for that. Visitors should put themselves firmly in the hands of their Spanish companions and let their meal be chosen for them. The food is likely to be better and the Spaniard will feel responsible and flattered. The unadventurous should nevertheless steer clear of offal dishes and also avoid the more esoteric delicacies such as hake gills, elvers or baby eels and squids stewed in their own ink.

It is worth bearing in mind that regional cooking is the greatest feature of domestic cuisine and that there is no Spanish restaurant as such. A restaurant will be Castilian (eg roast lamb and suckling pig), or it will be Basque (eg hearty cod concoctions and massive slabs of steak), or it will be Catalan (eg subtle mixes of sea food and poultry, mushrooms, nuts and fruit), Andalusian (eg deep fried fish and the ubiquitous gazpacho summer soup), Galician (eg potato sews and sea food) or from other parts of Spain. Some regions are strong on rice such as Valencia, and others on fresh vegetables such as Navarre.

Visitors will gain high marks if they seek out the local specialities. Spaniards, who invariably consider themselves Basque, Andalusian, Catalan or whatever first and Spanish second, will be appreciative of the visitor who makes a special effort at trying out the home grown fare. The same is true of the local wines a lot of which are bad travellers but very good when drunk near their source. The Catalans and the Galicians are rightly proud of their local wines. Garlic and olive oil are inevitable; they are de rigueur in every regional kitchen.

The gargantuan banquets seemingly contradict the tapas bar environment. If meals are so huge, what is the use of the famed Spanish snacks? The answer has to do with the lateness of the local eating hours. No Spaniard would consider tapas to be a substitute for a meal. The word comes from *tapar* which means to cover and what tapas do is to cover up an individual's hunger pangs until it is finally time for lunch, which is seldom earlier than 2.30 pm and for dinner which is frequently later than 10.30 pm.

Spaniards on the whole dislike bluntness and getting straight to the point. Business meals have their ritual and serious talking does not normally start until the coffee and brandies have been served. By this final stage of the long-drawn out meal, the recognition of mutual interests, which is the prerequisite for any good business deal, should be taken for granted.

6

DE VISITA

◆ Obtaining and giving information about a company
◆ Describing the production process

En el polígono industrial

In this section you are shown round a Spanish company.

> Modas Florencia S.A.,
> * Oficinas y fábrica, en un polígono industrial cerca de Gerona.
> * Compañía mediana, 120 empleados.
> * Fundada 1958.
> * Buena reputación.
> * Directora de Relaciones Públicas = Rosa Fernández

Louise Taylor and Ben Smith are visiting a small fashion company called Modas Florencia S.A. Here are some facts they gathered before their visit.

The public relations manager takes them on a tour of the premises.
Listen for the information they already have. What else do they learn about the company?

Rosa Fernández Estamos aquí en el polígono industrial desde hace treinta y un años. Estas son las oficinas y la fábrica de Modas Florencia S.A. La empresa fue fundada en 1958 y tiene 120 empleados. Es una empresa mediana.

Louise Taylor ¿Tienen sucursales?
Rosa Fernández Sí, la compañía tiene sucursales en dos ciudades de España.

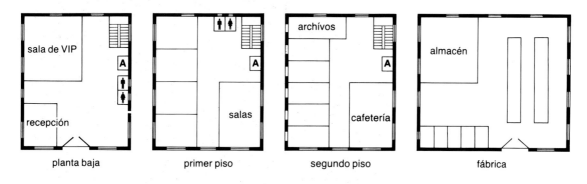

| planta baja | primer piso | segundo piso | fábrica |

The first part of the tour takes the visitors through the office building, floor by floor.

How does Sra Fernández describe the office building?

el almacén *warehouse*
los archivos *files, archives, records*
el ascensor *lift*
la cadena de producción *production line*
la cafetería *cafeteria, canteen*
el edificio *building*
la escalera *stairs*
el personal *staff*
el piso *floor*
la planta baja *ground floor*
la recepción *reception*
la sala de conferencias *conference room, auditorium*
la sala de juntas *boardroom*
los servicios *toilets*
el/la supervisor/a *supervisor*
la zona de embalaje *packing area*
cómodo/a *comfortable*
al fondo *at the end*
con capacidad *with a capacity*

En el edificio de oficinas – la planta baja
Rosa Fernández   El edificio de oficinas no es grande pero es muy cómodo y moderno. Aquí en la planta baja está la recepción, hay servicios cerca del ascensor y una sala de VIP con bar.

¿Verdad o mentira?
→ Sra Fernández Gastón has an office on the ground floor.
→ The boardroom is on the right-hand side.
→ There is a conference room which can hold up to 60 people.

En el primer piso
Rosa Fernández   En esta planta está mi despacho. Aquí a mano izquierda están los despachos de los directores de la compañía. Los servicios están al fondo cerca de la escalera. A mano derecha hay una sala de juntas y una sala de conferencias con capacidad para unas cincuenta personas.

What can be found on the second floor?

En el segundo piso
Rosa Fernández   En el segundo piso tenemos más oficinas, una cafetería grande para el personal, y al fondo están los archivos.

Sra Fernández takes her visitors on to the factory. What's on the left-hand side of the factory floor?

En la fábrica
Rosa Fernández   Aquí está la cadena de producción. Allí a la izquierda están el almacén, la zona de embalaje y los despachos de los supervisores y los diseñadores.

Desde hace...

Desde hace translates as *for* to refer to how long something has been established or how long an action has been taking place. Sra Fernández said: **Estamos aquí en el polígono industrial desde hace treinta y un años** (*We've been here on the industrial estate for thirty one years*).

Note that when an action which began in the past continues into the present, the present tense must be used, eg: **Soy Director de Marketing desde hace un año** (*I've been Marketing Director for a year*); **Estoy en España desde hace una semana** (*I have been in Spain for a week*); **Trabajo en esta compañía desde hace dos años** (*I have been working for this company for two years*).

¿Desde cuándo...?

When you want to know how long someone has been living, working, etc. somewhere, ask: **¿Desde cuándo...?** (*Since when...?*), eg **¿Desde cuándo es usted Director de Marketing?** (*Since when have you been Marketing Director?*).

Hace...

Hace... (on its own) means *ago*.

Use it to say when something happened, eg **hace una semana** (*a week ago*); **hace una hora** (*an hour ago*); **La compañía fue fundada hace cuarenta años** (*The company was founded forty years ago*).

Before moving to the next section make a note of these useful expressions in your notebook.

PRACTICA ▶ **1** You are welcoming a group of Spanish visitors to your workplace. Say who you are and what your position is, when the company was founded and how many branches and employees there are.

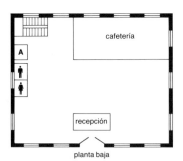

planta baja

primer piso

2 You are taking some visitors on a tour of these premises. Plan what you would say on your tour and use the following phrases: **en la planta baja está(n)..., en el primer piso hay/tenemos..., aquí está(n)..., a la izquierda está(n)..., a la derecha está(n)..., al fondo está(n)...**

3 A group is being given a guided tour round the Campofrío meat product factory. As you listen to the guide's commentary, put the English sentences in the correct order, to show what he's doing.

por peso *by weight*
la zona de deshuesado
    deboning area
¡Cuidado! *Careful!*
la empaquetadora *packaging machine*

☐ *a* Showing them where to go

☐ *b* Saying that they will also see the packaging machine

☐ *c* Explaining that they are going straight away to see the boning area

☐ *d* Warning people to be careful as they go in

☐ *e* Explaining how the hams are graded by weight

4 During a business trip to Spain, you and a Spanish business associate are going to visit a small shoe factory (**una fábrica pequeña de zapatos**) near Alicante. You are on the phone to your associate describing the itinerary below. Use expressions like: **Voy a...**, **Vamos a...**, **y después...**

This is the itinerary: arrive in Spain at Alicante on Tuesday 1 June; go to the Hotel; the hotel is called...; hire a car; travel to an industrial estate near Torrevieja; arrive at 11 a.m. at the small shoe factory.

Name of guide: _____

Name of Personnel Manager: _____

Name of firm: _____

Location of factory: _____

Length of time at this location: _____

Year of foundation: _____

Number of employees: _____

Location of showroom: _____

5 You are going on a tour of the shoe factory with your hosts.

a Listen to the guide and fill in this fact sheet.

b What are the three areas visited? Is this their only factory building?

c With the help of the data sheet prepare a short speech in Spanish about the factory.

6 Draw a sketch of your own place of work or your company headquarters. You are showing a Spanish visitor around. What would you say?

6   Una sociedad anónima

In this section you will practise describing the size and activities of a company.

FRASES ➤

Fabricamos...   *We manufacture...*
Usamos... We *use...*
No confeccionamos...   *We don't make...*
Compramos...   *We buy...*
Importamos...   *We import...*
Tenemos un buen porcentaje   *We have a good percentage (of the market)*
Queremos introducir...   *We want to introduce...*
Nos gustaría...   *We would like to...*

La compañía:

El producto:

Las materias primas:

Porcentaje del mercado:

Volumen de ventas:

Planes:

As you listen to Sra Rosa Fernández of Modas Florencia S.A. describing her company, fill in the fact sheet.

Rosa Fernández   Modas Florencia S.A. es una empresa mediana. Fue fundada en 1958 y tiene 120 empleados. Tenemos sucursales en dos ciudades de España.

Fabricamos exclusivamente ropa para damas: trajes, chaquetas, faldas, blusas y pantalones. Usamos principalmente fibras naturales: algodón, lana y seda. Nosotros no confeccionamos ropa de poliéster. Compramos algunos materiales en España e importamos otros de varios países dentro y fuera de la CE. Tenemos un buen porcentaje del mercado español. Nuestro volumen de ventas es de varios millones de pesetas. Queremos introducir nuestros productos en otros mercados. Nos gustaría vender también en Alemania y Francia.

¿Verdad o mentira?
➤ The company makes ladies' clothes.
➤ They use a variety of fibres, natural and synthetic.
➤ They buy all the raw materials outside the EC.
➤ They wish to expand into other markets.

---

el algodón   *cotton*
la blusa   blouse
la CE (Comunidad Europea)   *the EC*
la chaqueta   *jacket*
la falda   *skirt*
las fibras naturales   *natural fibres*
la lana   *wool*
las materias primas   *raw materials*
el mercado   *market*
el país   *country*
los pantalones   *trousers*
el poliéster   *polyester*
la ropa para damas   *ladies' clothes*

la seda   *silk*
la sociedad anónima   *public limited company*
el traje   *suit*
el volumen de ventas   *turnover*
confeccionar   *to make clothes*
algunos/as   *some*
nuevo/a   *new*
varios/as   *several*
exclusivamente   *exclusively*
principalmente   *principally*
dentro de   *within, inside*
fuera de   *outside*

Types of company

S.A. (Sociedad Anónima)
Public Limited Company
S.R.L. (Sociedad de
Responsabilidad Limitada)
Limited Liability Company
las compañías nacionales/
multinacionales *national/
multinational companies*
las PYMES (pequeñas y
medianas empresas) *small
and medium-sized companies*
la firma establecida *well-
established company, a
company of old standing*
la cooperativa *cooperative*
el concesionario, la concesionaria
franchise holder
la empresa fantasma
bogus company

Adverbs

You will have noticed the adverbs **exclusivamente** and **principalmente** in the dialogue. You can find out more about adverbs on pages 150.

More on adjective agreement

If you are talking about percentages, you will need to use these four adjectives: **bueno** (*good*); **alto** (*high*); **bajo** (*low*); **pequeño** (*small*). **Bueno**, when used before a noun, becomes **buen**. Practise with these sentences: **Setenta y cinco por ciento es un buen porcentaje; Noventa y dos por ciento es un porcentaje alto; Diez por ciento es un porcentaje bajo; Dos por ciento es un porcentaje pequeño.**

Queremos..., Nos gustaría...

Queremos... (*We want/wish/are planning to...*) and **Nos gustaría...** (*We would like to...*) are used with verbs in the infinitive, eg **Queremos trabajar en Europa. Nos gustaría viajar a España.**

García e Hijos (García and Sons)

Why **e Hijos** and not **y Hijos**? Because **y** is never used before words beginning with **hi** or with **i**, eg **José e Isabel.**

1 You are describing the activities of a shoe manufacturer. They make ladies' shoes and they use only quality materials, which they buy in Germany and Italy. They have no branches. Their turnover is good. Use the following phrases as a guide: **fabricamos; usamos; compramos; vendemos; no tenemos; nuestro volumen de ventas.**

la cuota *market share*
la tonelada *ton*
el turno *shift*
producimos *we produce*

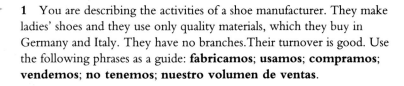

2 The guided tour at Campofrío continues... Listen to the guide's statistics, and try to work out the following:
a the shift system
b hourly production
c Campofrío's market share

If you are listening to a lengthy explanation, here are some useful expressions to break the monotony: **¡Excelente!; Sí, claro** (*Of course, sure*); **Muy interesante** (*Very interesting*).

3 During a visit to a company, you get the following answers to your questions. What did you ask?
a La firma fue fundada en 1963.
b Sí, tenemos seis sucursales en España y una en París.
c No. Solamente usamos fibras naturales.
d Vendemos nuestros productos en nuestro salón de ventas.

6

4 Look at the list of job titles in the margin and fill in the blanks.

a José Martínez Boix is in charge of the company's operation in the south of Madrid.

Es ..... de la compañía.

b There will be one of these presiding over the board meeting.

Es el/la ..... de la compañía.

c Sra Elena Martínez Rojas can sign on behalf of the managing director.

Es ..... de la compañía.

5 At a meeting with a group of Spanish business people, you are explaining your company's plans for the near future, eg **Queremos introducir nuestros productos en otros mercados. Nos gustaría vender nuestros productos en los países de la CE**. Say:

a We want to work in Spain and would like to have a branch in Madrid.

b We would like to sell our products in this country and we also want to introduce our products in France, Germany and Italy.

¿Cómo se fabrica?

This section is about describing the production process at a factory.

FRASES

Las materias primas principales son... *The main raw materials are...*
Si vale *If it is OK*
Tienen que ser... *They must be...*
No valen *They are worthless*

As you listen to the commentary given during this guided tour of Porcelana Santa Clara, a china factory, note what is said about the manufacturing and quality control stages. Tick the expressions in the fact sheet, as you hear them.

Se mezclan y se saca una muestra.
Se hacen churros de distintos diámetros.
Las piezas salen de los moldes.
Se preparan y van al horno.
Se ponen las piezas en esta cinta transportadora.
Se clasifican en calidades.

la arcilla	clay
el barniz	glaze
la calidad	quality
el caolín	kaolin
la cinta transportadora	conveyor belt
los churros	clay sausages
el defecto	defect
el diámetro	diameter
la esponja	sponge
el fallo	fault
la galleta	biscuit
el horno	oven
el molde	mould
la muestra	sample
la pieza	piece, item
el platillo	saucer
el plato	plate
la sección de retoque	retouching/finishing section
el tiempo	time
pasar	to pass
tirar	to throw away
cuarto/a	fourth
chico/a	small
distinto/a	different
quinto/a	fifth
perfectísimo/a	absolutely perfect

Raw materials, sampling and shaping

Guía   Las materias primas principales son caolín y arcilla. Se mezclan y se saca una muestra. Esa muestra se analiza y si vale, se prensa y se forman estas galletas. Luego se hacen churros de distintos diámetros, más diámetro para un plato grande o menos diámetro para un platillo chico.

Cleaning, polishing and firing

Guía   Las piezas salen de los moldes, se secan y pasan a la sección de retoque. Allí se pulen con unas esponjas, se preparan y van al horno. Algunas piezas necesitan más tiempo en el horno; otras menos.

Glazing

Guía   Esta es la sección de barniz. Se ponen las piezas en esta cinta transportadora y se revisan una por una. Si no hay fallos, van al segundo horno.

Quality control

Guía Después de cuarenta y ocho horas, cuando las piezas salen del horno, se clasifican en calidades: primera, segunda, tercera, cuarta y quinta. Las piezas de primera calidad tienen que ser perfectísimas; las de segunda, también; las de tercera y cuarta tienen defectos; las de quinta calidad no valen, son para tirar.

INFRAESTRUCTURA ➤

¿Cómo se fabrica?

se fabrica	*it is manufactured*
se mezcla	*it is mixed*
se saca	*it is taken out*
se analiza	*it is analysed*
se prensa	*it is pressed*
se forma	*it is shaped into*
se hace	*it is made*
se seca	*it is dried*
se pule	*it is polished*
se prepara	*it is prepared*
se pone	*it is put*
se revisa	*it is checked*
se clasifica	*it is classified*

¿Cómo se fabrica?

You may have seen signs in windows saying **Se habla inglés** (*English spoken here* or *We speak English*). To construct this expression we need **se + habla** which is the part of the verb **hablar** used for **él** or **ella**.

The expressions listed left follow a similar pattern. The plural is, eg **Se preparan** (*They are prepared*).

Look at the following examples: **La muestra se analiza** (*The sample is analysed*); **Las piezas se revisan una por una** (*The items are checked one by one*); **Se saca una muestra** (*A sample is taken*). Many more examples appear in the guided tour above. See also page 151.

More adverbs

When describing a production process, you can use adverbs to organise your explanations, eg **primero** (*first*); **luego** (*then*); **después** (*after that*); **finalmente** (*finally*).

Perfectísimo/a

Look at this sentence: **Las piezas de primera calidad tienen que ser perfectísimas** (*Top quality items must be absolutely perfect*). **Perfectísimo/a** is a superlative adjective. Superlatives describe something that is exceptionally large, good or appealing, etc.

If during a visit you become particularly interested in the manufacturing process of a product and wish to be given a quick demonstration of how it is made, ask **¿Cómo se fabrica?** (*How is it manufactured?*) or **¿Cómo se hace?** (*How is it made?*).

It is formed by joining **Perfect(o) + -ísimo(a).** Other useful superlatives are: **buenísimo/a(s)** (*really good*); **carísimo/a(s)** (*extremely expensive*); **pequeñísimo/a(s)** (*exceptionally small*); **grandísimo/a(s)** (*very large indeed*), eg **Este vino es buenísimo. La porcelana es carísima. Los despachos son pequeñísimos. Las fábricas son grandísimas.** Like all other adjectives these must agree with the noun they describe. See page 147.

PRACTICA

1 ¿Cómo se fabrica? Put the sentences in the right order:

a Se preparan y van al horno.

b Se revisan una por una.

c Se mezclan los ingredientes.

d Se hacen churros de distintos diámetros.

e La muestra se analiza.

f Se ponen las piezas en la cinta transportadora.

2 Steps to making an appointment. Provide a caption for each picture by matching the items below.

Se marca ...   (*You dial*)   ...en el diario.
Se apunta ...   (*You make a note of*) ...el número de teléfono.
Se dice ...   (*You say*)   ...el día y la hora para la reunión.
Se propone ... (*You suggest*)   ...el nombre (your own).

3 Sr Ricardo Bocanegra describes some of the things he does every day at the office. Two of the activities in his professional life are discussing individual cases with his sisters and employees, and preparing articles or lectures.
Find out which part of the day – morning, afternoon or evening – is given over to each activity.

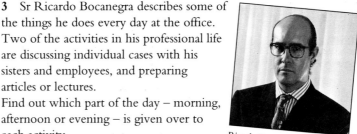

Ricardo Bocanegra

suelo   *I usually/I'm in the habit of*
una cita de hora en hora
   one meeting an hour
resuelvo   *I resolve*
los problemas que surgen
   matters arising
estudiar   *to study*

85

4 Change these sentences into the superlative, eg **El hotel es muy bueno** – **El hotel es buenísimo**.

a Su despacho es muy pequeño.

b Esta firma vende un producto muy interesante.

c El polígono industrial es muy grande.

d Tienen un piso muy caro en Madrid.

5 Put these sentences in order to describe a typical morning in an office then join them together using the following adverbs: **primero**; **luego**; **después**; **finalmente**.

Se toma el almuerzo.

Se dan citas.

Se toma una taza de café.

Se llega entre las ocho y media y las nueve menos cuarto.

Se hacen reuniones.

Se abren las cartas.

Chupa Chups

Read the magazine interview opposite with Sr Javier Bernat, owner of the lollipop company Chupa Chups.

It is possible to use the present tense to refer to something in the past. This is called the historic present. See how Javier Bernat uses the present tense as he answers the first question about the beginnings of the company.

La clave del éxito

los accionistas	*shareholders*
la clave	*key*
el éxito	*success*
el fabricante mundial	
	world manufacturer
el fundador	*founder*
la gama	*range*
los inconvenientes	
	disadvantages
la manzana	*apple*
el negocio familiar	
	family business
las ventajas	*advantages*
unido/a	*close, united*
basar	*to base*
buscar	*to look for*
iniciar	*to begin*
nacer	*to be born*
vender	*to sell*

Chupa Chups vende 1.500 millones de unidades al año. Hablamos con el Sr Javier Bernat y le preguntamos cuál es la clave del éxito de Chupa Chups.

Pregunta: ¿Cuándo se inicia Chupa Chups?

Respuesta: Chupa Chups se inicia en los años cincuenta, cuando el fundador de la empresa, que es mi padre, toma un cincuenta por ciento de participación de una empresa industrial de productos de la manzana, y decide que, de la gama de doscientos productos que allí hay, uno solamente tiene potencial. Los accionistas deciden venderle la compañía. Así nace Chupa Chups.

Pregunta: Chupa Chups es un negocio familiar. ¿Cuáles son las ventajas y cuáles los inconvenientes?

Respuesta: Sólo hay ventajas. Somos una empresa de segunda generación, muy unida. Somos muy rápidos, muy ágiles, tomamos decisiones rápidamente...

Pregunta: ¿En qué se basa el éxito de Chupa Chups?

Respuesta: El éxito está en buscar la perfección. Concretamente, pues, desde hace quince años que la empresa utiliza sola y exclusivamente productos naturales. Somos una empresa muy ecológica.

Pregunta: ¿La compañía es el primer fabricante mundial de 'lollipops'...?

Respuesta: Con 1.500 millones de unidades al año, somos la compañía que más fabrica y más vende caramelos lollipops del mundo.

Empresa:
Nombre del director:
Fundada:
Negocio familiar: ventajas/inconvenientes:
Producto:
Ventas:

a What's the key to the success of Chupa Chups? Explain in English.

b Summarize in English how the company came to be owned by the Bernats.

c Read the article again and complete this fact sheet.

6

Inventario

Describing a company

La compañía se llama... *The company is called...*

Fue fundada en... *It was founded in...*

Fue fundada hace diez años *It was founded ten years ago*

Está en el polígono industrial desde hace dos años *It's been on the industrial estate for two years*

Tenemos cuarenta empleados *We have forty employees*

Tenemos cinco sucursales *We have five branches*

¿Cuántas sucursales tiene(n)? *How many branches have you got?*

Aquí está la zona de embalaje *Here's the packing area*

Fabricamos... *We manufacture...*

Usamos... *We use ...*

Compramos... *We buy...*

Importamos... *We import...*

Vamos a introducir... *We are going to introduce...*

Describing the production process

¿Cómo se hace/fabrica? *How is it made?*

Primero...; luego...; después...; finalmente... *First...; then.... after that; finally...*

Se preparan... *They are prepared...*

Punto de Control

Make sure you can do the following in Spanish

➤ Describe your company: when it was founded; size; number of employees; product; raw materials used; number of branches and/or factories; market share (Spanish/European/British/world); annual turnover.

➤ Name half a dozen products you make and name the materials they are made of.

➤ Choose one product and explain how it is manufactured.

➤ Name as many different types of company as possible.

➤ Name as many job titles as possible.

De visita

Arguably one of the more surprising features foreign visitors will encounter as they work their way into the Spanish business scene is the strength and the extent of the family network. Spanish companies are overwhelmingly small, family-owned concerns. Doing business with a Spanish company frequently involves doing business with a family.

A very high proportion of Spanish business, both big and small, were created by self-made men in the so-called 'miracle' years of the late 1950s and the 1960s when the economy grew extremely rapidly. A familiar figure in Spanish companies is that of the *fundador*, the founder, who as often as not is the father or the grandfather of those who are currently in charge of running the company.

The company in question may have started in a small workshop in a village or, should it be a distribution business, the founder may have started by selling off the back of a donkey from village to village. There are numerous examples of corporate beginnings in Spain. Nowadays those businesses are to be found in the *polígonos industriales*, or industrial estates, that lie on the outskirts of most medium-sized towns.

The business will have grown over the years from its humble beginnings and its transfer to a *polígono* will be a sign of its consolidation. But it will remain close to its roots and be very proud of them.

A perceptive visitor to a Spanish family-owned business will note the subtle changes that succeeding generations have wrought on the company hierarchy and on the way the company runs its affairs. The contrast between the founder, who will be the company chairman, and say one of the grandchildren, who may be in charge of sales, will be a marked one.

The company's patriarch will, in the main, be a conservative and much revered personality, cautious about new ideas and potential partnerships, and authoritarian in style. Younger members of the family with responsibilities in the company will, in all likelihood, be very different; they will, in passing, illustrate the very fast social changes that Spain has undergone.

The children and grandchildren of the founding patriarch will hold university degrees and possibly have language skills. The jump between one generation and another in Spain can be a giddy one, a company's founder may be an entirely self-taught individual who has used natural intelligence to make up for the shortcomings of formal education, while immediate descendants could well hold MBA degrees from US universities.

Such quantum leaps between the background of the different family members inevitably lead to differences in style and attitudes within a family-owned business. The contrasts should not however lead the visitor into believing that a company might have divergent strategies.

Families form a compact unit in Spain, as is common in Mediterranean societies, and the hierarchical structure is strong. Younger members of the family, for instance, may be anxious to raise capital and expand but if the patriarch prefers to self-finance the business and to limit its scope, then these wishes are unquestioned.

The importance of understanding the nature of such loyalties cannot be overestimated when it comes to doing business with family-owned companies. The visitor should recognise that the decision-making remains at the top and take aboard the very close bonding that exists within such companies.

CIFRAS Y PORCENTAJES

◆ Describing performance ◆ Talking about figures and accounts

¿Qué porcentaje exportan?

This section practises talking about and comparing company figures.

FRASES ▶

¿Me puede contar...?   *Could you tell me...?*
¿A qué mercados exportan?   *Which markets do you export to?*
¿Qué parte/porcentaje de su producción está dedicada a la exportación?   *What proportion of your output do you export?*
En comparación con   *Compared with*
Hoy en día   *Nowadays, at present*
Se describe a sí misma   *It considers itself*
Al año   *Per year*
Podríamos...   *We could...*
Yo creo   *I believe, think*
Ni... ni   *Neither... nor*
A mi juicio   *In my view*

Javier Bernat

la cifra   *figure*
la facturación   *sales revenue*
el mundo   *world*
la unidad   *unit*
exportar   *to export*
aproximadamente
    approximately
pronto   *soon*

Chupa Chups is a Spanish company which makes and exports lollipops. This is Sr Javier Bernat of Chupa Chups talking about the company. How many factories do they have and where? How many lollipops a year do they produce?

Entrevistador   ¿Me puede contar un poco en líneas generales a qué mercados exportan y qué parte de su producción está dedicada a la exportación en comparación con el producto nacional?
Javier Bernat   Hoy en día Chupa Chups está exportando noventa por ciento de su producción, en aproximadamente cien países, contamos con siete u ocho fábricas: tres en España, dos en Francia, una en San Petersburgo, una pronto en China también.

You'll need to be very confident about using and understanding figures and percentages. If you haven't yet learned them, refer to the full list of numbers on page 158 and learn them, a few at a time.

la concentración de mercado
    market concentration
las empresas medianas
    medium-sized companies
la reestructuración
    restructuring
el tamaño   *size*
la ventaja   *advantage*
competir   *to compete*
dividir   *to divide*
sufrir   *to suffer*
ineficiente   *inefficient*
pequeño/a   *small*
por encima de   *over...*
por lo tanto   *therefore*
cualquier/a   *any*

Entrevistador   La compañía se describe a sí misma como el primer fabricante mundial de, bueno de Chupa Chups.

Javier Bernat   Sí, de Chupa Chups, de lollipops. Con nuestros 1500 millones de unidades al año, somos la compañía que más fabrica y más vende caramelos lollipops del mundo.

Pedro Ballvé

Answer in Spanish: **¿Qué porcentaje de su producción exporta Chupa Chups?**

Listen to Sr Pedro Ballvé Lantero, President of Campofrío, another large and successful Spanish company, talking about the present and future of large, medium-sized and small companies. What are the figures he mentions?

Pedro Ballvé   Podríamos dividir las compañías entre las muy pequeñas y especializadas, las medias que hacen un poco de todo, y luego las grandes. Cuando hablo de compañías grandes, hablo por encima, pues, de los 10.000 millones de pesetas de facturación. Bueno, yo creo que va a haber una concentración de mercado en las empresas grandes. Las empresas medianas son las que, a mi juicio, más van a sufrir en esta reestructuración ya que no tienen ni las ventajas de la grande ni las ventajas de las pequeñas, y por lo tanto su tamaño les hace ser ineficientes para competir en cualquiera de los dos mercados.

¿Verdad o mentira?
Medium-sized companies have all the advantages because they are neither too large nor too small to compete in today's market.

INFRAESTRUCTURA   ➤

Comparison of adjectives

To compare items you use **más... que** plus an adjective, eg **España es más grande que Inglaterra**. (*Spain is bigger than England.*)

   Comparisons are often used to talk about figures and percentages, eg **es más alto/a que...** (*is higher than*); **son más altos/as que...** (*are higher than*); **es más bajo/a que...** (*is lower than*); **son más bajos/bajas que...** (*are lower than*).

   To add that something is *a little* or *much* higher or lower, use **un poco más** or **mucho más**, eg **es un poco más alto que...** (*it's a bit higher than...*); **son mucho más bajos que...** (*they're much lower than...*).

   For example:
Las cifras correspondientes a este año son mucho más altas que las cifras correspondientes al año pasado (*The figures for this year are much higher than last year's figures*).

Superlatives

If you want to say that something is the highest, the lowest, the most expensive etc. use **es el más alto, es el más bajo, es el más caro**. These expressions must agree in gender and number with the noun. Use: **es la más alta/baja/cara** etc. in the feminine singular and **los más altos**, etc and **las más altas**, etc in the masculine plural and the feminine plural respectively.

Adverbs

Chupa Chups exporta *mucho*. (*Chupa Chups exports a lot*) **Chupa Chups exporta** *más que* **otras compañías.** (*Chupa Chups exports more than other companies*)   **Chupa Chups** *es la* **compañía** *que más* **exporta.**   (*Chupa Chups is the company that exports the most.*)

The following words have irregular comparatives and superlatives:
mucho (*much/a lot*)
   más que (*more than*)   (el/la/los/las)... **que más** (*the most*)
poco (little)
   menos que (*less than*)   (el/la/los/las)... **que menos** (*the least*)
   eg **Chupa Chups es la compañía que más fabrica y más vende.**

Numbers

In Spanish you don't need the word *a* with 100 or 1000, eg *a hundred pounds* – **cien libras**; *a thousand pounds* – **mil libras**.

Dates

A full stop is often used in writing the year, eg 1.973. Years are said as complete numbers. Dates must be read in full, eg 1973 – **mil novecientos setenta y tres**.

Percentages

There are three ways of writing percentages in Spanish: **12%; 12 por 100; 12 por ciento.**

These would be read out in the same way: 1,34% – **uno coma treinta y cuatro por ciento**; 2,11% – **dos coma once por ciento.**

Fractions
1/2 medio
1/3 un tercio
1/4 un cuarto
2/3 dos tercios
1/8 un octavo

Examples:
7 $^{1}/_{2}$ – **siete y medio**;
5 $^{2}/_{3}$ – **cinco y dos tercios**.

PRACTICA ➤ **1** ¿Más alto o más bajo? Compare the figures and percentages in column A with those in column B and say whether they are higher or lower. Use **más**; **un poco más**; **mucho más**; **alto/a(s)**; **bajo/a(s)**. Eg **Libros de cocina: El precio de catálogo es un poco más alto que el precio de venta al público.**

A
Libros de cocina
precio de
catálogo 5.787 ptas

Porcelana Marbella
exportaciones 78%

Restaurante Galdós
menú del día
Precio: 1.700 ptas

Tapices de Castilla S.A.
facturación
23.000.000 ptas

B
Libros de cocina
precio de venta al
público 5.575 ptas

Porcelana Málaga
exportaciones 35%

Restaurante Verbena
menú del día
Precio: 2.300 ptas

Alfombras Roselló S.A.
facturación
23.857.000 ptas

los beneficios   *profits*
la ganancia   *profit*
los gastos generales   *overheads*
la mano de obra   *workforce*
los materiales   *materials*
la pérdida   *loss*
las ventas   *sales*

2   ¿Pérdida o ganancia?
a   Add the figures for Zapatos y Accesorios S.A. in the text below to the chart to find out if they are making a profit or a loss.

Gastos generales: ochocientos setenta y cinco.

Materiales: seiscientos noventa y cinco.

Mano de obra: trescientos noventa.

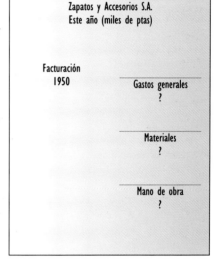

Zapatos y Accesorios S.A.
Este año (miles de ptas)

Facturación
1950

Gastos generales
?

Materiales
?

Mano de obra
?

Modas Florencia S.A.
El año pasado(miles de ptas)

Facturación
1950

Gastos generales
470

Materiales
695

Mano de obra
495

b   Would Modas Florencia S.A. still be making a profit if...? Change last year's figures in the graphic according to the information below and find out.

Este año los beneficios de Modas Florencia S.A. son quince por ciento más bajos que los beneficios del año pasado. Pero el coste de los materiales es diez por ciento más bajo.

93

7

la Bolsa   *Stock Exchange*
el bono   *bond*
la cotización   *quotation, price*
el indice Dax   *Dax Index*
el punto   *point*
el resultado final   *the final result*
la subida   *rise, increase*
indicar   *to indicate*
bajó   *it dropped*
ganó   *it gained*
subió   *it rose*

3*a*   Listen to the Stock Exchange report as you might hear it on the radio. By how many points did the Dax Index rise? The Nikkei Index dropped 1.32%; how many yen was that?

b   Listen again to the recording. This time there will be pauses to allow you to replace the original figures with the following ones:
18   37   2,7%   31,65 puntos   3 puntos   370 yenes   1,11%
2,7 puntos

4   You are asking a sales director from another company what proportion of their output they export. What question would you ask?

La empresa en cifras

In this section you'll learn to say more about company performance.

FRASES ➤   La distribución está todavía sin desarrollar   *Distribution is still undeveloped*

Sr Pedro Ballvé talks about Campofrío's sales outlets and export figures.

How many outlets do they have in Spain?

Which three countries does he mention as having more developed distribution systems?

What are Campofrío's present export figures?

la capacidad de compra del
    mercado   *market buying*
    capacity
la forma   *way*
el punto de venta   *sales outlet*
ver   *to see*
prometedor   *promising*
alrededor   *about*
a través de   *through*
del orden de   *in the region of,*
    around
sin embargo   *however*

Pedro Ballvé   En España tenemos del orden de 90.000 puntos de venta, donde sólo los grandes clientes se concentran a través de 150 ó 160 puntos del orden del 15% de la capacidad de compra del mercado, y por eso la distribución en España yo diría que está todavía sin desarrollar de la forma que lo podemos ver en Francia, en Alemania o en Inglaterra.

...Para darle a usted una idea, este año nos estaremos moviendo alrededor de los 2.500, que son 25 millones de dólares de producto en exportación, que dentro del total nuestro que son 500 ó 520 millones de dólares es una cifra pequeña. Sin embargo, el futuro es muy prometedor.

Adjectives

Remember that most adjectives usually come after a noun: **una cifra pequeña** (*a small figure*). But a few of the most frequently-used adjectives, including **bueno, malo, grande**, come before the noun eg **los grandes clientes**. See page 148.

Grande is shortened to **gran** before singular nouns of either gender, eg **una fábrica grande**: **una gran fábrica**; **un aparcamiento grande**: **un gran aparcamiento**.

Bueno (*good*), **malo** (*bad*)

These adjectives drop the final **o** when they are placed before a masculine singular noun, eg **es un buen producto**; **es un buen precio**; **es un mal momento para vender**.

The same applies to the following adjectives: **uno** (*one*); **primero** (*first*); **tercero** (*third*), eg: **el primer piso**.

No changes apply to the same words in the feminine: eg **es una buena/mala idea**; **está en la primera/tercera planta**, etc.

Comparative and superlative
Mayor (*bigger, larger*); **el/la mayor** (*the biggest, largest*).

La mayor parte means *most of*, as in **Chupa Chups exporta la mayor parte de su producción**.

1 Company performance.
Premium Goods Ltd

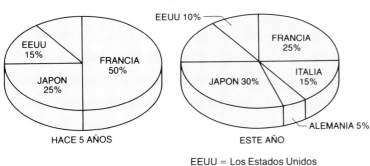

HACE 5 AÑOS

ESTE AÑO

EEUU = Los Estados Unidos

a Both of these charts show a breakdown by country of a company's exports. What percentage of output currently goes to each country? Where do they sell the largest proportion of their production? Make sentences, eg:

Esta compañía exporta el (x%) a Francia, el (x%) a ...
La compañía exporta la mayor parte de su producción a...

b Now compare the two charts. For each country, say whether the company exports more or less than it did five years ago, eg

La compañía exporta al Japón 5% más que hace cinco años.

7

Intergift en el Salón Internacional del Regalo de Ifema - Madrid

Este año el 61% de los expositores de Intergift son fabricantes, mientras que el 39% restante son mayoristas, distribuidores e importadores. De las pequeñas empresas españolas que tienen un mínimo de 29 empleados, solamente un 3% tiene participación de capital extranjero, pero esta participación es menos del 50% del capital social. El 45 por 100 de estas empresas son exportadoras, pero su volumen de ventas al exterior es de sólo 26 por 100 de su facturación total.

****

2 Read the newspaper cuttings and do the accompanying exercises.

¿Verdad o mentira? Correct any errors.

a Las importaciones han crecido este año sólo un 4,4%.

b Las exportaciones han crecido un 15,5%.

c El déficit del comercio exterior español es más alto este año que el año pasado.

Select the correct alternative to complete these sentences.

d El 39%/61%/29% de los expositores son importadores/fabricantes/mayoristas/distribuidores.

e Hay grandes/pequeñas/medianas empresas españolas que tienen un mínimo de 29 empleados.

f Un 29%/50%/3% de pequeñas empresas tienen participación de capital español/extranjero.

Comercio exterior español

Según las cifras de comercio exterior de los cinco primeros meses de este año, observamos que las importaciones han crecido un 8,2%, mientras nuestro nivel de exportación es muy débil y ha crecido sólo un 4,4%. A consecuencia de todo esto, nuestro déficit en este período es un 15,5% más alto que el déficit del mismo período del año pasado.

****

3 Complete the dialogue. Work with a colleague if possible.
You work for Roxy Textiles Ltd. During a visit to a Spanish company the marketing manager asks you some questions about the company.

Director de marketing ¿Cuáles son los productos de la compañía?
Usted (Say the products are: jackets, T-shirts [**camisetas**] and another textile product of your choice)
Director de marketing ¿Qué materias primas usan?
Usted (Say the company uses only natural fibres such as wool and cotton.)
Director de marketing ¿Dónde compran las materias primas?
Usted (Say the company buys the raw materials from several countries of the Commonwealth [La Mancomunidad])
Director de marketing ¿A qué países exporta Roxy Textiles Ltd?
Usted (Say the company exports to ten countries, five of them in the EEC: the Benelux countries [**los países del Benelux**], Italy and Germany.)
Director de marketing ¿Qué porcentaje de su producción exportan a la CEE?
Usted (23%)
Director de marketing ¿Qué productos nuevos van a introducir?
Usted (Choose a textile product)

el comercio exterior *foreign trade*
el nivel *level*
ha/han crecido *it has/they have grown*
débil *weak*
mismo/a *same*
sólo *only*

el capital social *shareholders' capital*
el distribuidor *distributor*
el expositor *exhibitor*
el importador *importer*
el/la mayorista *wholesaler*
el capital extranjero *foreign capital*
la participación de capital *capital investment*
el regalo *gift*
el volumen de ventas *sales revenue*
restante *remaining*

Ingresos y desembolsos

In this section you'll practise talking about accounts.

En relación con   *in relation to*
Han experimentado   *(they) show, have undergone*
Ha crecido   *(it) has grown*
El beneficio después de impuestos   *after-tax profit*
Creció   *(it) grew*
Ha alcanzado   *(it) has reached*

Listen to this speech about company performance made to Banesto shareholders.

Can you pick out the figures he gives for: growth in total assets, percentage growth in net results and after-tax profit?

Presidente Pues bien, los activos totales del Grupo han experimentado un crecimiento en 1.991 en términos absolutos de 1.778.402 millones de pesetas, que significa más de un 35 por 100 en relación con el año anterior.

...El resultado bruto de explotación, que mide la rentabilidad de las operaciones bancarias antes de dotaciones, ha crecido un 18,96%. Creemos que es un crecimiento superior a la media de los grandes bancos.

...El beneficio después de impuestos creció un 14,31%.

...Por último, significarles que en 1.991, la rentabilidad sobre recursos propios medios, que es como hay que medir la rentabilidad de las empresas, sean o no bancarias, ha alcanzado un 19,4%, con un crecimiento de 0,74 puntos porcentuales. En síntesis, desde 1.987 hasta el 31 de diciembre del pasado, los beneficios netos se han multiplicado por dos.

los activos   *assets*
el beneficio neto   *net profit*
los billones   *billions*
el crecimiento   *growth*
la dotación   *endowment*
la explotación   *running, exploitation*
los gastos   *expenditure*
los ingresos   *takings, income*
el período   *period*
el punto porcentual   *percentage point*
los recursos   *resources*
la rentabilidad   *profitability*
el resultado bruto   *gross income*
anterior   *previous*
total   *total*

INFRAESTRUCTURA ▶

'Las cuentas claras conservan la amistad'

Clear accounts keep friendship intact

Ha crecido, ha alcanzado

These are expressions in the perfect tense. In Spanish the perfect tense is generally used as in English, eg: **La rentabilidad ha crecido un 18%** (*Profitability has grown by 18%*).

You will find further explanations and examples of the perfect tense in Unit 9, and on page 155.

Un crecimiento de...

Note the use of **un crecimiento de 1.78 millones** (*an increase of 1.78 million*). You could also use **un aumento de...** to talk about an increase; and for a decrease, **una disminución de...**

These phrases are often used with **Se registra** to mean *There has been (an increase/decrease)...*

PRACTICA ▶

1   Study this section of a balance sheet and answer the questions which follow in Spanish.

el balance *balance sheet*
el activo circulante *assets*
la caja *cash*
los clientes *customers*
las existencias *stock*

PORCELANAS DENIA S.A.

Balance Comparativo	(en miles de pesetas)	
ACTIVO		
Activo Circulante	31.12.92	31.12.93
Caja y Bancos	2.400	2.000
Clientes	5.250	5.000
Existencias	7.850	8.500
Total	?	?

la cuenta *account*
los desembolsos *expenses*
los impuestos *tax*
el libro de caja *cash book*
el negocio *business*
las pérdidas y ganancias
    profit and loss
el presupuesto del cash flow
    cash flow forecast
el registro *register*

a   ¿Cuál es el total correspondiente a 1992 y cuál es el total correspondiente a 1993?
b   ¿Qué aumento o disminución de existencias se registra en 1993?
c   El total general de 1993, ¿es más alto o más bajo que el total general de 1992?

el alquiler rent
el beneficio bruto/neto *gross/net profit*
las contribuciones municipales *rates*
la depreciación *depreciation*
los honorarios profesionales *professional fees*
las reparaciones *repairs*
el salario *wages*
el seguro *insurance*
el sueldo *salary*

2 Read the following explanation of company finances. Answer the questions which follow, in Spanish.

Indique:

a las tres cuentas principales de un negocio

b los tres registros de un negocio.

3 Study this profit and loss account of a small business.

¿Verdad o mentira?

a The stock figures are higher than the sales figures.

b The amount paid in rent and rates is 750.000 ptas.

c This company spends more in insurance than repairs.

> Un negocio necesita mantener sus finanzas bajo control. Las tres cuentas principales de un negocio son: la cuenta de pérdidas y ganancias, el balance y el presupuesto del cash flow. Los tres registros que todo negocio debe llevar son: el libro de caja, el registro de ventas y el registro de compras. Estos libros indican principalmente los ingresos y desembolsos, las ventas, los beneficios y los impuestos que se deben pagar, como por ejemplo el IVA.

Pérdidas y Ganancias (miles de pesetas)

Existencias	300	
Compras	5.000	
	5.300	
Existencias finales	200	
Ventas		5.100
Sueldos		1.100
Beneficio bruto		4.000
Gastos generales		
Salarios	800	
Alquiler	400	
Contribuciones municipales	200	
Electricidad	180	
Teléfono	160	
Correos	60	
Seguro	80	
Reparaciones	95	
Depreciación	100	
Honorarios profesionales	225	2.300
Beneficio neto		1.700

7

4 You're seeking a loan and need to prepare a profile of your business to present to the bank. Answer the questions below as a way of structuring your talk. Use the profit and loss account in exercise 3 to provide any useful figures.

PREMIUM GOODS LTD
3 PLEASANT PLACE
SHEFFIELD
0742 45673 AND 0742 34529

las acciones *shares*
la garantía *guarantee, surety*
el historial *background*
el local *premises*
el préstamo *loan*

El negocio: ¿Qué producto vende?
¿A quién vende su producto?
Historial: ¿Como se llama el negocio.?
¿Cuándo fue fundado el negocio?
El mercado: ¿Qué tipo de cliente tiene?
Local: ¿Como es su negocio/oficina/fábrica?
Personal: ¿Tiene empleados/obreros? ¿Cuántos?

Pérdidas y ganancias: ¿Tiene las cifras correspondientes
- existencias, compras, existencias finales, ventas, sueldos, beneficio bruto
- gastos generales: ¿Cuánto paga en total?
- ¿Cuánto es el beneficio neto?

Préstamo: ¿Cuánto dinero necesita?
Garantía: ¿Qué garantía puede usted ofrecer al Banco (casa; existencias; acciones; etc)?

Campofrío – Informe anual

Here is an extract from the President's letter to shareholders, printed in the Campofrío annual report for 1991.

el accionista   *shareholder*
el ambiente   *atmosphere*
la empresa matriz   *parent company*
la estrategia   *strategy*
el desarrollo   *development*
la diversificación   *diversification*
el enfriamiento   *cooling*
la gama   *range*
el informe anual   *annual report*
la inversión   *investment*
IPC, Indice de Precios al Consumo   *RPI, Retail Price Index*
PIB, Producto Interior Bruto   *GDP, Gross Domestic Product*
Moscú   *Moscow*
el paso de... a...   *transfer of... to...*
el terreno   *field, arena*
ascendió   *it went up*
desarrollar   *to develop*
redujo   *it reduced*
amplio/a   *wide*
antes de impuestos   *before tax*
durante   *during*

Carta del Presidente

*D*istinguidos accionistas:

Durante el pasado año, el ambiente de enfriamiento económico redujo el crecimiento del PIB al 3,7%. Con respecto al Indice de Precios al Consumo (IPC) terminamos el año con 6,5%.

El crecimiento de nuestra facturación fué en 1990 del 11,8% alcanzando una cifra neta de 40.529 millones de pesetas. El cash flow bruto ascendió a 5.783 millones de pesetas antes de impuestos.

Junto al desarrollo de la empresa matriz que acabo de exponerles brevemente, hemos creado, dentro de nuestra estrategia de diversificación, una 'Joint Venture' (51% Campofrío) con la firma francesa 'Société des Caves et producteurs réunis de Roquefort' al objeto de desarrollar un negocio de producción y venta de una amplia gama de quesos.

En el terreno internacional, el pasado 14 de diciembre inauguramos la Sociedad Mixta, al 50%, CAMPO-MOS en Moscú. Con respecto a AGROCARNE (40%, a través de Tenki BV), en la República Dominicana, el paso de la fábrica piloto a una nueva planta de 7.500m² de avanzada tecnología ha supuesto una inversión global de 1.100 millones de pesetas.

¿Verdad o mentira?

a   El cash flow neto ascendió a 5.783 millones de pesetas.

b   Campofrío tiene el 51% de la 'Joint Venture' con 'Société des Caves... de Roquefort'; el 50% es de CAMPO-MOS y el 45% es de AGROCARNE.

c   La nueva planta de AGROCARNE en la República Dominicana tiene 7.600m².

Inventario

Discussing company finances

¿A qué mercados exportan? *Which markets do you export your products to?*

¿Qué porcentaje de su producción exportan? *What proportion of your output do you export?*

Las cifras correspondientes a este año son mucho más altas/bajas que... *This year's figures are much higher/lower than...*

Describing performance

¿Cuántos puntos de venta tienen? *How many sales outlets do you have?*

La empresa exporta la mayor parte de su producción a... *The company exports most of its output to...*

Talking about accounts

La rentabilidad ha crecido un 18% *Profits have grown by 18%*

¿Qué aumento o disminución se registra? *What increase or decrease has there been?*

¿Cuánto es el beneficio bruto/neto de la compañía? *What's the company's gross/net profit?*

¿Qué garantía puede usted ofrecer? *What surety can you offer?*

Punto de Control

Make sure you can do the following in Spanish:

- Read these figures and percentages:
  347.778 ptas   el año 1997   64%   35,8% $18.721 $15^1/2$ 34 $3/4$ 1.300 $1/8$

- Say the following:
  The gross profit is 53 million pesetas.
  Sales have increased by 7%.
  Your cash flow has increased by 6.2 %.

- Talk about your company's exports: what products are exported, which countries they go to, what percentage goes to the EEC.

- Say these words and phrases:
  profit and loss account expenses stocks salaries insurance figures turnover gross/net profits shares capital investment

Cifras y porcentajes

A few years back British business executives examining the financial documents of a Spanish company would have understood next to nothing. Quite apart from language difficulties, they would have been stumped by the presentation of data, or rather of the little data which was available to an outsider.

Fortunately, European Community directives have prompted greater transparency and propelled domestic reporting systems into more recognisable models. Increasingly, the corporate environment and the balance sheet procedures are looking comparable. Spain, nevertheless, has still a way to travel along the convergence road and for the time being business visitors are likely to encounter unexpected problems as they peruse Spanish companies.

Foreign visitors will soon be perplexed by reporting procedures. They should forget about the familiar vertical financial statement format that is headed with the companies sales and is followed by the cost of those sales, then the gross profit and thus continues downwards to the net profit bottom line. Procedure in Spain is in accordance with the so-called East-West format that lists, separately and on facing sheets, expenses and income.

Visitors will eventually find the bottom line in the traditional format of a Spanish profit and loss account but they may often wonder quite how they arrived at this end point. To a newly arrived British business executive the procedure will not make immediate sense. Frequently the visitor will require the skills of those who are well versed in the domestic procedures. Locally-based accountants will be able to reshuffle the figures and make them comprehensible.

Further frustrations will occur as it transpires that there is, in fact, little published and readily available information. Often the data that is readily at hand is unlikely to be reliable and it will almost certainly be outdated. Until recently, companies which were not quoted on the stock exchange were only obliged to deposit a copy of their statutes and a brief resumé of their annual results with the *Registro Mercantil*, Spain's equivalent of Companies House.

Transparency is at least in the works. In order to comply with EC directives, the authorities have, since the beginning of the 1990s, insisted on detailed, independently audited accounts. Under the new rules equity held in a company by its directors must now be declared and significant changes in share capital and in trading conditions must also be immediately notified to the Registro.

The problem is that the companies register is heavily overburdened. The standards that British business executives may be accustomed to expect at home will still take a time to become the norm in an environment such as Spain's. An interested party could take as long as a week to obtain information and when the data is finally delivered it might well be a year old.

A third surprise appears in the form of procedures for meetings. It is quite impossible in Spain to stage a quick meeting of a given company's shareholders in order to decide on an important development. Delays, however, have nothing to do with the *mañana* stereotype or with the alleged procrastination that afflicts Spaniards. The problem is caused by the manner in which Spanish companies have traditionally issued bearer shares, instead of registered paper and thus do not genuinely know who their shareholders might be. In order to ensure that equity holders attend shareholder meetings, companies must accordingly notify the event a month in advance by publishing details of the meeting in the official gazette and in a national newspaper. Such legal requirements obviously act against quick acquisition strategies.

8

AL CONTADO

◆ Talking about prices and discounts ◆ Ordering goods and writing letters ◆ Payment and delivery terms

Hablemos de Precios

In this section you will practise asking about prices and discounts.

Tenemos una selección de *We have a selection of*
Ahora mismo *Right now*
¿Cuál es el precio por unidad? *What's the unit price?*
Por pedidos de 250 unidades *For orders of 250 units*
Cada uno *Each*
Se pueden hacer pedidos sueltos *One can make small or individual orders*
¿Qué descuento hay por pago al contado? *What's the discount for cash payment?*
Le puedo hacer 12% de descuento *I can give you a 12% discount*
¿Cuál es el plazo de entrega? *What's the delivery period?*
Entrega inmediata *Immediate delivery*

el artículo *article, item*
el bolígrafo *ballpoint pen*
la calculadora *calculator*
la camiseta publicitaria *promotional T-shirt*
la idea *idea*
el llavero *keyring*
el pedido mínimo *minimum order*
el regalo publicitario *promotional gift*
el reloj pequeño de mesa *small table clock*
seleccionar *to select*
económico/a *economic*
suelto *single, individual*

Two customers are enquiring about promotional gifts.

–How many gift ideas are listed in the company catalogue?
–What's the price of the keyrings for orders of 250 and 500 units?

Jefe de ventas Bueno. Tenemos una selección muy grande de regalos publicitarios. Ahora mismo tenemos en catálogo aproximadamente 1.000 ideas para regalos. ¿Qué artículos van ustedes a seleccionar?
Cliente 1 Queremos calculadoras, camisetas publicitarias, bolígrafos, llaveros y relojes pequeños de mesa.
Cliente 2 Estos llaveros son muy atractivos. ¿Cuál es el precio por unidad?

Jefe de ventas Aquí tiene la lista de precios. Por pedidos de 250 unidades, el precio de estos llaveros es de 70 pesetas cada uno; por 500 unidades, 59 pesetas y por 1000 unidades 55 pesetas.

¿Verdad o mentira? Correct any errors.

–The company sells stationery articles for publicity companies.
–The company has a catalogue but no price list.

The customers would like to place an order. Is there a minimum order? What's the delivery period?

Cliente 2 ¿Hay un pedido mínimo?
Jefe de ventas Sí. El pedido mínimo es de 40.000 pesetas. Pero luego se pueden hacer pedidos sueltos más pequeños.
Cliente 2 ¿Qué descuento hay por pago al contado?
Jefe de ventas Le puedo hacer 12% de descuento.
Cliente 1 ¿Cuál es el plazo de entrega?
Jefe de ventas Entrega inmediata.

INFRAESTRUCTURA ➤

Le puedo hacer 12% de descuento
You heard this expression in the dialogue. In a less formal conversation you'd be told: **Te puedo hacer 12% de descuento**. Notice the use of **le** and **te** for *you/to you/for you.*

PRACTICA ➤

el comprador *buyer*
el/la detallista/minorista *retailer*
el ejemplar *copy*
el libro de arte *art book*
el precio al consumo/al consumidor *consumer price*
el precio al detalle/al por menor *retail price*
el precio al por mayor *wholesale price*
valer *to cost*
el vendedor *seller*
hablemos *let's talk*
valer *to cost*
sobre *about, on*

1 Pablo, a sales representative, is discussing prices with Raúl, the buyer for VIPS books in Madrid.

a How much is the catalogue price of the books on Dalí, Henry Moore and González?
b How many copies of the book on Julio González has Raúl got and what discount is he prepared to offer the buyer?

2 Match the questions with the answers.
a ¿Cuál es el plazo de entrega?
b ¿Hay descuento por pago al contado?
c ¿Cuál es el precio de las camisetas por unidad?
d ¿Tienen una lista de precios?
e ¿Cuál es el precio total de los bolígrafos por 500 unidades?

1 Sí. Aquí tiene la lista de precios.
2 Las camisetas pequeñas y medianas, 600 pesetas cada una; las grandes, 700 pesetas.
3 Es de cuatro semanas.
4 El precio total es de 4.000 pesetas.
5 Sí, hay un descuento del 15%.

3 You'd like to buy some promotional gifts... if the price is right. Complete this dialogue and practise with a colleague if possible.

Sales Manager Aquí tiene el catálogo de regalos de empresa.
Usted (Say thank you. Tell the Sales Manager that you'd like the diaries.)
Sales Manager Estas agendas son de primerísima calidad.
Usted (Ask how much they are per unit.)
Sales Manager Estas cuestan 7.000 pesetas cada una. Por pedidos de 100 agendas le puedo hacer un descuento del 9%.
Usted (Ask him if there is an additional discount for cash payment.)
Sales Manager Sí. Hay un 5% de descuento adicional por pago al contado, con entrega inmediata.

4 What discounts are these opticians offering? Compare prices and answer the questions in Spanish.
a ¿Cuál es el descuento que ofrece Optica Roma en gafas graduadas?
b ¿Dónde son más caras las lentillas rígidas?
c ¿Qué diferencia de precio hay entre las lentillas blandas en Rola y en Optica Roma?
d ¿Dónde se ofrece un descuento más alto en el precio de los audífonos?
e ¿Dónde se ofrece un descuento del 20% en el precio de las gafas de sol?

los audífonos/el aparato auditivo
  hearing aid
las gafas de sol   *sunglasses*
las gafas graduadas
  prescription glasses
las lentillas/los lentes de contacto
  contact lenses
blando/a   *soft*
rígido/a   *hard*

Pedido

In this section you will practise placing an order and making enquiries by letter.

FRASES ➤

¿Qué precio tiene(n)...?   *What's the price of...?*
¿Qué forma de pago utilizan ustedes?   *What method of payment do you use?*
Acabamos de empezar   *We've just begun*
Contra reembolso   *Cash on delivery/COD*

At the Intergift trade fair in Madrid, a customer who owns a tobacconist's places an order for some articles on display on one of the stands.

¿Verdad o mentira?
–The customer is allowed to place small individual orders below 10.000 ptas.
–The firm accepts several methods of payment.
–The first item on the order form will be the keyrings.

el espejo   *mirror*
el estanco   *tobacconist's*
el género   *merchandise*
la hoja de pedido   *order form*
los pedidos posteriores
    subsequent orders
interesado/a   *interested*
por supuesto   *of course*

Collective numerals
un par de....   *a pair of*
una decena   *about ten*
una docena   *a dozen*
una veintena   *about twenty*
una treintena   *about thirty*

100   un centenar/una centena
100s   cientos/centenares
1000   un millar
1000s   miles/millares

media docena   *half-a-dozen*
la mitad de   *a half*
un kilo y medio   *1½ kilos*
una hora y media   *an hour and a half*

Vendedor Hola, buenas tardes.
Cliente Buenas tardes. Yo estaba interesada... mire, tengo un estanco en el centro de transportes de Madrid y me gustaría introducir este género tan bonito que tienen ustedes aquí. ¿Qué precio tienen estos espejos, por ejemplo?
Vendedor Pues los espejos son 850 pesetas ¿eh?
Cliente ¿Se pueden hacer pedidos sueltos?
Vendedor Sí, bueno. Ahora mismo tenemos un pedido mínimo que son 35.000 pesetas.
Cliente Y ¿qué forma de pago utilizan ustedes habitualmente?
Vendedor Pues nosotros, como acabamos de empezar, lo que estamos haciendo es hacerlo contra reembolso.
Cliente Contra reembolso. También para los pedidos posteriores, ¿también será contra reembolso?
Vendedor Sí, sí, por supuesto.
Cliente Pues si le parece a usted, podemos empezar a rellenar la hoja de pedido.
Vendedor Muy bien. Muy bien. ¿Qué es lo que le interesa? ¿Qué artículos?
Cliente Pues yo pienso que podríamos empezar por los llaveros.
Vendedor Muy bien. ¿Me puede dar sus datos?
Cliente Sí. Le daré también una tarjeta.
Vendedor Muy bien, sí.

8

Carta Comercial
A business letter

Here's how to write a letter in Spanish to obtain information, place an order, and change or cancel it.

```
                                        Cardiff, 21 de julio



Muy Sr mío/Distinguido Sr        Dear Sir
Muy Sra mía/Distinguida Sra      Dear Madam
Distinguido/Estimado Señor X     Dear Mr X
Distinguida/Estimada Señora Y    Dear Ms Y
Señores           Dear Sirs (to  a company)


Ref. Ref.
Asunto: Subject.
```

Use **Les** when writing to a company or more than one person, but **Le** to a single addressee eg: **Le agradeceremos**. Similarly, replace **agradeceremos** by **agradecería** in a more individual personal letter. (*I'd be grateful...*)

Asking for something

Les agradeceremos el envío de *We'd be grateful if you could send us*

– la siguiente información *the following information*
– información sobre condiciones de pago *information on payment terms and conditions*
– su catálogo más reciente *your latest catalogue*
– una lista de precios *a price list*
– detalles sobre los siguientes productos *details about the following products*

Placing an order

Les agradeceremos el envío de los siguientes productos: list the products with details such as **modelo** (*model*), **número de catálogo** (*catalogue number*), **tamaño** (*size*), **material** (*material*), **color** (*colour*).

Address for delivery

Por favor enviar a la siguiente dirección... (*Please send to the following address.*)

Changing, or cancelling an order

Les agradeceremos se sirvan *We'd be grateful if you could...*
– cambiar/modificar el pedido de fecha (*date*)...de la siguiente forma:
 change/modify our order of (date) as follows:
– cancelar el pedido de fecha *cancel our order of (date)*

**Types of written
 communication**
Petición de información *Letter
 of enquiry*
Cotización *Quotation*
Pedido *Order*
Acuse de recibo
 Acknowledgement
Aviso de envío *Advice Note*
Factura *Invoice*

Closing En espera de sus gratas noticias, le/les saluda muy atentamente. *Looking forward to hearing from you.* *Yours sincerely* Atentamente *Yours faithfully/sincerely*

PRACTICA

1 Match the statements 1–3 with the documents they refer to.
a Cotización; *b* Pedido; *c* Petición de información.

1 El comprador pide información a la empresa sobre precios, descuentos, condiciones de pago y entrega.
2 El vendedor envía lista de precios, catálogo y detalles sobre sus productos al comprador.
3 El comprador envía una carta a la empresa con los detalles del pedido: número de unidades, tamaño, color, material, precio y la dirección donde el pedido debe ser enviado.

2 Fill in the blanks in this letter of enquiry.
Choose from: **agendas, Asunto, camisetas, el envío, llaveros, le saluda.**

```
                        Manchester, 12 de Junio de

Sr Francisco Mascaró
Director de Ventas  MRP
Mascaró Regalo Publicitario S.A.
Av. España 25,
MADRID


Estimado Señor:


................: Petición de información.


Le agradeceremos..................de la siguiente
información: lista de precios, tamaños y colores,
descuentos por pago al contado y plazo de entrega de
los siguientes regalos de empresa .................
..................,.......................... .


En espera de sus gratas noticias, .................
..............atentamente.
(signature)
```

8

Keep a list of basic formulae and phrases for letter-writing in your notebook. Some of these expressions will also prove useful when speaking or telephoning.

3 Write a letter to each of these companies.

a asunto: petición de información

A.Segoviano S.L.
A.S. Complementos Decorativos
Ferraz, 80
28008 - Madrid

Productos: bolsas publicitarias, cintas de fantasía (ribbons), papel de regalo (gift wrapping paper), pegatinas (stickers).

b asunto: pedido

Artenudo
Artesanía de cuadros marineros
Mártires, 109
02630-La Roda
Albacete

Productos: cuadros, decoración náutica (pictures, nautical ornaments)

Condiciones de pago y de entrega

This section will help you discuss payment and delivery terms.

FRASES ▷

Estás hablando de muchos ejemplares *You're talking about a lot of copies*
¿Qué te parece? *What do you think?*
Nuestros precios incluyen... *Our prices include...*
Esta letra de cambio vence... *This bill of exchange falls due...*

★This is one of a list of international shipment terms called Incoterms. See page 160 for a more comprehensive list.

 Raúl and Pablo are talking about terms of payment. Listen and find two reasons why Raúl thinks Pablo will be able to sell the books easily. What advantage to Raúl does Pablo point out?

Pablo Sí, pero el precio es importante. Por ejemplo, en este caso, con unos descuentos de 70 y 75% podemos pagar un 10% por ejemplar.
Raúl Un 10% es muy poco. Estos libros de arte son libros de gran

las condiciones de pago
  payment terms
el crédito documentario
  irrevocable *irrevocable letter*
  of credit
el espacio *space, room*
FAS* *free alongside ship*
  (Franco-Costado del buque)
el giro bancario *bankers draft,*
  bank transfer
los problemas de almacenaje
  storage problems
el puerto *port*
la recepción de *the receipt of*
llevar *to carry*
por ejemplo *for example*
en este caso *in this case*

calidad. La calidad es tan importante como el precio.

Pablo Estás hablando de muchos ejemplares Raúl... Y necesitas espacio en el almacén... ¿verdad? A 10% por ejemplar, puedo comprar todos estos libros y tú no tienes más problemas de almacenaje, ¿qué te parece?

 Three sales reps are talking about their company's payment terms for overseas customers. What is included in the prices mentioned by the first speaker? What discount is mentioned? What terms does the second speaker describe? According to the third speaker, when is the bill of exchange due?

Representante 1 Nuestros precios incluyen F.A.S. puerto de Barcelona diez días después de la recepción del pedido. Nuestras condiciones de pago son el crédito documentario irrevocable a 30 días. Los precios al por mayor llevan un descuento del 20% por pago al contado.

Representante 2 Nuestras condiciones de pago son giro bancario a la presentación de la factura.

Representante 3 Esta letra de cambio vence a los 45 días.

Ventas *sales*

el/la comerciante a domicilio   *door-to-door salesperson*
el/la comerciante individual   *sole trader*
el día bajo   *off-peak day*
la temporada baja   *off-peak season*
los días laborables   *working days*
el lugar de ventas   *point of sale*
la oferta   *offer*
el presupuesto   *estimate, tender, quotation*
las rebajas   *cut price/marked down goods*
el saldo   *bargain*
agotado/a   *sold out, out of stock*
la garantía en depósito   *security*
la muestra   *sample*
el pedido de muestra   *sample order*
franco almacén   *ex-warehouse*
franco fábrica   *ex-works*
la factura de flete   *freight note*
el envío *shipment,   dispatch*
el certificado de origen   *certificate of origin*
los permisos de importación   *import and export licences*

Formas de pago *methods of payment*
la letra de cambio   *bill of exchange*
el cobro revertido   *C.O.D.*
la carta de crédito irrevocable   *irrevocable letter of credit*
el cheque; el talón   *cheque*
la tarjeta de crédito   *credit card*
pago por adelantado   *payment in advance*
la remesa documentaria   *documentary collection*
el cobro contra reembolso   *cash on delivery (COD)*
cuenta abierta   *open account*
el conocimiento de embarque   *bill of lading*
el registro de consignación   *consignment note*
el pagaré   *promissory note, IOU*

Tan importante como...
Tan...como (*As...as*) is used with adjectives to describe and compare items, eg **Modas Florencia S.A. es tan grande como Porcelanas Denia S.A. El producto A es tan bueno como el producto B. Los precios de este año son tan competitivos como los precios del año pasado.**

Did you know?
Bills of exchange are frequently used in Spain as means of payment in the retail trade as well as in everyday business transactions. An initial payment (**el pago inicial**) is usually made, to be followed by monthly instalments (**las mensualidades**) with interest (**el interés**). A booklet of vouchers (**las letras de cambio**) is issued at the time of purchase.

1 Choose an adjective from the list below and then complete the sentences.

alto-atractivo-bueno-caro-competitivo

a Estos libros sobre los Impresionistas son tan..... como.....

b Nuestros precios son tan ..... como.....

c El precio de los bolígrafos por unidad es tan..... como.....

d La calidad de los productos de Estudios Madrid es tan..... como.....

2 Study the phrases titled 'ventas' and find one to use in each of the following situations.

a There is no more of a particular product range left for sale.

b A store has end-of-range goods to sell quickly.

c You need to specify a number of days excluding the weekend.

d Hotels on the coastal areas in Spain don't do much business in winter.

3 Your company has placed orders with two different companies in Spain. You receive letters from both companies confirming the delivery of the goods. Explain in English the meaning of the last paragraph in each letter.

adjunto *attached, enclosed*
adjuntamos *we enclose*
la factura por duplicado
   duplicate invoice
f.c.g.v. (ferrocarril gran velocidad)
   fast goods train
f.c.p.v. (ferrocarril pequeña
   velocidad) *slow goods train*

Adjunto enviamos factura por ferrocarril y factura comercial por duplicado. Las mercancías serán enviadas por f.c.g.v.

Adjuntamos factura de envío por Transportes Altamirano S.L. y factura comercial.

12% anual   *12% pa (per annum)*
la fecha de libramiento   *date of issue*
el interés   *interest*
el lugar de libramiento   *place of issue*
las mensualidades   *monthly instalments*
el pago inicial   *down payment*
el vencimiento   *maturity*

4 You are selling a machine worth 500.000 ptas to a Spanish customer.

Explain the payment terms in Spanish: 40% down payment; ten monthly instalments payable through bills of exchange at 12% pa. Work out the amount and tell the customer how much each instalment will cost for this machine. Fill in the Bill of Exchange.

Lugar de libramiento

Importe

Fecha de libramiento

Vencimiento

CLASE 14ª

10 PTA

HASTA 4.000 PTA

Por esta LETRA DE CAMBIO *pagará usted al vencimiento expresado*

0 A 8000017

a ....
la cantidad de ....

C. C. C.

D. C.

en el domicilio de pago siguiente:

PERSONA O ENTIDAD ....
DIRECCION .... Núm. de cuenta ....

Cláusulas

Firma, nombre y domicilio del librador

Nombre y domicilio del librado

Acepto .... de ....
A .... de 19 ....

No utilice este espacio, por estar reservado para inscripción magnética

Artículos de regalo

Answer in Spanish:

-¿A qué países exporta España la mayor cantidad de artículos de regalo?
-¿Qué cifras corresponden al volumen de ventas al exterior de ropa de cama, mesa y tocador?
-¿Qué productos han experimentado un aumento en sus exportaciones? Indique los porcentajes correspondientes.

El mercado de artículos de regalo

El principal país receptor de los productos fabricados en España es Estados Unidos, seguido a continuación por países de la Comunidad Económica, con una mayor incidencia de Francia, Alemania, Italia y Portugal. El mercado estadounidense se encuentra especialmente interesado en una producción de gran tradición y prestigio en España, como es la cerámica y porcelana decorativa y de uso doméstico.

El capítulo más importante dentro de las exportaciones es el dedicado a estatuillas y más objetos y adornos de céramica con un volumen de ventas al exterior de 10.672.105 miles de pesetas. Esta cifra le sitúa con un 28 por 100 sobre el total de exportaciones realizadas.

Le sigue la partida referida a la ropa de cama, mesa y tocador, con 7.845.132 miles de pesetas. Francia, Estados Unidos, y Portugal son los mayores receptores de las ventas de este apartado. El vidrio se exporta en su mayor parte a Francia, Alemania e Italia, mientras que las alfombras se destinan principalmente a Estados Unidos, Italia y Francia.

Los productos que han experimentado un aumento en sus exportaciones son los objetos de escritorio (+ 25,40 por 100), los objetos de vidrio (19,39 por 100) y la ropa de cama y mesa (+ 2,3 por 100). En el capítulo dedicado a las importaciones se aprecia un incremento en todas las partidas, exceptuando la dedicada a material de escritorio que ha reducido sus compras al exterior en un 12 por 100.

Finalmente, se observa que la balanza comercial del mercado del regalo del año arroja un saldo a favor de las importaciones de 45.955.264 miles de pesetas.

CREDIT: INTERGIFT/GABINETE DE PRENSA DE IFEMA

el adorno   *decorative object*
la alfombra   *rug*
el apartado   *section*
el capítulo   *section*
la estatuilla   *statuette*
la partida   *section*
la ropa de cama   *bed linen*
la ropa de mesa   *table linen*
la ropa de tocador   *towels, bath robes, etc*
el vidrio   *glass*
el saldo a favor   *credit balance*
demás   *other*
estadounidense   *American*
de uso doméstico   *domestic, household*
arroja   *throws*
le sitúa   *it places it*

Inventario

Prices, orders and discounts

Hablemos de precios   *Let's talk about prices*

¿Tiene(n) una lista de precios?   *Have you got a price list?*

¿Tiene(n) un catálogo?   *Have you got a catalogue?*

¿Cuál es el precio por unidad?   *What's the price per unit?*

¿Qué precio tiene(n)...?   *What's the price of...?*

¿Hay un pedido mínimo?   *Is there a minimum order?*

¿Se pueden hacer pedidos sueltos?   *Could we place orders for small amounts/single items?*

¿Qué descuento hay por pago al contado?   *What's the discount for cash payment?*

Hay un descuento de...   *There is a discount of...*

Le/Les puedo hacer 10 por ciento de descuento   *I can give you a discount of 10%*

¿Cuál es el precio total?   *What's the total price?*

Payment terms and delivery

¿Cuál es el plazo de entrega?   *What's the delivery period?*

¿Cuáles son las condiciones de entrega/pago?   *What are the delivery/payment terms?*

¿Qué forma de pago utilizan ustedes?   *What method of payment do you accept?*

Punto de Control

Check you can do the following in Spanish:
- Ask how much something is per unit, retail and wholesale.
- Ask for a price list and a catalogue.
- Ask how much T-shirts are for orders of 250 and over.
- Ask if there is a discount for cash payment.
- Put together a short letter of enquiry asking for the price of two articles, stating colour, size, material and quantity required.
- Say you'd like to place an order, to modify an order, to cancel an order.
- Tell someone in Spanish how much he/she would have to pay per month using bills of exchange in the following situation: price 45.000 ptas; deposit 10%; 5 instalments at 10% interest.

Al contado

The main idea that British visitors must keep in mind as they set out to do business in Spain is that they are dealing with an intensely legalistic society whose legislative umbrella is entirely different to what is the norm in the UK. The basis of this contrast is the gulf that separates Britain's Common Law practice from the written law system which, based on the Napoleonic code, forms the basis for standard legal procedure in Continental Europe.

In Spain company law and the civil code form a light set of rules with a lot of fine print that any newcomer ignores at its peril. What the British executive takes for granted in the UK may well cause financial embarrassment when applied to Spain.

The issue concerning *poderes*, or the power of attorney, and the *apoderado*, or the individual who has such powers, is a case in point. These powers and the person in which they are invested must be duly spelt out in a legal document and specifically outlined. A business executive who is a director of a firm, or even its chairman, and who has long been used to taking decisions, acting on them and allocating resources at home, may find hands tied in Spain.

Unless the powers of a director are specifically set out in a legal document that has been drawn up by a lawyer and duly authorised by a public notary, it is impossible to do proper business in Spain and the director cannot, for example, sign a bill of exchange. It is vital to understand such a legal intricacy because the financial viability of a company will normally depend on bills of exchange.

Visiting British business executives will soon realise that the system of financing in Spain is radically different from what they are used to in the UK. In Spain the bill of exchange is a key financial instrument and trade discount lines - at 30, 60, 90 or 180 days - are all important.

Instead of overdraft facilities, Spain uses credit lines. In the UK everybody uses cheques but in Spain the norm is to use the bill of exchange. This credit instrument allows a certain amount of room for manoeuvre but it is within authorised limits set out in an underlying contract which specifies an agreed rate.

British business executives used to UK norms, should be especially wary of the casual overdraft. They will find the situation extremely uncomfortable. The treatment meted out by banks, both the domestic ones and the foreign ones based in Spain, on the debtor is, at least from the point of view of the individual on the receiving end, little short of usury.

Bank charges of 24 per cent and more on an overdraft, however temporary the borrowing might be, may seem

extraordinary in the UK but they are common practice in Spain. A business executive with a short-term problem in liquidity, because a payment or a transfer has been delayed, could face acute difficulties.

The most important financial lesson that the visitor must learn in Spain is to apply in good time for the *póliza de crédito*, or the credit line, and to forget about cheques and to use bills of exchange, or *letras de cambio*, instead. In order to make use of such finance by way of this instrument, the foreign businessman must have properly recognised powers, or *poderes*.

The system is not overtly complicated, although it can be stultifyingly legalistic. It is just a question of playing by an existing set of rules. Once the procedures are properly understood, the domestic banking system should in normal circumstances be found to be supportive.

FERIAS

◆ Exhibiting at a Trade Fair ◆ Benefits of exhibiting your products ◆ Setting up a stand

Estamos aquí para vender.

This section is about introducing your company and product at a trade fair.

FRASES ▶

¿Qué hace(s) aquí en la feria?   *What are you doing at this fair?*
Los españoles ¿aceptan bien un producto extranjero?   *Do the Spanish take to foreign products?*
¿Está(s) contento con el stand?   *Are you happy with the stand?*
Pasar pedidos pequeños   *To pass on small orders*

el/la colega   *colleague*
la imagen   *image*
la loza   *china*
la marca   *trademark*
la sociedad   *company*
la tienda   *shop*
vender   *to sell*
conocido/a   *well-known*
un poco   *a bit*
porque   *because*
todavía   *still, yet*

At the Feria de Madrid, one of the exhibitors explains the purpose of exhibiting products at a trade fair.

Listen and find: the product, the name of the exhibitor, two of their reasons for exhibiting at the fair. Explain in English the expression 'dar un poco de imagen de marca.'

Russell Willmoth Hola, buenos días. Soy Russell Willmoth, de la sociedad Churchill de Inglaterra. Somos fabricantes de loza inglesa de

Stoke-on-Trent, the Midlands.

Entrevistador ¿Y qué haces aquí en la feria?

Russell Wilmoth Estamos aquí principalmente con mi colega Martín Doro para vender loza. Para vender el producto a mayoristas o también para tener contacto con el detallista, la tienda pequeña y para pasar los pedidos pequeños a los mayoristas y también para dar un poco de imagen de marca porque no somos muy conocidos todavía en España.

Russell Wilmoth

Now listen to the rest of the interview and find the following information:

– The reaction of the average Spanish customer to foreign products.

– What the exhibitor thinks of the stand he has been given at the fair.

Entrevistador Y... los españoles, ¿aceptan bien un producto extranjero?

Russell Willmoth Hoy en día yo creo que el mercado español es como el resto de Europa: el español tiene mucha costumbre de ver productos de fuera, tanto como el inglés, o el francés, o de donde sea.

Entrevistador ¿Estás contento con el sitio que tienes para el stand aquí en la feria?

Russell Willmoth Bueno, el sitio para mí es muy conveniente. Estamos muy cerca de la cafetería. Tenemos un servicio al lado y estamos en un rinconcillo por donde la gente puede pasar sin problemas. Para mi está bien el sitio.

la costumbre de *the habit of*
la gente *people*
el resto *rest*
el rinconcillo *corner*
el servicio *toilet*
el sitio *place*
conveniente *convenient*
de donde sea *wherever from*
de fuera *from outside*
tanto como *as well as*

INFRAESTRUCTURA ➤

Somos, estamos

Look at the following words: **somos** (*we are*); **estamos** (*we are*); **tenemos** (*we have*).

They refer to actions performed by two or more people, eg **estamos aquí, con mi colega** (*here we are, my colleague and I*) or to activities carried out by a company, eg **estamos aquí para vender nuestros productos** (*we (the company) are here to sell our products*).

Here are a few more: **exponemos** (*we exhibit*); **fabricamos** (*we manufacture*); **queremos** (*we want*); **vendemos** (*we sell*); **tenemos contacto con** (*we are in touch with*).

PRACTICA ▶

1 Say these sentences in Spanish:
a We manufacture and sell English china.
b We want to exhibit in Madrid and Valencia next year.
c We are happy with the stand.

2 Here the exhibitors talk about the advantages of speaking Spanish at trade fairs. What are the four good reasons mentioned?

el expositor *exibitor*
el/la visitante *visitor*
la vajilla *crockery*
establecer *to establish*
hacer conocer *to make known*
no tengo que moverme *I needn't move*
ya *already*

 – El expositor debe hablar español en la feria porque hay muchos visitantes que no hablan inglés y entonces es difícil establecer contacto con ellos. Hoy, por ejemplo, después de cinco o seis horas de hablar un poco con los visitantes, tenemos ya una lista de treinta tiendas pequeñas que quieren información sobre Churchill y quieren comprar nuestra vajilla.
 – Es muy importante tomar pedidos, pero es más importante hablar con la gente y hacer conocer el nombre de la compañía.
 – En una feria se puede hablar con mucha gente, con muchos mayoristas, y no tengo que moverme del stand. Yo aquí en la feria puedo hablar con mucha gente y no tengo que viajar por todas las carreteras de España.

Try and immerse yourself in things Spanish. Take every opportunity to buy – and read – newspapers, magazines, booklets, books; go to films, concerts, lectures; and talk back to people who talk to you!

3 Make complete sentences by matching the phrases in columns A and B.

A	B
a Vendemos	mayoristas.
b La compañía se llama	un catálogo.
c Nuestros clientes son	muebles.
d Tenemos	cien mil pesetas.
e El precio de un sofá es de	Furni.

4 You are representing a company at a trade fair. Choose a product and a name for the company and answer the visitor's questions:

Visitante ¿Qué producto venden ustedes?
Usted (Say the company sells china or crockery.)
Visitante ¿Cómo se llama la compañía?
Usted (Say your company name, from Staffordshire, England.)
Visitante ¿A quiénes venden ustedes?
Usted (Say you sell to retailers and wholesalers.)
Visitante ¿Son fabricantes?
Usted (Say you are.)
Visitante ¿Venden ustedes por correo? ¿Tienen catálogo?
Usted (Say you have a catalogue but you do not sell by post in Spain; only in England and Germany.)
Visitante Me gustan mucho estos productos. ¿Tiene usted una lista de precios a mano?

Usted	(Say yes; the prices are very reasonable.)
Visitante	Me gustaría recibir un catálogo.
Usted	(Say with pleasure. Ask for his/her name, address and telephone number.)

5 Martín Doro is introducing a visitor to the Churchill Tableware stand at the Feria de Madrid to his colleague Russell Willmoth.

a Why is she visiting the fair?

b What type of articles does her company sell through a catalogue?

c What is she currently selecting for her company's catalogue?

d Why is she interested in Portuguese tableware?

e When is she thinking of buying for the next catalogue?

6 Find the right phrase.

a You want to ask a company representative if they manufacture what they sell. You ask:

¿Son representantes?/¿Son vendedores?/¿Son fabricantes?

b You would like to receive a catalogue. You say:

Me gustaría enviar un catálogo/recibir un catálogo/solicitar un catálogo.

la cosa *thing*
las cristalerías *glassware*
ofrecer *to offer*
portugués/a *Portuguese*
por ahí *thereabouts*
quizá *perhaps*

121

La Feria es un escaparate

This section looks at the benefits of exhibiting at a trade fair.

La comercialización del producto   *The marketing of the product*
Ya le digo   *As I am saying*
No se estila aquí   *It's not the way things are done here*
Casi nunca   *Hardly ever*

FRASES

Listen to Sr Rafael Prieto of Empresas Alvarez, at the Feria de Madrid, as he explains the benefits of exhibiting at a trade fair. Can you pick out the two main areas of benefit he mentions?

Entrevistador   ¿Me podría decir su nombre y a qué compañía representa, por favor?

Rafael Prieto   Bueno, yo soy Rafael Prieto, soy Director Adjunto del Grupo de Empresas Alvarez: es un conjunto de empresas en las que se caracterizan varias marcas, entre ellas son Santa Clara en porcelana y Pontesa en loza.

Entrevistador   ¿La feria es importante para la comercialización del producto?

Rafael Prieto   Bueno, sí por supuesto. La feria es un escaparate de lo que haces durante todo el año, durante períodos de tiempo entre feria y feria. Aquí pues sabes que es un centro de reuniones de todos los profesionales tanto de la venta como de la compra del producto cerámico, y es una exposición temporal muy determinada en la que ya le digo converge todo el profesional de este sector.

el centro de reuniones   *meeting place*
el conjunto de empresas   *group of companies*
el Director Adjunto   *Assistant Manager*
el escaparate   *shop window*
la exposición temporal   *temporary exhibition*
la venta   *sales*
durante   *during*

Answer these questions in Spanish:

¿Quién es el Sr Prieto y a qué grupo comercial representa?

¿A qué se dedica el grupo comercial?

¿Por qué dice el Sr Prieto que la feria es importante para el producto?

Comprando...
You have read or heard words like: **comprando**, **vendiendo**, **exponiendo**. They are the equivalent of the English *buying, selling, exhibiting.*

They are used with the verb **estar** (*to be*), to say what is happening at a given moment. With regular verbs, replace -**ar** with -**ando**, and -**er** or -**ir** with -**iendo**,

eg **compr(ar)** ➔ **comprando**; **vend(er)** ➔ **vendiendo**; **expon(er)** ➔ **exponiendo**.

For example: **Este mes estamos exponiendo y vendiendo nuestros productos en la Feria de Valencia**. (*This year we are exhibiting and selling our products at the Valencia fair.*)
Los clientes están comprando más productos tradicionales este año. (*Clients are buying more traditional products this year.*)

PRACTICA ➤

1 Change the following sentences to explain that usually you do one thing, but just now you're doing something else...
eg **Normalmente, vendo artículos de piel**.
Ahora, estoy vendiendo artículos de piel.

a Normalmente, represento a una compañía española. ➔ colombiana
b ¿Haces mucho deporte? ➔ poco
c Cogemos ideas de otros expositores. ➔ clientes
d Fabricamos loza decorativa. ➔ de uso doméstico

2 Listen to Srta Gala Sánchez at the Intergift exhibition in Madrid.

First listen for the following information:
a Who does she represent?
b Where exactly is the stand?
c Are the products being well received?

el pabellón *block, pavilion*
la reacción *reaction*
la serie *selection*
en este caso *in this case*

Now explain the following expressions in English:
somos distribuidores; **es bastante aceptable**

3 You are in charge of a stand at a fair and are being interviewed for a magazine. Answer the questions, talking about a product of your choice.

¿Cómo se llama y qué hace aquí en la feria?
¿Cómo es el stand que tienen aquí?
¿Cómo es la reacción de la gente ante el producto que ofrecen ustedes?

9

la casa   *home*
la restricción   *restriction*
gastar   *to spend*
llevo   *I have been*
nuevo/a   *new*

4 Elizabeth Lord is describing her import/export business. What does it consist of? As you listen, find out what makes the Spanish want to spend more money now and on what products.

5 Read now what Elizabeth Lord tells her interviewer about doing business in Spain.

a Find the meaning of the expression: **no se usan los cheques**

Entrevistador   ¿Hay problemas para vender aquí en España? ¿Las formas de pago son diferentes?
Elizabeth Lord   Sí. No se usan los cheques aquí. Casi nunca. Nosotros solamente hacemos cobro revertido, que es C.O.D. Pagar con cheques y tarjeta no se estila aquí.

b How many forms of payment do you remember besides C.O.D.? Look back at Unit 8 to revise them!

124

¿Dónde está el stand?

This section looks at the technical aspects of exhibiting at a fair.

Four exhibitors are discussing whether they are happy with the location of their stands.

What does Russell Willmoth think is different about exhibiting in Spain?

Find out what 'se puede regatear' means.

Entrevistador   Y en España, ¿puedes elegir dónde quieres poner el stand?
Russell Willmoth Yo creo que nosotros no. Por ejemplo en Birmingham o Francfort somos muy fuertes. Compramos un espacio enorme. Entonces en este caso se puede regatear un poco. Pero aquí tenemos solamente veinte metros cuadrados. Bueno, el sitio está bien para mí.
Entrevistador   ¿Es caro exhibir en España, en Madrid?
Russell Willmoth Es caro... pero...(*talking to his colleague*) ¿cuánto vale el metro cuadrado?... no estoy seguro. Salía algo como dos mil libras para veinte metros cuadrados. Es menos que en Alemania o Inglaterra. En Inglaterra es muy caro, por ejemplo.
Entrevistador   Sí.
Russell Willmoth Pero lo que es caro aquí, no es el sitio, son los hoteles.

caro   *expensive*
fuerte   *strong*
seguro   *sure*
elegir   *to choose*
regatear   *to bargain*

What does 'se han portado muy bien conmigo' mean?

Entrevistador   ¿Estás contenta de donde está el stand y todo eso?
Elizabeth Lord   Sí, sí, sí. Se han portado muy bien conmigo.

What does Gala Sánchez think makes her stand attractive?

Entrevistador   ¿Por qué piensas que este stand atrae la atención?
Gala Sánchez   Pues por la forma en que está montado. Después también encuentro que es un producto que llama mucho la atención.

125

la avalancha *avalanche*
la red *network*
la ubicación *location*
físico/a *physical*
al comienzo *at the beginning*
al menos *at least*

Rafael Prieto represents a Spanish company. What's special about his stand?

Entrevistador ¿Estáis contentos con el sitio que tenéis aquí?
Rafael Prieto Sí. Nos han ofrecido otro pero creemos que es un sitio con una ubicación física muy buena.
Entrevistador Yo noto que tienes un pequeño bar aquí y cae mucho personal que trabaja aquí, ¿esto es importante?
Rafael Prieto Bueno, sí. Es importante al menos al comienzo de una feria. Entonces normalmente los dos, tres primeros días, hay una avalancha de compradores buscando cosas nuevas. Entonces eso te obliga a prácticamente tener toda la red de vendedores en el stand.

¿Verdad o mentira?
a Exhibitors can choose the location of their stand.
b Exhibitors pay around one hundred pounds per square metre.
c Exhibiting in Spain is as expensive as exhibiting in Britain.

INFRAESTRUCTURA ➤

Look at the following expressions:
  Hemos instalado (*We have set up*)
  Se han portado bien (*They've behaved well*).
  They are expressions in the perfect tense, used to say what someone *has done*. The perfect is generally used as in English. It is made up of the verb **Haber** and a past participle.
  With most verbs, -**ar** is replaced by -**ado** and -**er** or -**ir** by -**ido**.
  eg mont(**ar**) mont**ado**;
  ten(**er**) ten**ido**;
  asist(**ir**) asist**ido**.

he montado
has montado
ha montado
hemos montado
habéis montado
han montado

126

Hemos montado un stand muy bonito (*We've set up a very pretty stand*).

Nos han ofrecido un buen descuento (*They've offered us a good discount*).

Note: **portarse** (*to behave*) is a reflexive verb – see page 151.

PRACTICA ➤

1 You have been exhibiting your products at a trade fair in Spain. Fill in the blanks to explain what you've done. Use **hemos vendido/hemos representado/hemos montado/hemos estado**.

a Este mes..........en la Feria de Valencia.
b ....una exposición de nuestros productos.
c ....mucho durante la Feria.
d Este año no ....a otras empresas: solamente nuestros productos.

la columna *column*
las escaleras *stairs*
la puerta *door*
preguntar *to ask*
subir *to go up*
al fondo *at the end*

2 This visitor to Interfashion is asking for information at the reception desk.
a Where will he find the Collie stand?
b Find out as much as you can about the location of the public telephone and the fax machine. What are the contents of the catalogue?

127

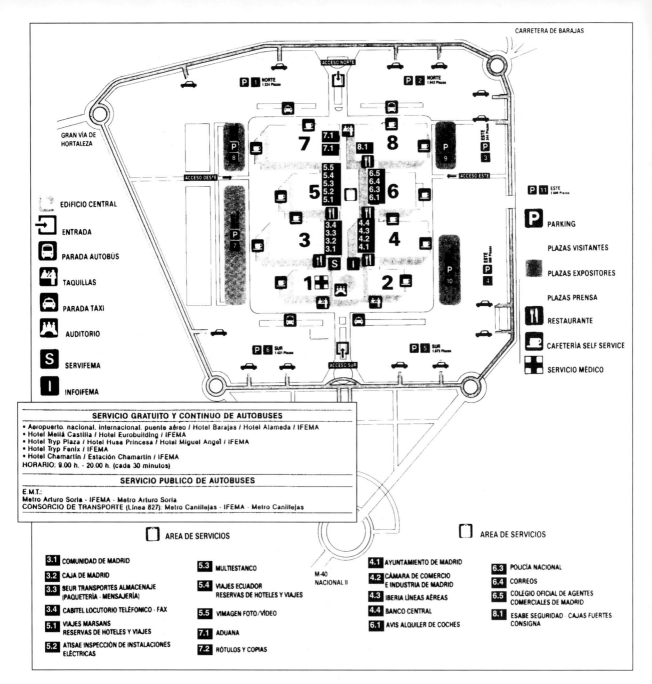

CARRETERA DE BARAJAS

P 1 NORTE 1.324 Plazas
P 2 NORTE 1.843 Plazas
ACCESO NORTE

GRAN VÍA DE HORTALEZA

ACCESO OESTE

7   7.1
    7.1
        8.1   8
ESTE
P 9   P 3 344 Plazas

ACCESO ESTE

P 11 ESTE 3.580 Plazas

5.5
5.4
5.3
5.2
5.1
5   6.5
        6.4
        6.3
        6.1
        6

3   3.4
        3.3
        3.2
        3.1
            4.4
            4.3
            4.2
            4.1
            4

P 7
P 8

ESTE
P 4 500 Plazas

1   S   2

P 10

P 6 SUR 1.431 Plazas
P 5 SUR 1.673 Plazas
ACCESO SUR

Key / Leyenda

- EDIFICIO CENTRAL
- ENTRADA
- PARADA AUTOBÚS
- TAQUILLAS
- PARADA TAXI
- AUDITORIO
- S SERVIFEMA
- I INFOIFEMA

- P PARKING
- PLAZAS VISITANTES
- PLAZAS EXPOSITORES
- PLAZAS PRENSA
- RESTAURANTE
- CAFETERÍA SELF SERVICE
- SERVICIO MÉDICO

SERVICIO GRATUITO Y CONTINUO DE AUTOBUSES

- Aeropuerto, nacional, internacional, puente aéreo / Hotel Barajas / Hotel Alameda / IFEMA
- Hotel Meliá Castilla / Hotel Eurobuilding / IFEMA
- Hotel Tryp Plaza / Hotel Husa Princesa / Hotel Miguel Angel / IFEMA
- Hotel Tryp Fenix / IFEMA
- Hotel Chamartín / Estación Chamartín / IFEMA

HORARIO: 9.00 h. - 20.00 h. (cada 30 minutos)

SERVICIO PUBLICO DE AUTOBUSES

E.M.T.:
Metro Arturo Soria · IFEMA · Metro Arturo Soria
CONSORCIO DE TRANSPORTE (Línea 827): Metro Canillejas · IFEMA · Metro Canillejas

AREA DE SERVICIOS

AREA DE SERVICIOS

M-40 NACIONAL II

3.1 COMUNIDAD DE MADRID	5.3 MULTIESTANCO	4.1 AYUNTAMIENTO DE MADRID	6.3 POLICÍA NACIONAL
3.2 CAJA DE MADRID	5.4 VIAJES ECUADOR RESERVAS DE HOTELES Y VIAJES	4.2 CÁMARA DE COMERCIO E INDUSTRIA DE MADRID	6.4 CORREOS
3.3 SEUR TRANSPORTES ALMACENAJE (PAQUETERÍA · MENSAJERÍA)	5.5 VIMAGEN FOTO/VÍDEO	4.3 IBERIA LÍNEAS AÉREAS	6.5 COLEGIO OFICIAL DE AGENTES COMERCIALES DE MADRID
3.4 CABITEL LOCUTORIO TELÉFONICO · FAX	7.1 ADUANA	4.4 BANCO CENTRAL	8.1 ESABE SEGURIDAD · CAJAS FUERTES CONSIGNA
5.1 VIAJES MARSANS RESERVAS DE HOTELES Y VIAJES	7.2 RÓTULOS Y COPIAS	6.1 AVIS ALQUILER DE COCHES	
5.2 ATISAE INSPECCIÓN DE INSTALACIONES ELÉCTRICAS			

3   The Parque Ferial Juan Carlos 1, also known as IFEMA, is a large, modern trade fair centre in Madrid. Look at the plan and answer the questions in Spanish, in full. Use **tiene**, **está**, **hay** and **se puede** as necessary.

el acceso *entrance*
el multiestanco
  tobacconist's/newsagent's
el pabellón *pavilion*
¿en qué...? *in which...?*

eg **¿Dónde está Correos? Correos está en el pabellón 2**.

a ¿Hay una parada de autobuses en el acceso sur? Está a la derecha o a la izquierda?

b ¿Cuántas cafeterías self-service tiene IFEMA?

c ¿Dónde está el multiestanco?

d ¿El pabellón 2 está cerca o lejos del acceso norte?

e ¿En qué pabellón hay servicio de teléfono y fax?

f ¿En qué pabellón se puede alquilar un coche?

g ¿En qué pabellón está el servicio médico?

h ¿Dónde está la oficina de la Cámara de Comercio e Industria de Madrid?

i Describe in Spanish the facilities at IFEMA.

Ifema has eight blocks with five restaurants, twelve cafeterias, a post office, banks, telephones and fax service and car rental service. Iberia and the Madrid Chamber of Commerce and Industry have offices at IFEMA. There is also a modern auditorium.

Now answer these questions on the transport facilities at IFEMA.

j There is a shuttle service to and from which airport, which railway station and which hotels?

k What's the timetable?

l Which main bus line and which two underground stations serve IFEMA?

Sala de prensa

Estas facilidades están agrupadas en una Sala de Prensa dotada de teléfono y fax, terminales de ordenador con acceso directo a la información de las bases de datos de uso público y las propias bases de datos de IFEMA, pantallas de TV, y todo lo que puedan necesitar los informadores para el mejor desarrollo de su labor.

Y todo ello en una Sala de Prensa bien situada (en la primera planta del Edificio Central), perfectamente equipada, puestos individuales de trabajo, cabinas telefónicas, sala de reuniones..., en la que arquitectura y decoración contribuyen a crear un espacio donde trabajar a gusto.

A las bases de datos al servicio de los participantes en los certámenes —ya mencionados en SERVIFEMA e INFOIFEMA— hay que añadir una de especial interés para los medios de comunicación: la FOTOTECA.

La Sala de Prensa

IFEMA offers special facilities for members of the media.

a On which floor is the room for members of the press?

b What facilities are available?

c What special service is also available?

la base de datos *database*
la pantalla *screen*
trabajar a gusto *to enjoy working*

9

Inventario

¿Qué hace(s) aquí en la feria?
What are you doing at the fair?
Los españoles, ¿aceptan bien un producto extranjero? *Do the Spanish take to foreign products?*
¿Está(s) contento/a con el stand? *Are you happy with the stand?*
¿Tienen ustedes una lista de precios a mano? *Have you got a price list handy?*
Me gustaría recibir un catálogo. *I would like to receive a catalogue.*
Vendemos por correo. Aquí tiene un catálogo. *We sell by mail order. Here is a catalogue.*
¿Dónde están los teléfonos? *Where are the telephones?*
¿La feria es importante para la comercialización del producto? *Is the fair important for the marketing of a product?*

¿Las formas de pago en España son diferentes? *Are payment terms different in Spain?*
¿Cuánto vale el metro cuadrado? *How much is it a square metre?*
¿Puedes elegir dónde quieres poner el stand? *Can you choose where you want to put your stand?*
¿Por qué piensas que este stand atrae la atención? *Why do you think this stand is attractive?*
Un producto que llama mucho la atención *A very attractive product*
Nos han ofrecido *We've been offered*

Punto de Control

Check you can do the following in Spanish:

- Ask exhibitors at a fair what product they are selling.

- Ask an exhibitor for a description of the product, a catalogue, a price list and payment terms.

- Explain the advantages of a stand close to the cafeteria as opposed to one in a quiet corner.

- Describe a product (your choice): say what it is, its size, price and payment terms.

- Ask potential customers for their name, address, telephone and fax numbers, and address for delivery of catalogues or merchandise.

- Ask if there is a telephone, a fax machine, a press room.

Ferias

Trade fairs in Spain are very important, much more so than in the UK. As in Germany they are a must for any entrepreneur seeking to make contacts, to explore partnerships and to study the competition. Business executives thinking of visiting Spain would be very wise to check first whether a trade fair is scheduled that deals with their particular line of business and, should this be the case, plan their trip around it.

Business people broadly involved in the food sector, for example, should know that an agricultural fair, Agroexpo, which is weighted towards processed meat products is held early in February in the Extremaduran town of Don Benitor and that round about that same date Gelat, an international fair dedicated to ice-cream manufacturing, is held in Alicante.

A high-quality food fair, the Salon Internacional del Gourmet, is held in late April in Madrid and the following month Seville stages an international Mediterranean Food Exhibition and Silleda, in Galicia, holds one that combines cattle, forest and agricultural food. The year's calendar of major food sector fairs winds up in late September at Lerida, Catalonia, with Eurofruit which specialises in sweet fruit and at Valencia in early October with Euroagro which deals with agricultural production, transformation and marketing.

On the consumer goods front there are fairs which highlight products that are well-established in Spain both because they are manufactured locally and because they draw on a large domestic market. This is the case with the international tourism fair, Fitur, held in Madrid in late January, with Valencia's mid-February international toys fair,

Feju, with Expocalzado, a footwear fair that is held in Alicante in two editions, in April and again in October, and with Modatec, an international show of footwear fashion and technology that is also held in two phases in Alicante, in May and in November.

Trade fairs in Spain run the full range, from children's fashions (Fimi, Valencia, January and June) to iron and steel (Siderometalurgica, Bilbao, September) and from international printing (Graphispag, Barcelona, February) to playground equipment, gambling machines and accessories (Induferias, Valencia, November).

In all, nearly 100 major exhibitions are staged in Spain every year - the 1993 official calendar had 94 international fairs - and so there is virtually something for everyone. At each of these fairs, the visitor can expect to meet just about anyone who matters in a given domestic sector as well as a considerable number of fellow foreigners who will likewise be intent on doing business in Spain.

As is so often the case in Spain, language ability is low. If the purpose is to do business with Spaniards then visitors ought to have good Spanish or have themselves accompanied by an interpreter.

Increasingly, the big exhibition halls and areas are moving out of town. Madrid's organising body, the Instituto Ferial de Madrid, IFEMA, has recently established itself in huge grounds near the airport. Transport from the inner city is not however a problem for IFEMA and the other city bodies lay on frequent bus services from hotels and from pre-established pick-up points to the exhibition site. A feature common to all the Spanish fairs, and a comment on their importance which is afforded to them, is that they tend to be extremely well run.

A full list of the year's Feria calendar - dates change every year and some fairs are held every two years - is available from the commercial office of the Spanish Embassy in London (24 Belgrave Square, SW1X 8OA, telephone 071 - 235 5555, fax 071-235 9905) or from the Association of Spanish Trade Fairs, Asociación Ferial Española (General Pardiñal 112, 28006-Madrid, telephone 34-1-262 1022, fax 564 4273).

British business executives who are interested in the possibility of exhibiting at any particular *feria* should also contact the Department of Trade and Industry, which helps the organisation of group exhibits in a select number of Spain's fairs.

10

HABLEMOS DE NEGOCIOS

◆ Describing a company and its products ◆ Discussing
promotional activities ◆ Ideas and proposals

¿Qué fabrica su empresa?

This section will help you talk about your company and the product or
service it supplies

¿Dónde se ubica su empresa?   *Where is your company located?*
La distribución, ¿cómo la llevan?   *How do you carry out the distribution?*
¿Es una agencia española?   *Is it a Spanish agency?*
¿Qué papel juega la publicidad?   *What's the role of publicity?*
Lo que pretende es vender   *What it tries to do is to sell*

At Interfashion, Antonio Audi from Audi Diseño talks to Josep Maltes,
Managing Director of Collie S.A. What are Sr Maltes' responsibilities as
managing director?

la compañía participada   *joint venture*
el ejercicio anterior   *the last fiscal year*
el género de punto   *knitwear*
el pueblo   *small town*
llevar   *to carry*
mover   *to move*
geográficamente   *geographically*

Antonio Audi   Hola buenos días, soy Antonio Audi de la empresa Audi
Diseño. Su nombre por favor.
Josep Maltes   Me llamo Josep Maltes y soy director gerente de la
empresa Collie S.A.
Antonio Audi   Geográficamente, ¿dónde se ubica su empresa?
Josep Maltes   En Cataluña, en el área de Barcelona, en un pueblo que
se llama Cabrea de Mar.

Antonio Audi   Sí.

Josep Maltes   ...que tiene un polígono industrial, cerca de Mataró.

Antonio Audi   ¿Y su posición dentro de esta empresa?

Josep Maltes   Soy director gerente, mi función es coordinar las distintas áreas de dirección, marketing, administración.

Antonio Audi   ¿Y qué productos fabrica su empresa?

Josep Maltes   Nos dedicamos a la fabricación de artículos de género de punto.

Choose the right option:

Cabrea de Mar is an industrial estate/a factory/a town.

Collie S.A. manufactures footwear/knitwear/beachwear.

Sr Audi goes on to ask questions about Collie S.A. Listen for the number of employees and the company sales revenue. State these in Spanish, using **la compañía tiene...**

Antonio Audi   ¿Qué número de empleados tienen Vds?

Josep Maltes   Cincuenta empleados.

Antonio Audi   ¿La empresa es totalmente nacional o es participada?

Josep Maltes   Es una empresa catalana, con capital 100% nacional.

Antonio Audi   ¿La facturación anual que mueven Vds?

Josep Maltes   En el ejercicio anterior, pues, la facturación fue de 800 millones de pesestas.

Antonio Audi   La distribución de los artículos ¿como la llevan?

Josep Maltes   Pues a través de agentes comerciales, que nos representan en las diferentes provincias, las diferentes partes del mercado.

Antonio Audi   O sea en el mercado nacional.

Josep Maltes   El mercado nacional, sí.

Answer in Spanish:
– How do they distribute their products?
– Do they export their products?

 Listen to Rosa Caminal from Contrapunto, a successful Spanish publicity company. How long has the company been in business? What is its main strength?

Rosa Caminal   Contrapunto que ya tiene 17 años en España, se creó con una empresa de seis, siete personas, ahora somos más de cien, somos un grupo, pero en este momento ocupamos un lugar en el ranking de facturación, somos la empresa número diez del ranking.

Entrevistador   ¿O sea que Contrapunto es una agencia puramente española?

Rosa Caminal   Sí. Contrapunto es una agencia española. Nuestros clientes son básicamente clientes españoles y nuestro mercado natural es ése: clientes españoles, aunque también tenemos clientes

los cambios   *the changes*
el conocimiento   *knowledge*
el estilo de vida   *lifestyle*
los hábitos   *habits*
el lenguaje   *language*
se creó   *it was set up*
o sea   *that is to say*
aunque   *although*
sobre todo   *above all*

133

internacionales. Contrapunto sobre todo tiene un conocimiento del consumidor español verdaderamente privilegiado. Conocemos muy bien al consumidor, en los cambios que ha experimentado el consumidor, en hábitos, en lenguajes, en estilos de vida.

Entrevistador ¿Qué papel juega la publicidad?

Rosa Caminal Está clarísimo que lo que pretende es vender.

In what way does Contrapunto understand the average Spanish customer?

INFRAESTRUCTURA ➤

This is a good time to check your knowledge of items introduced in previous Infraestructura sections, especially those in Units 6 – 9.

Expressing opinions
Pienso que... (*I think that...*)
¿Qué piensa usted? (*What do you think?*)
El/ella piensa que (*He/she thinks that...*)
Pensamos que (*We think that...*)
¿Qué piensan ustedes? (*What do you think?*)
Creo que (*I believe/think that...*)
Creemos que (*We think/believe that...*)
¿Qué creen ustedes? (*What do you think?*) (*to two or more people*)
eg **Creo que es un buen descuento. ¿Qué piensan ustedes?** (*I believe it's a good discount. What do you think?*)

Expressing objections
Pienso/Creo que... pero... (*I think (that)... but...*)
eg **Pienso/Creo que el producto es bueno pero los colores no son atractivos.** (*I think the product's good, but the colours aren't appealing.*)

PRACTICA ➤

1 Some companies manufacture products; others offer a service. Match the different types of company listed in column *A* with the right product or service from column *B*.

A	*B*
a an insurance company	*1* un servicio de comidas
b a pottery	*2* loza de uso doméstico
c a consultancy firm	*3* un servicio de asesoramiento
d a catering firm	*4* pólizas de seguros

2 Say what these companies do. Use **fabrica**, **vende**, **ofrece un servicio de...**
a Porcelanas Santa Clara S.A. (Unit 6) *b* Campofrío S.A. (Unit 6)
c Contrapunto.

3 Talk about your company. Explain the following in Spanish:
The company is located in .... It is near (major town). It is
.... kilometres from London. We manufacture .... We
have .... (number) employees. It is a British company. The capital is
... % British. We have an annual turnover of £..... We sell our
products in the United Kingdom and export a small percentage to
....

4 You are introducing a product or service to a group of Spanish-
speaking business people. Choose a service/product of your own, or
select from: publicity services, hand-made furniture, ready to cook
meals.
a Name the product or service.
b Select three appropriate features from those listed to include in your
presentation.

- It is a new/good/high quality product/service.
- It measures (**mide**) x centimetres/metres by x cm/m.
- The materials are wood/china/aluminium/PVC/steel/plastic/wool/
  cotton/metal/polyester/natural fibres.
- it is heavy/light (**pesado/a**, **ligero/a**).
- This product/service is a bit expensive/is not expensive/the price is
  reasonable.
- Your customers are British (and/or other nationalities).

5*a* Say what you think of a product. Use **Pienso que...** or **Creo
que**... eg **Pienso que el producto es bueno.**
- You think the product is attractive.
- You believe there is a market for this product.
- You think publicity is very important to sell the product.

b There are details you don't quite like about the product. Use **Lo
siento, pero**... eg **Lo siento, pero pienso que el color no es
atractivo.**
- You think the product is too expensive.
- You think there is a distribution problem.

6 Talk about the company's plans for the immediate future with
regard to the product or service you described in question 4. Combine
your choice of expressions, verbs and phrases from the list below to
structure your talk:
- Quisiéramos/Nos gustaría/Vamos a...
- *Verbs:* introducir; exportar; aumentar; invertir; seleccionar.
- *Phrases:* las actividades de promoción; un nuevo producto/servicio;
  nuevos clientes; nuevos mercados; un nuevo catálogo; nuevos folletos
  informativos; a/en España, a/en la Comunidad Europea.

Los materiales   *Materials*
el acero   *steel*
el algodón   *cotton*
el aluminio   *aluminium*
las fibras naturales   *natural
    fibres*
la lana   *wool*
la loza   *china*
la madera   *wood*
el metal   *metal*
el plástico   *plastic*
PVC/uPVC   *PVC/uPVC*
hecho a mano   *hand-made*

When speaking a foreign language,
some people become uncertain and
reserved. Think positive and give it
your best attempt. Nobody will
expect you to be perfect in Spanish
and most will sympathise from their
own experience of foreign
languages.

10   La publicidad es importante

This section will help you talk about promotional activities.

FRASES ▶

Cómo funciona el producto   *How the product works*
Depende del mercado   *It depends on the market*
Organizamos   *We organize*
Asistimos   *We attend*
Compartimentamos   *We divide/share*

Sr Josep Selles at Banco de Sabadell promotes the bank's services to the business community. The interviewer asks Sr Selles about their range of promotional activities.

el abanico   *fan/range*
el promotor de ventas   *sales promoter*
los promotores   *promoters*
encaminado/a   *directed towards*

Name three kinds of promotional activity carried out by the Banco de Sabadell.

Josep Selles   Sí, sí. Tenemos prácticamente todo el abanico completo de lo que se suele hacer para promocionar productos. Pues tenemos lo que te digo, las simples listas, las promociones a través de Bancos, y luego, pues organizamos misiones comerciales, asistimos a ferias... ¿Cómo asistimos a ferias? Pues alquilamos

un stand nosotros y luego compartimentamos entre varias empresas. Misiones comerciales, ferias... luego tenemos los promotores, es decir una persona que viene aquí, se va a ver a una empresa, se entera de cómo funciona el producto y luego, en su país, hace una acción comercial que, bueno, encaminada a introducir ese producto ahí que puede durar tres, cuatro, cinco o seis meses, incluso algunos han llegado a un año, depende del mercado, depende del producto.

preparáis   *you prepare*
el mismo sector   *same sector*
nos conviene   *it's a good idea, it suits us*
uniforme   *standard*
en vez de   *instead of*

Explain in English the three stages of operation of a sales promoter, as described by Sr Selles. How do they save money when they take part in trade fair activities?

Sr Selles goes on to describe the catalogues produced by the bank on behalf of their clients. How do they make catalogue production more economical?

Interviewer ¿Preparáis algún tipo también de materiales promocionales, como puede ser catálogos, etcétera?

Josep Selles Evidentemente, cuando hacemos una misión o vamos a una feria se prepara; como por ejemplo en los showrooms, siguiendo con el ejemplo, tenemos un grupo más o menos del mismo sector, entonces nos conviene hacer un catálogo uniforme en vez de hacer cuatro catálogos o cinco catálogos de diferentes empresas, ¿no?.

INFRAESTRUCTURA ▶

la publicidad   *publicity*
la promoción por correo   *direct mail*
la lista de direcciones   *mailing list*
la promoción por teléfono   *direct marketing by telephone*
las misiones comerciales   *commercial missions*
la feria   *trade fair*
las demostraciones   *demonstrations*
el salón de ventas/el showroom   *showroom*

It would be useful at this point to consolidate your knowledge of verbs in Spanish. Turn to pages 152–157.

More useful expressions
Saying what you or your company would like to do:

Me gustaría *(I would like)*   **Nos gustaría** *(We would like)*
Use these expressions in combination with verbs in the infinitive.
eg **Me gustaría visitar su stand.** *(I would like to visit your stand.)*
Nos gustaría pagar con cheque. *(We would like to pay by cheque.)*

¿Por qué? Porque...
Why? Because...

eg **¿Por qué es importante la publicidad? Porque ayuda a vender.** *(Why is publicity important? Because it helps you to sell.)*
¿Porqué piensan que el descuento no es suficiente? Porque es un pedido al por mayor muy importante. *(Why do you think the discount is not enough? Because it is a very important wholesale order.)*

PRACTICA ▶

no hace maravillas   *it doesn't work miracles*
ayuda a vender   *it helps to sell*
tenemos contacto con   *we are in contact with*
en el extranjero   *abroad*
vienen a visitarnos   *they come to visit us*
responde   *it responds*
el soporte   *support*

 1 Listen to Sr Miguel Muñoz Alonso from Tandem DDB Needham. What does he say about the role of publicity?

2 ¿Por qué? Porque... Answer these questions in Spanish.
a ¿Por qué es importante la publicidad?
b ¿Por qué es una buena idea exponer los productos en una feria industrial?

3 Sr Pablo Moreno from VIPS Books explains how the company carries out the selection and purchase of books.

a Where do they establish contact with publishers and suppliers?

b What are the characteristics of the average VIPS Books customer?

c What type of books do they sell?

4 A sales promoter is visiting your company and wants to know how the company promotes its products.

a Mention some of your promotional activities, using **Hacemos:** publicity; direct mail; direct marketing by telephone; trade fairs.

b Say three things your company has done to promote its products. Use **Hemos** followed by **exportado, montado, vendido**, eg **Hemos exportado el 5% al Japón**.

c Say something your company would like to do, using **Nos gustaría**, eg **Nos gustaría exportar este producto**.

5 Giving the company view. Use **Pensamos que...** or **Creemos que**... and make the following claims:

a Trade fairs are a good idea.

b The product is appropriate for the European market.

c Our prices are competitive.

los editores *editors/publishers*
el/la proveedor/a *supplier*
tener en mente *to have in mind*
joven *young*
medianamente culto *reasonably educated*

¿Cuál es su propuesta?

This section will help you discuss ideas and proposals.

Cuál sería el plan de trabajo   *What the plan of work would be*
Haríamos   *We would do*
Invitaríamos   *We would invite*
Tenemos la propuesta preparada   *We have the proposal ready*
Tenéis un producto muy bueno   *You have a very good product*
Pero tenéis un problema con el precio   *But you have a problem with the price*

6 Promoting and selling a product means effective presentations and meetings.

Jaime Tresserra, a furniture designer, discusses with an executive from Banco de Sabadell the possible introduction into the American market of his specially designed cocktail cabinet. Banco de Sabadell is offering its showroom in New York as a venue to exhibit his furniture. What's special about this cocktail cabinet? What's the Bank representative's idea for the promotion of this product?

Jaime Tresserra
Este es un mueble bar. Las botellas van en los espacios de abajo, para reforzar la idea de peso, y arriba los vasos. Su forma es elíptica, con lo cual se adapta a cualquier rincón, cualquier esquina, no hay ningún problema de espacio, cabe en el mínimo de espacio entre dos sofás.

Representante   Se puede poner en cualquier tipo de espacio.
Jaime Tresserra   Sí, exactamente. Le llaman incluso pues el mueble totem, el mueble escultura, el mueble columna.
Representante   Muy bien. Si quieres pasamos a la reunión.
Jaime Tresserra   Estupendo.
Representante   Sacamos los papeles. Ya tenemos aquí la propuesta preparada. Bueno, para empezar, tenéis un producto muy bueno pero tenéis un problema con el precio. Entonces la idea sería aprovechar lo que se llama en Estados Unidos los open showrooms.

el/la decorador/a   *interior decorator*
la duración   *duration*
la forma   *shape*
el mueble   *piece of furniture*
el mueble bar   *cocktail cabinet*
los muebles   *furniture*
el peso   *weight*
aprovechar   *to take advantage of*
caber   *to fit*
reforzar   *to reinforce*
sacar (los papeles)   *to get (the documents) out*
con lo cual   *with which*
cualquier rincón/esquina   *any corner*

139

Listen to the next part of the meeting. What's the Bank's proposal?

Representante   Haríamos un mailing a los 150 decoradores más importantes presentando Tresserra, con un catálogo y los invitaríamos a venir a nuestro showroom a ver el producto.

Jaime Tresserra   Perfecto.

Representante   Esto es un poco la propuesta. Aquí te explico un poco cuál sería el plan de trabajo, la duración y el precio.

INFRAESTRUCTURA ➤

You might find it useful to learn expressions in groups collected by their function, such as the ones given here.

Making a suggestion
Sugerimos (*We suggest*)
Preferimos (*We prefer*)
Proponemos (*We are proposing*)
Ofrecemos (*We are offering*)

Agreeing
No hay problema (*No problem*)
Perfecto (*Of course/perfect*)
De acuerdo (*Agreed*)
Vale (*OK*)
Me gusta/Me gustan (*I like (it/them)*)
Estoy/Estamos de acuerdo (*I am/We are in agreement*)

Disagreeing
No me gusta/No me gustan (*I don't like it/them*)

No estoy/No estamos de acuerdo (*I am not/We are not in agreement*)

To disagree firmly but politely, you could say **Lo siento, pero...** (*I'm sorry, but...*); or try **Desafortunadamente...** (*Unfortunately ...*), eg **Lo siento, pero no estoy de acuerdo con las condiciones de pago.** (*I'm sorry, but I don't agree with the payment terms.*)

¿Cuál sería el plan? La idea sería...
Sería means *would be*: it's conditional tense of the verb **ser** (*to be*). Similarly, **haríamos** and **invitaríamos** are conditionals, meaning *we would do* and *we would invite*. You've already come across **me gustaría** for *I'd like*. For more on the conditional, see page 155.

1 Agreeing and disagreeing. Use **Estoy de acuerdo** or **No estoy de acuerdo**, and correct where necessary.

a Los representantes están en la feria para vender sus productos.

b En España la venta por correo es bastante importante.

c Muchas empresas expositoras son pequeñas empresas familiares.

d El showroom es más importante que la feria.

e El diseño es más importante que la calidad.

2 Sr David Balcells from Mobel Línea explains the different characteristics of a showroom and a trade fair.

El showroom ofrece un contacto más personal porque la gente que viene es gente seleccionada, gente que está interesada y que viene a ver nuestro producto y a colaborar con nosotros. En la feria es gente que pasa, que te deja su tarjeta, pero es diferente; es todo más impersonal. La ventaja que tiene la feria es que puedes ver mucha más gente que en el showroom.

Answer in Spanish: **¿Cuál es la ventaja del showroom**? **Cuál es la ventaja y cuál la desventaja de la feria**?

3 Choose a product and answer the customer's questions. Use the suggestions given if you wish.

a ¿Qué son?   (Cuadros de Inglaterra)

b ¿Qué precio tienen? (Los grandes/los pequeños cuestan)

c ¿Tienen un pedido mínimo? (10)

d ¿Qué forma de pago utilizan ustedes?   (C.O.D.)

e ¿Se puede pagar con tarjeta de crédito? (Sorry,no)

4 Pros and cons. List the qualities of your product: it's a tea set – **un juego de té de porcelana**.

a It's light; *b* It's attractive; *c* The design is good; *d* It's microwave-resistant (resistente al microondas) *e* It's not too expensive.

As a potential customer, point out the drawbacks of a product: this time it's a telephone – **un teléfono**.

a It's heavy; *b* The design is not very good; *c* It's much more expensive than the old model.

5a Complete the sentences with any one of **preferimos**, **proponemos**, or **ofrecemos**.

.... un descuento de 12% por pago al contado.

.... presentar el producto en una feria o en un showroom.

.... un servicio de asesoramiento financiero.

.... vender estos productos a plazos.

la gente   *people*
la gente que pasa   *passers-by*
la ventaja   *the advantage*
la desventaja   *the disadvantage*
colaborar   *to cooperate*
impersonal   *impersonal*
seleccionado/a   *selected*

The Spanish for *people* is **la gente**. It is singular, so instead of saying *people are* you have to say **la gente es** (literally 'people is').

b Match the following verbs with infinitives to make three complete sentences: eg **Preferimos pagar con letra de cambio**.

– preferimos   .../importar/exportar
– proponemos   .../comprar/vender
– ofrecemos   .../pagar/firmar un contrato

6 Your opinions are being challenged. Disagree with each statement and give your opinion:

eg **Pensamos que el precio es adecuado.**
Lo siento, no estamos de acuerdo. Pensamos que es un poco caro.

a Pensamos que el descuento del 6% es suficiente.
b Creemos que el plazo de entrega de dos meses es adecuado.
c Pensamos que el pago de un depósito no es necesario.

 ## Servicio Pensión del Banco de Sabadell

Read the publicity material from Banco de Sabadell giving details of a long list of benefits available to pensioners.

● **Aproveche todo lo que le ofrecemos.**
Por ser titular del Servicio Pensión, Usted tiene más ventajas.

● **Seguro de accidentes gratuito.** 1.000.000 de pesetas en caso de muerte por accidente. Además, puede contratar otras pólizas de seguro de vida, accidente y hogar, gestionados por BanSabadell Correduría de Seguros S.A., a precios especiales.

● **Tarjeta 4B.** Para obtener dinero en efectivo las 24 horas del día en la mayoría de cajeros automáticos del país y en horas de oficina en todas las oficinas bancarias que exhiban el distintivo 'TELECASH', así como en las redes asociadas del extranjero (Andorra, Portugal, Bélgica y Reino Unido). También podrá pagar en efectivo en todos los establecimientos donde vea el distintivo 'TELEPAGO 4B'.

> ● Además, la tarjeta 4B le ofrece la posibilidad de contratar, por un importe mínimo, el seguro 'EUROP ASSISTANCE', que le permitirá disfrutar de una gran variedad de prestaciones de asistencia en viaje.
>
> ● Con nuestro Servicio Pensión, las imposiciones a plazo fijo obtienen un elevado interés mensual. Para sacarle todo el provecho a su pensión.
>
> ● Y con un poco de suerte, viaje gratis.
> Cada año sorteamos 30 viajes de lujo a las principales ciudades europeas entre todos los titulares del Servicio Pensión. Este año, usted puede ser uno de los afortunados.

los cajeros automáticos *cash dispenser/ATM*
el hogar *home*
el importe mínimo *minimum amount*
al plazo fijo *fixed-term*
las prestaciones *facilities*
las redes asociadas *associated networks*
el seguro de vida *life insurance*
el viaje *trip/journey*
en caso de muerte por accidente *in case of accidental death*
además *besides*

Work with one or more fellow students or colleagues if possible. In turns, take the role of the sales rep and a customer. Follow this format:

➤ Introduce yourself by name and job title to your potential customers.

➤ Introduce your colleague(s) if you are working as a team and make sure you know the correct names of your potential customers.

➤ Name the institution you are working for.

➤ Introduce the service you are selling.

➤ Spell out the advantages to your customers. Use **Se puede comprar/obtener…**

– free personal accident insurance (state the amount)
– cash card (name it and say when and where it can be used)
– extra services that can be purchased with the card
– higher interest on their savings
- what they could win if they are lucky!

10

Giving opinions

¿Qué piensa usted?   *What do you think?*

Pienso que/Pensamos que   *I/We think*

Creo que/Creemos que   *I/We believe/think*

Expressing objections

Pienso que... pero   *I think ... but ...*

¿Por qué?   *Why?*   Porque... *Because ...*

No me gusta(n)/No nos gusta(n)... *I/We don't like*

No estoy/No estamos de acuerdo *I/We don't agree*

Lo siento, pero...   *I'm sorry, but ...*

Putting forward proposals

Me gustaría/Nos gustaría   *I/We would like*

Sugerimos   *We suggest*

Preferimos   *We prefer*

Proponemos   *We propose*

Ofrecemos   *We are offering*

¿Cuál es su propuesta?   *What's your proposal?*

Nuestra propuesta es la siguiente: *Our proposal is as follows:*

Agreeing

Me gusta(n)/Nos gusta(n)   *I/We like*

Estoy/Estamos de acuerdo   *I /We agree*

No hay problema   *No problem*

Perfecto   *Perfect/Of course*

De acuerdo   *Agreed*

Vale   *OK*

Punto de control

Check you can do the following in Spanish:

- Talk briefly about the company you represent: its location, size, number of employees, turnover, exports.

- Describe your company's product or service.

- Say that you like a product but you think it is a bit expensive.

- Disagree firmly but politely with statements.

- Talk about the advantages and disadvantages of a product or service.

Hablemos de negocios

Foreigners intent on setting up a company in Spain may soon come to the conclusion that they are in a country that is run by lawyers for the benefit of lawyers. Periodically the administration announces legislative changes that aim to cut through the bureaucratic red tape and to simplify the procedures that are required to open for business. Old business-in-Spain hands claim that nothing really changes and that the legal jungle remains as impenetrable as ever.

A consequence of this situation is that prospective business executives will need a lawyer they can trust and work with. The lawyer will guide them through the labyrinthine bureaucracy and will also introduce them to two all-important figures - the *gestor* and the *notario*.

The existence of the *gestor* profession is in itself a comment on the reels of red tape that exist in Spain. The *gestor* is in reality nothing more than a fix-it, middleman. Operating from a *gestoría*, they will queue up at the myriad of central government, local government and municipal government offices, in order to obtain and assemble the numerous permits required to authorise a business venture.

Once the documentation is in order, the *notario*, or the public notary, takes over. A counter-signature by a *notario* is necessary to convert any commercial transaction or any official permit into a legal document. Even the most mundane paperwork will frequently require the notary's sanction.

The lawyer, the *gestor* and the *notario* make a formidable trio whose support is essential to any business executives operating in Spain, foreigners as much as local Spaniards. The other key ally is, obviously, an accountant. Visitors should not rely on their own ability to read a balance sheet but should employ someone who is well-versed in the local book keeping lore.

Together with the legal jungle trio, the accountant comes into play when a foreign business is seeking to establish a partnership with an existing domestic company or to acquire it outright. Usually the quickest way into business in Spain is through the acquisition route. This will save on the paperwork involved in setting-up from scratch.

While due diligence is a watchword everywhere, it should be borne in mind in Spain more than in most places. *Lo Negro* is the code word for business that belongs to what is called the submerged economy and for income that is hidden from the authorities, and in particular from the tax authorities.

Until relatively recently the norm among many Spanish companies was to keep two sets of books: a cosmetic one for the benefit of outsiders and a second one that was for the directors' eyes only and which gave a true picture of the company's business. Double book-keeping is officially now a feature of the past but it has not disappeared - it is just more hidden than before.

An unintended consequence of the introduction of Value Added Tax (IVA in Spanish) in the wake of European Community entry in 1986 and of new auditing regulations inspired by the Commission, has been to submerge undeclared operations still further. They are very much a feature of industries based on out-work such as shoes and textiles. An outsider, much like the tax inspector, will be hard put to fathom what such businesses are really about; sales and income could be quite fictitious.

PRONUNCIATION

Learning to pronounce Spanish should be reasonably easy because with just a few exceptions, pronunciation and spelling go closely together. The best way to improve your pronunciation is to listen to the recordings that accompany the book as often as possible and imitate the speakers. The following is a guideline to the sounds:

CONSONANTS

Letter and sound		Example
b	like *b* in *bar*	**b**uenos días
c	before **a**, **o** and **u** and any other consonant, like *c* in *cost*	en**c**antado, **c**rudo
	before **e** and **i** like *th* in *thin*	pre**c**io, por**c**elana
ch	like *ch* in *chair*	mu**ch**as
d	at the beginning of a word, like *d* in *day*	**d**ías, **d**os
	between vowels or after **r**, like *th* in *them*, pronounced very lightly	a**d**iós, buenas tar**d**es
	at the end of a word, **d** is hardly pronounced at all	ciuda**d**, uste**d**
f	like *f* in *for*	**f**eria
	(Note: The combination **ph** does not exist in Spanish eg *foto*.)	
g	before **a**, **o** and **u** and any other consonant, like *g* in *go*,	**g**usto, **g**rande
	before **e** and **i** like a strong *h* (as in *loch*)	**g**erente
	In the combinations **gue** and **gui** the **u** is silent	Mi**gu**el, **gu**itarra
h	is silent	**h**ora, ¡**H**ola!
j	like the *ch* in *loch*	**j**amón, a**j**o
l	like *l* in *love*	**l**a, ing**l**és
ll	like the *lli* in *million*	Me **ll**amo, ¿cómo se **ll**ama?
m	like *m* in *man*	**m**is**m**o, **m**añana
n	like *n* in *none*	**n**o, **n**ombre
	However, when **n** comes before **v** it is pronounced as *m*. The two letters together are pronounced *mb*	e**nv**iar
ñ	like *ni* in *onion*,	espa**ñ**ol, a**ñ**o
p	like *p* in *put*	**p**or favor
qu	like the *c* in *cake*	¿**qu**é?, **qu**isiera
r	within or at the end of a word is slightly rolled	seño**r**ita, llama**r**
	at the beginning of a word and **rr** strongly rolled	**r**estaurante, Medite**rr**áneo
s	like *s* in *same*	**s**oy, co**s**a
	Before a voiced consonant (**b**, **d**, **g**, **l**, **m**, **n**) like *s* in *rose*	de**s**de, mi**s**mo
t	like *t* in *ten*	res**t**aurante, direc**t**ora
v	like *b* in *bar* (see **b** above)	fa**v**or, **v**igilia

VOWELS

a	like the *a* in *pat*	g**a**mb**a**, p**a**t**a**t**a**
e	like the *e* in *pen*	g**e**r**e**nt**e**
i	like *ee* in *seen*	V**i**go, Sev**i**lla
o	like the *o* in *often*	h**o**mbre, c**o**sta
u	like the *oo* in *cool*	g**u**sto

See also notes on **g** and **q** above.

DIPHTHONGS

The vowels **a**, **o** and **e** are strong vowels and **i** and **u** are weak vowels. A combination of strong and weak forms a diphthong.

ai/ay	like the *i* as in *tide*	**ai**re, h**ay**
au	like the *ou* in *sound*	M**au**ricio
ei/ey	like *ay* in *hay*	r**ei**na, r**ey**
ie	like *ye* in *yet*	c**ie**n, Torrev**ie**ja
oi/oy	like *oy* in *boy*	s**oy**, v**oy**
eu	like *e* in *pen* and *oo* in *cool*	**Eu**ropa

Note: with the combination **ee** each letter is pronounced separately, eg l**ee**r, cr**ee**r.

GRAMMAR SUMMARY

Note about punctuation

In written Spanish you must always include an inverted question mark at the beginning of a question: **¿En qué puedo servirle?** The same applies to the exclamation mark: **¡Sí!**

NOUNS AND ARTICLES

el mercado	*the market*	**un** mercado	*a market*
la compañía	*the company*	**una** compañía	*a company*

In the phrases above the words **mercado** and **compañía** are nouns. A noun is a word that tells you what something is or who someone is. **José** is a noun, so is **Madrid.**

El/la mean *the*; **un/una** mean *a/an*; **el** and **un** are masculine and **la** and **una** are feminine. These words are called articles. **El/la** are definite articles and **un/una** are indefinite articles.

Gender

Every noun in Spanish is either masculine or feminine whether it refers to people, animals, things or abstract ideas. As a general rule, nouns ending in **-o** are masculine and in **-a** are feminine, eg **el mercado** is masculine; **la compañía** is feminine.

There are exceptions: a few masculine nouns end in **-a**: eg **el día** (*the day*); **el mapa** (*the map*); **el problema** (*the problem*); **el tema** (*the topic/theme*); and a very small number of feminine nouns end in **-o**: eg **la mano** (*the hand*). Also there are a few nouns which are uni-sex; they have the same ending in both genders: eg **el/la colega, recepcionista, telefonista, turista.**

El/la are used before titles: eg **El Sr Pérez, La Sra García,** when you refer to people (**El Señor Pérez habla inglés**) though not when you address them (**Buenos días, Sr Pérez**).

It's best to learn each noun with its corresponding article.

Number

los mercados	*the markets*
las compañías	*the companies*

When there is only one of something it is called singular and when there are two or more of something it is called plural. In Spanish there is a simple way to make a noun plural: for nouns ending in a vowel, add **-s** and for nouns ending in a consonant add **-es.**

empresa → empresa**s**   señor → señor**es**

When the noun is plural, the article will also be plural. The plural of **el** is **los** and the plural of **la** is **las:**

la empresa → **las** empresas **el** señor → **los** señores

Un/una also have a plural form but in the plural the meaning changes to *some*:

una compañía *a company*; **unas** compañías *some companies.*

Note: In Spanish **un/una** are not used before occupations:

Soy arquitecto.   Soy gerente de márketing.

The diminutive

The diminutive in Spanish is formed like this:

la gamba (*prawn*) → **la gamb(a)** + **ita** → **la gambita**

In Spanish the diminutive is used when referring to small things and also when trying to emphasize the quality or the particularly pleasing characteristics of something, eg **un cochecito precioso** (*a lovely little car*). In Spanish, as in English, diminutives should be used only occasionally when they seem appropriate to the speaker.

ADJECTIVES

el mercado **europeo**	*the European market*
una compañía **británica**	*a British company*

In the examples the words **europeo** and **británica** are adjectives. Adjectives describe nouns.

Agreement of nouns and adjectives

Adjectives have to agree with the nouns they describe. If the noun is feminine, the adjective will be feminine; if the noun is singular, the adjective will be singular, and so on. This is called 'agreeing in gender and number'. In the phrase **una compañía británica,** *compañía* is feminine and singular so the describing word *británica* is also feminine and singular.

El mercad**o** europe**o** → **Los** mercad**os** europe**os**
Una compañí**a** británic**a** → **Unas** compañí**as** británic**as**

If an adjective is used for a mixture of feminine and masculine nouns, the adjective should be used in the masculine plural. **La Directora de márketing, el apoderado, los representantes y la secretaria son español**es**.

Most adjective endings are similar to noun endings, so the plurals are formed in the same way: if the adjective ends in a vowel add **-s,** if it ends in a consonant, add **-es:**

moderno → moderno**s**	pequeña → pequeña**s**
fácil → fácil**es**	francés → frances**es**.

147

Position of adjectives

When used together with a noun the adjective normally comes after it, eg **los productos españoles; una compañía británica**. Possessives (**mi socio**), demonstrative adjectives (**este producto**), and numerals (**un año; primer año; cien pesetas**) go before the noun, as do a small number of short, frequently used adjectives: **bueno, malo, grande**.

bueno/malo

These adjectives drop the final **-o** when they are placed before a masculine/singular noun. The same applies to these adjectives: **uno** (*one*), **primero** (*first*), **tercero** (*third*).

un **buen** mercado	el **primer** piso
el **tercer** despacho	un **mal** momento

No changes apply to the same words in the feminine:

> Es una **buena/mala** idea.
> Está en la **primera/tercera** planta.

Ciento becomes **cien** when it is a round hundred: **cien pesetas; cien mil pesetas**. Otherwise it is unchanged: **ciento uno, ciento veintidós**.

Grande is shortened to **gran** before singular nouns of either gender:

una fábrica **grande**	una **gran** fábrica
un aparcamiento **grande**	un **gran** aparcamiento

> La compañía A **es grande.** *A is a large company.*
> La compañía A **es más grande que** la compañía B.
>   *Company A is larger than company B.*
> La compañía C **es la más grande.** *C is the largest company.*

To say something is a bit higher/lower; much higher/lower than add **un poco** (*a bit*); **mucho** (*much*) before the word **más**.

un poco más alto/a(s) que	*a bit /slightly higher than*
un poco más bajo/a(s) que	*a bit/slightly lower than*
mucho más alto/a(s) que	*much higher than*
mucho más bajo/a(s) que	*much lower than*

Las cifras correspondientes a este año son **más altas que/un poco más altas que/mucho más altas que** las cifras correspondientes al año pasado. *This year's figures are higher/a bit higher/much higher than the figures for last year.*

Saying that something is good/bad; better/worse; the best/the worst.

> El producto A **es bueno.** *Product A is good.*
> El producto A **es mejor que** el producto B. *Product A is better than Product B.*
> El producto A **es el mejor.** *Product A is the best.*

	comparative	superlative
grande(s)	**más grande(s) que**	**el/la/los/las más grande(s)**
big	*bigger than*	*the biggest*
pequeño/a(s)	**más pequeño/a(s) que**	**el/la/los/las más pequeño/a(s)**
small	*smaller than*	*the smallest*
alto/a(s)	**más alto/a(s) que**	**el/la/los/las más alto/a(s)**
high/tall	*higher/taller than*	*the highest/tallest*
bajo/a(s)	**más bajo/a(s) que**	**el/la/los/las más bajo/a(s)**
low	*lower than*	*the lowest*

	comparative	superlative
bueno/a(s)	**mejor(es) que**	**el/la/los/las mejor(es)**
good	*better than*	*the best*
malo/a(s)	**peor(es) que**	**el/la/los/las peor(es)**
bad	*worse than*	*the worst*
grande(s)	**mayor(es) que**	**el/la/los/las mayor(es)**
big, large	*bigger, larger*	*the biggest, largest*

Mayor and **el/la mayor** come before the noun and are mainly used to express degrees of importance and abstract size, eg **la mayor parte de** *the majority of:*

> Chupa Chups exporta **la mayor parte de** su producción; Modas Florencia S.A. vende **la mayor parte de** sus productos en España.

ni…ni… *neither…nor…*

no + verb +	ni…		ni…	
La compañía **no** es	**ni**	grande	**ni**	pequeña.

The company is neither big nor small.

José	**no** vive	**ni** en Madrid **ni** en Vigo.

José lives neither in Madrid nor in Vigo.

Los precios	**no** son	**ni**	altos	**ni**	bajos.

Prices are neither high nor low.

Note: **Ni…..ni…** can appear before rather than after a verb – in which case **no** is not used:

> **Ni** Pedro **ni** Miguel trabajan aquí.
> *Neither Pedro nor Miguel work here.*
> Este producto **ni** se vende **ni** se exporta.
> *This product is neither sold nor exported.*

tan…como… *as…as…*

> El producto A **es tan bueno como** el producto B.
> *Product A is as good as product B.*
>
> El producto C **no es tan bueno como** el producto A.
> *Product C is not as good as product A.*

Very is expressed in Spanish by **muy** + adjective:

Es **muy** grande.	Es **muy** bueno.
It is very large.	*It is very good.*

Es **muy** caro.
It is very expensive.

Adding **-ísimo/a/os/as** to the adjective when it ends in a consonant or to its stem when it ends in a vowel means *extremely* or *very…indeed:*

bueno + **-ísimo** → **buenísimo** *extremely good*

caro → **carísimo** *extremely expensive*
pequeño → **pequeñísimo** *exceptionally small*
fácil → **facilísimo** *extremely easy*

Este vino es **buenísimo**.
La porcelana es **carísima**.
Estos despachos son **pequeñísimos**.

Demonstrative adjectives

este m. **esta** f. *this*	**estos** m. **estas** f. *these*
ese m. **esa** f. *that*	**esos** m. **esas** f. *those*

These adjectives come *before* the noun and must agree with it in gender and number.

> **este** mercado **esta** compañía
> **estos** mercados **estas** compañías
> **ese** despacho **esos** restaurantes

There is also a neutral form, **esto/eso** to use with expressions like: **¿Qué es esto?** *What's this?* **¿Qué es eso?** *What's that?*

Possessive adjectives (weak forms)
These adjectives also come before the noun.

Singular	Plural	
mi	**mis**	*my*
tu	**tus**	*your*
su	**sus**	*his, her, its (your formal with* usted*)*
nuestro/a	**nuestros/as**	*our*
vuestro/a	**vuestros/as**	*your*
su	**sus**	*their (your formal plural with* ustedes*)*

Mi compañía es muy grande.
¿Dónde está **su** hotel?

Strong forms

mío/a(s) *mine*	**nuestro/a(s)** *ours*
tuyo/a(s) *yours*	**vuestro/a(s)** *yours*
suyo/a(s) *his, hers, its, yours*	**suyo/a(s)** *theirs, yours*

These adjectives come after a noun in expressions like: **una amiga mía** *(a [female] friend of mine)*; **un colega mío** *(a colleague of mine)* or after the verb *ser*. **Esta habitación es suya** *(This room is yours)*. When the strong forms are used after the verb the definite article can be placed in front for emphasis: **Este despacho es el mío; Esta habitación es la suya.**

Because **suyo/a(s)** can mean *his, hers, yours* (usted/ustedes), and *theirs* clarification is very often needed. This can be easily done by saying **de él, de ella, de usted, de ustedes, de ellos,** instead.

	Este despacho es **de él**.
Este despacho es **suyo**.	Este despacho es **de ella**.
	Este despacho es **de ustedes**.

Expressing possession

In Spanish, possession is expressed using the word **de** (*of*):
el diario de Peter *Peter's diary*
el coche de Susana *Susana's car*

ADVERBS

The majority of adverbs are formed by adding **-mente** to the feminine form of the adjective:

> lento (*slow*) → lenta+**mente** (*slowly*)
> franco (*frank/honest*) → franca+**mente** (*frankly*)

Any accents on the adjectives are retained.

When two adverbs go together joined only by **y** or **pero** the ending **-mente** is omitted in the first of the two: **lenta pero eficazmente** (*slowly but efficiently*).

A few useful adverbs

exactamente (*exactly*); precisamente (*precisely*); fácilmente (*easily*); difícilmente (*with difficulty*); claramente (*clearly*); rápidamente (*quickly*); exclusivamente (*exclusively*); principalmente (*mainly*).

Other adverbs

The ending **-mente** is not added to the following adverbs:

bien (*well*); mal (*badly*); alto (*loudly*); bajo (*softly*).
Habla alto *He/She speaks loudly*; **Habla bajo** *He/She speaks softly*.

place: **aquí** *here*; **allí** *there*; **afuera** *outside*
time: **ahora** *now*
degree: **demasiado** *too*; **bastante** *quite/rather/fairly*;
son **demasiado** caros; está **bastante** cerca.
expressing doubt: **quizá(s)** *maybe*; **tal vez** *perhaps*.

Conjunctions

y means *and*

> La compañía española **y** la compañía británica.

Before words beginning with **i** or **hi**+consonant, **y** becomes **e**:
Francia **e** Italia; Pérez **e** Hijos S.A.

o means *or*

> La compañía española **o** la compañía británica.

Before words beginning with **o** or **ho,** the conjunction **o** becomes **u**: siete **u** ocho; minutos **u** horas.

In written Spanish, an accent is needed when **o** is placed between numerals to make a distinction between the conjunction and a zero: 35 **ó** 36.

o…o… *either…or…*

> **o** Francia **o** Italia

pero means *but*

> Vivo en Guildford **pero** trabajo en Londres.
> *I live in Guildford but I work in London.*

Pero is replaced by the word **sino** after a negative:
Mi apellido **no** es López **sino** García. *My surname is not López but García*; El billete **no** cuesta 10 pesetas **sino** 12 pesetas. *The ticket does not cost 10 Pesetas but 12 Pesetas.*

PREPOSITIONS

a de en

a *to; at*	Voy **a** Londres (*to*); **a** las 8 (*at*)
de *of; from*	La Directora **de** la compañía es **de** Londres. (*of the company / from London*)
en *in; at; on*	**en** el despacho (*in/at the office*)
	en la mesa (*on the table*)

a before **el** becomes **al**: **al hotel Hilton**
de before **el** becomes **del**: **Banco del Mediterráneo**

por
for; in (the morning/afternoon,etc); *along*
in: **por** la tarde *in the afternoon*
along: **por** la calle *along the street*, **por** el despacho *up and down the office*
for: gracias **por** la carta *thank you for the letter*

para
for: **para** mí una cerveza; **para** mañana
in the direction of: **para** Madrid

QUESTION WORDS

¿Qué? (*What?*)	**¿Qué** hora es?
¿Cómo? (*How?*)	**¿Cómo** estás?
¿Dónde? (*Where?*)	**¿Dónde** está su despacho?
¿De dónde? (*Where from?*)	**¿De dónde** es usted?
¿Adónde? (*Where (to)?*)	**¿Adónde** vamos?
¿Quién? (*Who?*)	**¿Quién** es su socio?
¿Cuándo? (*When?*)	**¿Cuándo** sale el avión?
¿Cuál? (*Which one? What?*)	**¿Cuál** es su nombre?
¿Cuánto? (*How much?*)	**¿Cuánto** cuesta el billete?
¿Cuántos/as? (*How many?*)	**¿Cuántos** socios tiene?
¿Por qué? (*Why?*)	**¿Por qué** viaja el lunes por la tarde?
Note: **porque** (*because*)	**porque** tengo una reunión por la mañana.

A statement can be changed into a question without changing the order of the words:

Está en el Hotel. ¿Está en el Hotel?
Vamos al bar. ¿Vamos al bar?

THERE IS/ARE

¿Hay?	Is there?/Are there?
Sí, hay	Yes, there is./Yes, there are.
No, no hay	No, there isn't/No, there aren't.

¿Hay una habitación disponible?
¿Hay un autobús para la estación de Atocha?
¿Hay una oficina de Correos cerca de aquí?
The usual answer is **Sí, hay uno/una** or **No, no hay**.

PRONOUNS

Subject pronouns

Yo *I*	**nosotros/as** *we*
tú *you* [informal]	**vosotros/as** *you* [informal plural]
usted *you* [formal]	
él *he*	**ustedes** *you* [formal plural]
ella *she*	**ellos/as** *they*

The words *I, you, he, she, it, we, you, they*, are called subject pronouns. In Spanish these words are not used very often, as the verb ending usually shows who is being referred to.

El and **ella** are the words to be used when referring to male and female animals and things.

The word **tú** should be used when talking to friends, relatives, children, young people, someone you know well, or when invited to do so. Otherwise, always use **usted**.

In written Spanish, for example on signs in public buildings, **Vd** or **Ud** – the shortened form of **usted** – is often used, and **Vds** or **Uds** for **ustedes** (the plural).

Object pronouns

These are the objects of verbs and stand in the place of nouns. They can be direct (*I'll buy it*; *I'll visit them*) or indirect (*Send it to him*). They are normally placed in front of the verb.

me	*me/to me*	**nos**	*us/to us*
te	*you/to you*	**os**	*you/to you*
le	*you/to you* [formal], *him/to him, her/to her*	**les**	*you /to you* [formal, plural]; *them/to them*
la	*her/it/you*, [fml] fem.	**las**	*them/you* [fml] fem.
lo	*him/it/you* [fml] masc.	**los**	*them/you* [fml] masc.

¿Me llama a las diez?   *Could you call me at ten?*
¿Qué me recomienda?   *What would you recommend (to me)?*

Te llamaré.   *I'll call you.*
¿Qué te dijo?   *What did he/she say to you?*

Le llamaré.   *I'll call you* [formal].
Le escribiré.   *I'll write to you.*

Le diré.   *I'll tell him/her.*

Lo compro.   *I'll buy it* [masculine object].
La compro.   *I'll buy it* [feminine object].

Nos llama.   *He/she calls us.*
Nos escribirá. *He/she'll write to us.*

Os llamaré.   *I'll call you* [plural].
Os escribiré.   *I'll write to you* [plural].

Les llamaré.   *I'll call you* [formal, plural], *them.*
Les escribiré.   *I'll write to you* [formal]/*to them.*

Notice the following expressions:

¿Me dice...? *Could you tell me?*
¿Me da...? *Could you give me?*
¿Me llama...? *Could you call me?*

Dice, **firma**, **deja**, **da**, **rellena** and **llama** are the form used to ask somebody politely to do something.

The verb **gustar** is used with the following object pronouns **me**, **te**, **le**, **nos**, **os**, **les** to mean *like*.

Me gusta. *I like it.* **Le gusta** la cerveza. *He likes beer.*

Reflexive pronouns

In Spanish some verbs are used with the personal pronoun referring back to the subject. These verbs are reflexive verbs and the accompanying pronouns are: **me**, **te**, **se**, **nos**, **os**, **se**. Verbs with an infinitive ending in **-se** are reflexive, eg **llamarse** (*to be called*); **levantarse** (*to get up*); **prepararse** (*to get ready*).

(yo) **me** llamo	(nosotros/as) **nos** llamamos
(tú) **te** llamas	(vosotros/as) **os** llamáis
(usted, él, ella) **se** llama	(ustedes, ellos/as) **se** llaman

Se plus the 3rd-person singular of the verb is used to talk about what people in general do or to talk about what is done without saying who is doing it.

Aquí **se habla** español. *Spanish is spoken here.*
Se trabaja mucho *One works hard; people work hard*
Se come tarde *One eats late; people eat late*

Expressions like these are also used when explaining process and/or procedure:

La muestra **se analiza**. *The sample is analysed.*
Las piezas **se revisan una por una**. *The items are checked one by one.*

¿Se puede? is a useful expression which follows a similar pattern. It means *Is it possible?/Can one?*, eg **¿Se puede** enviar un fax? (*Is it possible to send a fax?*). The answer would be **Sí, se puede** (*Yes, it is possible*) or **No, no se puede** (*No, it is not possible.*).

Verbs can be regular or irregular. Regular verbs follow a pattern; irregular verbs break the pattern in some places.

Regular verbs fall into three groups according to the last two letters of the infinitive: **-ar**, **-er** or **-ir**. To use the verb, this ending is removed and replaced by a different ending.

The Present tense
Regular verbs

-ar trabajar *to work*	**-er comer** *to eat*	**-ir vivir** *to live*
(yo) trabaj**o**	(yo) com**o**	(yo) viv**o**
(tú) trabaj**as**	(tú) com**es**	(tú) viv**es**
(Vd/él/ella) trabaj**a**	(Vd/él/ella) com**e**	(Vd/él/ella) viv**e**
(nosotros) trabaj**amos**	(nosotros) com**emos**	(nosotros) viv**imos**
(vosotros) trabaj**áis**	(vosotros) com**éis**	(vosotros) viv**ís**
(Vds/ellos/ellas) trabaj**an**	(Vds/ellos/ellas) com**en**	(Vds/ellos/ellas) viv**en**

Irregular verbs
A few verbs are irregular only in the first person singular:

-ar		**-er**	**-ir**
dar *to give*	**estar** *to be*	**hacer** *to make*	**salir** *to depart*
doy	**estoy**	**hago**	**salgo**
das	est**ás**	haces	sales
da	est**á**	hace	sale
damos	est**amos**	hacemos	salimos
dais	est**áis**	hac**éis**	salís
dan	est**án**	hacen	salen

Radical changing verbs
In some verbs all the words except for the **nosotros/as** and **vosotros/as** forms have an alteration in the middle of the word.

These verbs can be placed in three basic categories regardless of the ending of the verb itself.

Category A	Category B	Category C
The **e** changes to **ie**	The **e** changes to **i**	The **o** changes to **ue**
invertir *to invest*	**pedir** *to ask for*	**poder** *to be able to*
inv**ie**rto	p**i**do	p**ue**do
inv**ie**rtes	p**i**des	p**ue**des
inv**ie**rte	p**i**de	p**ue**de
invertimos	*pedimos*	*podemos*
invertís	*pedís*	*podéis*
inv**ie**rten	p**i**den	p**ue**den

Other useful radical changing verbs:

Category A

cerrar (*to close/to shut*) c**ie**rro, c**ie**rras, c**ie**rra, *cerramos/áis*, c**ie**rran.

comenzar (*to start/to begin*) com**ie**nzo/as/a, *comenzamos/áis*, com**ie**nzan.

empezar (*to start*) emp**ie**zo/as/a, *empezamos/áis*, emp**ie**zan.

entender (*to understand*) ent**ie**ndo/es/e, *entendemos/éis*, ent**ie**nden.

extender (*to extend*) ext**ie**ndo/es/e, *extendemos/éis*, ext**ie**nden.

preferir (*to prefer*) pref**ie**ro/es/e, *preferimos/ís*, pref**ie**ren.

querer (*to want*) qu**ie**ro/es/e, *queremos/éis*, qu**ie**ren.

Category B

decir (*to say*) d**i**go, d**i**ces, d**i**ce, *decimos/ís*, d**i**cen.

conseguir (*to obtain*) cons**i**go, cons**i**gues, cons**i**gue, *conseguimos/ís*, cons**i**guen

seguir (*to follow*) s**i**go, s**i**gues, s**i**gue, *seguimos/ís*, s**i**guen.

Category C

almorzar (*to have lunch*) alm**ue**rzo, alm**ue**rzas, alm**ue**rza, *almorzamos/áis*, alm**ue**rzan.

contar (*to count*) c**ue**nto/as/a, *contamos/áis*, c**ue**ntan.

encontrar (*to find*) enc**ue**ntro/as/a, *encontramos/áis*, enc**ue**ntran.

jugar (*to play [sports or games only]*) j**ue**go/as/a, *jugamos/áis*, j**ue**gan.

Verbs **ser** (*to be*) and **ir** (*to go*) are irregular throughout:

ser		ir	
soy	somos	voy	vamos
eres	sois	vas	vais
es	son	va	van

ser, estar, tener

ser (*to be*)	estar (*to be*)	tener (*to have*)
soy	estoy	tengo
eres	estás	tienes
es	está	tiene
somos	estamos	tenemos
sois	estáis	tenéis
son	están	tienen

In Spanish there are two verbs **ser** and **estar** which translate as *to be*. They are not interchangeable.

Ser is used only in the following situations: i) when followed by a noun, ii) when followed by an adjective referring to a permanent or inherent quality such as origin and nationality, or things that identify someone or something.

name: **Soy** Elvira Sánchez;
nationality: **Es** una compañía española;
origin: **es** de Madrid;
occupation, job title, other titles: **Soy** apoderada;
possession: **es** mi despacho;
time: ¿**Qué** hora es? **Son** las 7 de la mañana;
date: **es** el 12 de febrero; **es** lunes;
price: ¿Cuánto **es**? **Son** 25 pesetas;
quantity: **es** mucho, poco, bastante;
size and height: **es** grande, pequeño/a, alto/a, bajo/a.
Use **ser** also when referring to political or religious persuasion.

Some set expressions using **es**:

es igual	*it's the same*	es aburrido	*it's boring*
es temprano	*it's early*	es interesante	*it's interesting*
es tarde	*it's late*	es simpático/a	*he/she is nice*
es verdad	*it's true*	es caro	*it's expensive*
es fácil	*it's easy*	es barato	*it's cheap*
es difícil	*it's difficult*	es gratis	*it's free of charge*

Estar is used with a preposition to indicate:

location: el Sr Pérez no **está** en su despacho; **estoy** en el Hotel Hilton;
position: **está** arriba, abajo (*upstairs, downstairs*); **estoy** de pie (*standing*).

It is also used for moods, well-being and state of health: ¿**Cómo estás, Pablo?** and with an adjective to express a temporary state or quality: **está ocupado**; **estamos completos**.
    It is also used as part of the present continuous (see below).

Some set expressions using **está**:

está bien	*fine/it's OK*	está cerrado	*it's closed*
está mal	*it's wrong*	está completo	*it's full* (bus, hotel)
está cerca	*it's near*	está libre	*it's free/not*
está lejos	*it's far*		*taken* (seat, etc)
está abierto	*it's open*	está ocupado	*it's engaged/taken*

Note: for *to be late*: just say **llego tarde** (*I'm late*) or **voy a llegar tarde** (*I'll be late*).

Tener (*to have*)
Here are some expressions that use parts of **tener**:

Tengo una habitación reservada.
¿Qué cargo **tiene** usted en la compañía?
Aquí **tiene**.
Use **tener** to talk about your age: **Tengo 25 años** (*I'm 25 years old*; literally 'I have 25 years'). The corresponding question is: ¿**Cuántos años tiene?** (*How old are you?*)

Other expressions using **tener**:

tener frío *to be cold*   tener sed *to be thirsty*
tener calor *to be hot*   tener prisa *to be in a hurry*
tener miedo *to be afraid*   tener suerte *to be lucky*
tener hambre *to be hungry*
eg **tengo prisa** (*I'm in a hurry*); **tiene sed** (*He is thirsty*)

Desde hace...

Desde hace translates as *for* to refer to how long something has been established or how long an action has been taking place:

> **Estamos aquí en el polígono industrial desde hace 31 años.** *We've been here in the industrial estate for 31 years.*
> **Soy Director de Márketing desde hace 1 año.** *I have been Marketing Manager for a year*
> **Trabajo en esta compañía desde hace dos años** (*I have been working for this company for two years*).

The phrase **¿Cuánto tiempo llevas aquí?** is also frequently used to mean *How long have you been here?*

The present continuous tense

The present continuous tense is used to emphasise an action that is literally happening at a given moment.

> ¿Qué **estás comiendo**? **Estoy comiendo** paella.
> *What are you eating? I am eating paella.*

It is a combination of the verb *estar* and the present participle. With regular verbs you form the participle by replacing **-ar** by **-ando** and **-er**, **-ir** by **-iendo**. **-ando/iendo** are the equivalent of **-ing** in English.

> (Yo) estoy trabaj**ando**. *I am working (right now).*
> (Yo) estoy com**iendo**. *I am eating (right now).*

-ar	-er	-ir
estoy trabaj**ando**	estoy com**iendo**	estoy viv**iendo**
estás trabaj**ando**	estás com**iendo**	estás viv**iendo**
está trabaj**ando**	está com**iendo**	está viv**iendo**
estamos trabaj**ando**	estamos com**iendo**	estamos viv**iendo**
estáis trabaj**ando**	estáis com**iendo**	estáis viv**iendo**
están trabaj**ando**	están com**iendo**	están viv**iendo**

The continuous tense is used less in Spanish than in English.
    Notice that unlike in English the continuous tense in Spanish is not used for describing things you are planning to do in the immediate future. Use **voy a** (*I am going to*) or **vamos a** (*we are going to*) followed by a verb in the infinitive:

> **Voy a ir a España.** *I am going to Spain/I'm planning to go to Spain.*
> **Vamos a alquilar un coche.** *We are hiring a car.*

The present simple tense, not the continuous tense, is used in the following expressions when talking on the phone:

> **Le llamo** por lo siguiente... *I'm calling about the following...*
> **Le llamo** a pedido del señor/de la señora x... *or* **Le llamo** en nombre del **señor/de la señora x...** *I'm calling on behalf of Mr/Mrs x...*
> **XX al habla. ¡Dígame!** *It's xx speaking...*

The past tense

Regular verbs

Imperfect
Use the imperfect to refer to incomplete actions in the past or actions not restricted by time limits:

> **Trabajaba** en Valencia. *I used to work in Valencia.*
> **Tenía** un piso pequeño en Madrid. *I had /I used to have a small flat in Madrid.*

The imperfect is also used to describe habitual actions or settings in the past:

> Siempre **iba** en autobús al trabajo. *I always travelled to work by bus.*

Preterite (Simple past)
Use the preterite when you are talking about events, or completed actions in the past.

> **Trabajé** un año en Bilbao. *I worked in Bilbao for a year.*
> **Vendí** las acciones el año pasado. *I sold the shares last year.*

Imperfect		
-ar	**-er**	**-ir**
trabaj**aba**	com**ía**	viv**ía**
trabaj**abas**	com**ías**	viv**ías**
trabaj**aba**	com**ía**	viv**ía**
trabaj**ábamos**	com**íamos**	viv**íamos**
trabaj**ábais**	com**íais**	viv**íais**
trabaj**aban**	com**ían**	viv**ían**

Preterite		
-ar	**-er**	**-ir**
trabaj**é**	com**í**	viv**í**
trabaj**aste**	com**iste**	viv**iste**
trabaj**ó**	com**ió**	viv**ió**
trabaj**amos**	com**imos**	viv**imos**
trabaj**ásteis**	com**ísteis**	viv**ísteis**
trabaj**aron**	com**ieron**	viv**ieron**

Imperfect		
ser	**estar**	**tener**
era	estaba	tenía
eras	estabas	tenías
era	estaba	tenía
éramos	estábamos	teníamos
erais	estabais	teníais
eran	estaban	tenían

Preterite		
ser	**estar**	**tener**
fui	estuve	tuve
fuiste	estuviste	tuviste
fue	estuvo	tuvo
fuimos	estuvimos	tuvimos
fuisteis	estuvisteis	tuvisteis
fueron	estuvieron	tuvieron

ser, estar, tener : past tenses

Yo era *I used to be;*
Yo estaba *I used to be (location, mood,etc)*
Yo tenía *I used to have.*
Era estudiante en Sevilla. *I used to be a student in Seville (at one time).*
Teníamos un piso cerca de la Giralda. *We used to have a flat near the Giralda tower.*

Fui *I was;*
Estuve *I was (in a particular place, etc);*
Tuve *I (once) had*
Fui secretaria durante un año. *I was a secretary for a year.*
Estuve dos días en Brighton. *I was in Brighton for two days .*
Tuve un diario como éste. *I once had a diary like this one.*

The perfect tense

he trabaj**ado**	**hemos** trabaj**ado**
has trabaj**ado**	**habéis** trabaj**ado**
ha trabaj**ado**	**han** trabaj**ado**

In Spanish the perfect tense is generally used as in English. It's formed from the appropriate part of the verb **haber** (*to have*) and a past participle. To form the past participle of regular verbs, all you have to do is replace **-ar** by **-ado** and **-er, -ir** by **-ido**:

trabaj**ar** → trabaj**ado**
com**er** → com**ido**
viv**ir** → viv**ido**

Hemos montado una exposición en Madrid. *We have set up an exhibition in Madrid;*

He cancelado la cita con el Señor Rodríguez.
I have cancelled the appointment with Sr Rodríguez.
Hemos estado de vacaciones. *We have been on holiday.*

The future

llamar**é**	llamar**emos**
llamar**ás**	llamar**éis**
llamar**á**	llamar**án**

With regular verbs the future is formed by adding the following endings to the infinitive: **-é, -ás, -á, -emos, -éis, -án**.

trabaj**ar** → trabaj**aré**
com**er** → com**eré**
viv**ir** → viv**iré**
llamar**é** más tarde. *I'll call later.*

The conditional

trabajar**ía**	trabajar**íamos**
trabajar**ías**	trabajar**íais**
trabajar**ía**	trabajar**ían**

With regular verbs the conditional is formed by adding the following endings to the verb in the infinitive: **-ía; -ías; -ía; -íamos; -íais; -ían**

trabaj**ar** → trabaj**aría** (*I would work*)
com**er** → com**ería** (*I would eat*)
viv**ir** → viv**iría** (*I would live*)

Me gustar**ía** pagar con cheque. *I would like to pay by cheque.*
Nos gustar**ía** hablar de precios. *We would like to discuss prices.*

¿Le gustar**ía** tomar una cerveza? *Would you like to have a beer?*
¿Les gustar**ía** visitar nuestro stand? *Would you like to visit our stand?*
¿Te gustar**ía** tomar una cerveza? *Would you like to have a beer?*

Ser	**Estar**	**Tener**
ser**ía**	estar**ía**	tendr**ía**
ser**ías**	estar**ías**	tendr**ías**
ser**ía**	estar**ía**	tendr**ía**
ser**íamos**	estar**íamos**	tendr**íamos**
ser**íais**	estar**íais**	tendr**íais**
ser**ían**	estar**ían**	tendr**ían**

Sería una buena compra. *It would be a good purchase.*
¿Tendría un coche más pequeño? *Would you have a smaller car?*

155

Regular verbs

-ar

Present	Present continuous	Imperfect	Preterite	Future	Conditional	Present perfect
-o	estoy -ando	-aba	-é	-aré	-aría	he -ado
-as	estás -ando	-abas	-aste	-arás	-arías	has -ado
-a	está -ando	-aba	-ó	-ará	-aría	ha -ado
-amos	estamos -ando	-ábamos	-amos	-aremos	-aríamos	hemos -ado
-áis	estáis -ando	-abais	-asteis	-aréis	-aríais	habéis -ado
-an	están -ando	-aban	-aron	-arán	-arían	han -ado

-er

Present	Present continuous	Imperfect	Preterite	Future	Conditional	Present perfect
-o	estoy -iendo	-ía	-í	-eré	-ería	he -ido
-es	estás -iendo	-ías	-iste	-erás	-erías	has -ido
-e	está -iendo	-ía	-ió	-erá	-ería	ha -ido
-emos	estamos-iendo	-íamos	-imos	-eremos	-eríamos	hemos -ido
-éis	estáis -iendo	-íais	-isteis	-eréis	-eríais	habéis -ido
-en	están -iendo	-ían	-ieron	-erán	-erían	han -ido

-ir

Present	Present continuous	Imperfect	Preterite	Future	Conditional	Present perfect
-o	estoy -iendo	-ía	-í	-iré	-iría	he -ido
-es	estás -iendo	-ías	-iste	-irás	-irías	has -ido
-e	está -iendo	-ía	-ió	-irá	-iría	ha -ido
-imos	estamos-iendo	-íamos	-imos	-iremos	-iríamos	hemos -ido
-ís	estáis-iendo	-íais	-isteis	-iréis	-iríais	habéis -ido
-en	están -iendo	-ían	-ieron	-irán	-irían	han -ido

Some regular verbs:

-ar

A ahorrar *to save*; almacenar *to store*; alquilar *to hire/rent*;
C calcular *to calculate*; cambiar *to change*; cancelar *to cancel*; cenar *to have dinner*; comprar *to buy*; concentrar *to concentrate*; confirmar *to confirm*; contestar *to answer*; contratar *to hire (someone)*; crear *to create*;
D dejar *to leave behind*; deletrear *to spell*; desayunar *to have breakfast*;
E enseñar *to show*; evitar *to avoid*; exportar *to export*;
F firmar *to sign*; fomentar *to encourage*;
G gastar *to spend*; girar *to turn*;
H hablar *to speak*;
I importar *to import*; iniciar *to initiate/start*; instalar *to install*; integrar *to integrate*;
L lanzar *to launch*;

LL llamar *to call*; llevar *to carry/to wear*;
N necesitar *to need*; negociar *to negotiate*;
P presentar *to introduce*;
Q quitar *to remove/take off*;
R rellenar *to fill in*; representar *to represent*; reservar *to reserve*; revisar *to look over*;
S seleccionar *to select*; solicitar *to ask for/to order*; superar *to exceed*;
T telefonear *to telephone*; terminar *to finish*; tirar *to throw away*; tomar *to take/to have (some food or drink)*;
U usar *to use/utilize*;
V viajar *to travel*; visitar *to visit*;

-er

beber *to drink*; comer *to eat*; depender *to depend*

-ir

permitir *to allow*; recibir *to receive*

Irregular verbs

Present tense					
dar	**hacer**	**ir**	**querer**	**obtener**	**poder**
to give	*to make*	*to go*	*to want*	*to obtain*	*to be able to*
doy	hago	voy	quiero	obtengo	puedo
das	haces	vas	quieres	obtienes	puedes
da	hace	va	quiere	obtiene	puede
damos	hacemos	vamos	queremos	obtenemos	podemos
dais	hacéis	vais	queréis	obtenéis	podéis
dan	hacen	van	quieren	obtienen	pueden

Note: for the conjugation of the following verbs in the present tense please see 'Radical changing verbs' section: **almorzar, cerrar, comenzar, conseguir, contar, empezar, encontrar, entender, extender, decir, invertir, jugar, preferir, querer, seguir, tener.**

Imperfect					
daba	hacía	iba	quería	obtenía	podía
etc.	*etc.*	*etc.*	*etc.*	*etc.*	*etc.*

Preterite					
di	hice	fui	quise	obtuve	pude
diste	hiciste	fuiste	quisiste	obtuviste	pudiste
dio	hizo	fue	quiso	obtuvo	pudo
dimos	hicimos	fuimos	quisimos	obtuvimos	pudimos
disteis	hicisteis	fuisteis	quisisteis	obtuvisteis	pudisteis
dieron	hicieron	fueron	quisieron	obtuvieron	pudieron

Future					
daré	haré	iré	querré	obtendré	podré
etc.	*etc.*	*etc.*	*etc.*	*etc.*	*etc.*

Conditional					
daría	haría	iría	querría	obtendría	podría
etc.	*etc.*	*etc.*	*etc.*	*etc.*	*etc.*

Present perfect					
he dado	he hecho	he ido	he querido	he obtenido	he podido
etc.	*etc.*	*etc.*	*etc.*	*etc.*	*etc.*

Useful combinations

The following expressions can be combined with both regular and irregular verbs in the infinitive, eg **Quisiera cancelar…/Debemos telefonear…**

Quisiera… Quisiéramos…	*I would like to/We would like to…*
Voy a… Vamos a…	*I am going to/ We're going to …*
Proponemos…	*We propose…*
Me gustaría… Nos gustaría…	*I'd like to… /We'd like to…*

Tengo que… Tenemos que…	*I have to…/We have to…*
Prefiero… Preferimos…	*I prefer to…/We prefer to…*
Debo… Debemos…	*I must/ought to… /We must/ought to…*
Espero… Esperamos…	*I hope to/we hope to…*
Hay que…	*It is necessary to…*
¿Se puede…?	*Is it possible to…?*
Suelo… Solemos…	*I am/ we are in the habit of…*

HELPFILE

NUMBERS

1 uno/un/una	31 treinta y uno
2 dos	32 treinta y dos, etc
3 tres	40 cuarenta
4 cuatro	50 cincuenta
5 cinco	60 sesenta
6 seis	70 setenta
7 siete	80 ochenta
8 ocho	90 noventa
9 nueve	100 cien
10 diez	200 doscientos/as
11 once	300 trescientos/as
12 doce	400 cuatrocientos/as
13 trece	500 quinientos/as
14 catorce	600 seiscientos/as
15 quince	700 setecientos/as
16 dieciséis	800 ochocientos/as
17 diecisiete	900 novecientos/as
18 dieciocho	1000 mil
19 diecinueve	2000 dos mil
20 veinte	3000 tres mil
21 veintiuno/a	4000 cuatro mil
22 veintidós	5000 cinco mil
23 veintitrés	6000 seis mil
24 veinticuatro	7000 siete mil
25 veinticinco	8000 ocho mil
26 veintiséis	9000 nueve mil
27 veintisiete	10.000 diez mil
28 veintiocho	100.000 cien mil
29 veintinueve	1.000.000 un millón
30 treinta	

Examples:
110 ciento diez
159 ciento cincuenta y nueve
2.345 dos mil trescientos cuarenta y cinco

ORDINAL NUMBERS   NUMEROS ORDINALES

primero/a	*first*	sexto/a	*sixth*
segundo/a	*second*	séptimo/a	*seventh*
tercero/a	*third*	octavo/a	*eighth*
cuarto/a	*fourth*	noveno/a	*ninth*
quinto/a	*fifth*	décimo/a	*tenth*

DECIMALS   DECIMALES

3,4 tres coma cuatro [= 3.4 in English]
0,05 cero coma cero cinco [= 0.05 in English]

FRACTIONS   FRACCIONES

1/2 medio/media
1/3 un tercio/la tercera parte de
1/4 un cuarto/la cuarta parte de
1/5 un quinto/la quinta parte de
1/6 un sexto/la sexta parte de
3/4 tres cuartos/ las tres cuartas partes
3/6 tres sextos/ las tres sextas partes
1/100 un centésimo/la centésima parte
1/1000 un milésimo/la milésima parte

PERCENTAGES   PORCENTAJES

3% tres por ciento/tres por cien
15% quince por ciento/quince por cien

SIGNS   SIGNOS

+ signo de más   − signo de menos   x signo de multiplicación
÷ signo de división   > es mayor que   < es menor que

2+2=4 dos más dos son cuatro
4−2=2 cuatro menos dos son dos
2x5=10 dos por cinco son diez
10÷2=5 diez dividido por dos son cinco
10>5 diez es mayor que cinco
5<10 cinco es menor que diez

WEIGHTS AND MEASURES   PESOS Y MEDIDAS

1 mm un milímetro
1 cm un centímetro
1 m un metro
1 km un kilómetro   el kilometraje   mileage

litre el/un litro   eg 10 litros

1 gr el/un gramo   gramos
1kg el/un kilo/kilogramo
2 kg dos kilos
1/2 kg medio kilo

THE TIME   LA HORA

1 a.m. es la una de la madrugada
7 a.m. son las siete de la mañana
8.15 a.m. son las ocho y cuarto de la mañana
2.20 p.m. son las dos y veinte de la tarde
5.30 p.m. son las cinco y media de la tarde
9.45 p.m. son las diez menos cuarto de la noche
11.50 p.m. son las doce menos diez de la noche

DAYS OF THE WEEK   LOS DIAS DE LA SEMANA

lunes *Monday*
martes *Tuesday*
miércoles *Wednesday*
jueves *Thursday*

viernes *Friday*
sábado/s *Saturday*
domingo/s *Sunday*

MONTHS OF THE YEAR   LOS MESES DEL AÑO

enero *January*
febrero *February*
marzo *March*
abril *April*
mayo *May*
junio *June*

julio *July*
agosto *August*
septiembre/setiembre *September*
octubre *October*
noviembre *November*
diciembre *December*

In Spanish, the days of the week and the months of the year are written in lower case.

THE FOUR SEASONS   LAS CUATRO ESTACIONES

el otoño *autumn*
el invierno *winter*
la primavera *spring*
el verano *summer*

YEARS   AÑOS

In Spanish, years are read as complete numbers. A full stop and not a comma separates the thousands and hundreds.

> eg 1.812 mil ochocientos doce [= 1812]
> 1.993 mil novecientos noventa y tres [=1993]

DATE   LA FECHA

In Spanish *cardinal* numbers are used for all dates, except for the *first* of each month:

1° (el primero) de enero *1st January*
2 (dos) de enero *2nd January*
3 (tres) de enero *3rd January*
4 (cuatro) de enero *4th January*
22 (veintidós) de enero *22nd January*

While in English it is possible to say 'the 4th of January' or 'January the 4th', in Spanish it is always said in the same order: el 4 de enero.

PUBLIC HOLIDAYS   DIAS DE FIESTA

Spain has a number of national public holidays, as well as various holidays particular to individual regions. In addition, there are *Días puente* [literally 'bridge days', the day before or after a public holiday].

Puentes are something that should always be taken into account when making appointments in Spain. If a public holiday falls on a Tuesday, for instance, Monday often becomes part of a long weekend; likewise, if the holiday falls on a Thursday, Friday will be taken as a holiday too.

National public holidays

1° de enero Día del Año Nuevo *New Year's Day*
6 de enero Día de los Reyes Magos *Epiphany*
19 de marzo San José *St Joseph's Day*
marzo/abril jueves santo/viernes santo *Maundy Thursday, Good Friday*
1° de mayo Fiesta del Trabajo *Labour Day*
24 de junio San Juan *St John's Day*
25 de julio Día de Santiago *St James' Day* [Patron Saint of Spain]
12 de octubre Día de la Hispanidad *Columbus Day*
1° de noviembre Todos los Santos *All Saints' Day*

COLOURS   LOS COLORES

rojo *red*
amarillo *yellow*
morado *purple*
azul celeste *light blue*
blanco *white*
rosa *pink*
castaño *brown/hazel*

azul *blue*
verde *green*
naranja *orange*
azul marino *navy*
negro *black*
marrón *brown*

Colours are adjectives and so must agree in number and gender, eg:

> la casa blanca   los ojos verdes   las blusas rojas

The only exceptions are: *naranja, azul celeste* and *rosa* which remain unchanged in the plural.

EC [European community]
CE [Comunidad Europea]
el Benelux the Benelux countries
el Magreb the Maghreb

Nationality	Country	Currency
belga *Belgian*	Bélgica	franco/s
holandés *Dutch*	Holanda	florín/es
luxemburgués		
Luxembourger	Luxembourg	franco/s
alemán *German*	Alemania	el marco alemán
británico *British*	Reino Unido	la libra esterlina
escocés *Scottish*	Escocia	la libra esterlina
galés *Welsh*	País de Gales	la libra esterlina
inglés *English*	Inglaterra	la libra esterlina
danés *Danish*	Dinamarca	la corona

español *Spanish*	España	la peseta
francés *French*	Francia	el franco francés
griego *Greek*	Grecia	el dracma
italiano *Italian*	Italia	la lira
portugués *Portuguese*	Portugal	el escudo
irlandés *Irish*	República de Irlanda	el punt

Non EC countries

americano *American*	Estados Unidos [EEUU]	el dólar
australiano *Australia*	Australia	el dólar australiano
austríaco *Austrian*	Austria	el chelín austríaco
canadiense *Canadian*	Canadá	el dólar canadiense
chino de Hong Kong *Hong Kong Chinese*	Hong Kong	el dólar de Hong Kong
japonés *Japanese*	Japón	el yen
noruego *Norwegian*	Noruega	la corona noruega
sueco *Swedish*	Suecia	la corona sueca
suizo *Swiss*	Suiza	el franco suizo

INCOTERMS

Incoterms are a set of rules for the interpretation of the most-commonly used terms of delivery (ie shipment terms). They are not embodied in law, but are binding if the exporter and importer so agree.

Some incoterms:

EXW Ex Works; **FCA** Free carrier; **FAS** Free alonside ship; **FOB** Free on Board; **CFR** Cost and Freight; **CIF** Cost, Insurance and Freight; **DDP** Delivered Duty Paid.

SOME PRACTICALITIES

1 How to get free or reduced cost medical care in Spain and Gibraltar.
You should obtain a form E111 from a Post Office and make several photocopies of it. Find out also whether it is possible to exchange it on arrival for a more convenient book of vouchers.

Medical treatment will be provided under the EC regulations by doctors practising under the Spanish health care system at a surgery (*consultorio*), health centre (*centro sanitario*) or hospital clinic [*ambulatorio*]. If you have to call a doctor to your hotel in an emergency, produce your E111 and give the doctor a photocopy, never the original. If you need hospital treatment, the doctor can arrange it at a state hospital. Again produce another photocopy immediately or you will be charged. If you are charged by a doctor then the treatment will be considered private and you will not receive a refund.

If you are in Gibraltar, health care will be provided at the health centre or St Bernard's hospital. You must produce your E111 if you are not a UK national; otherwise, just produce your UK passport. In any case make sure you have good private health insurance cover before you go to Spain.

2 To call the UK from Spain
Dial 07, then dial 44 followed by the UK area code leaving out initial 0 and the rest of the number.

3 Travelling by car
Some useful words for buying petrol: gasolina *petrol*; lleno *full tank*; 25 litros, etc. de súper *4-star*; de normal *2-star*; de gasolina sin plomo *unleaded*

Breakdowns: carry two warning triangles in the car. Use the emergency telephones by the road or call the RACE [Real Automóvil Club de España] which has an arrangement with the AA.

If you are involved in an accident: call the police; call the number in your car rental agreement; don't admit liability; exchange names, addresses, car and insurance details and if the accident is serious notify your consulate.
Fines: if you are caught speeding or commiting a traffic offence, the fine must be paid on the spot. Fines tend to be heavier than in the UK.

Useful phrases:
¡Socorro! *Help!*;
¡Un médico, por favor! *A doctor, please*
¡Una ambulancia, por favor! *An ambulance, please!*
¡La policía, por favor! *Police!*

4 Information for exporters to Spain.
Contact the Department of Trade and Industry.

DTI Spanish Desk	DTI Fairs and Promotions Branch
8th Floor	Dean Bradley House
Kingsgate House	52 Horseferry Road
66-74 Victoria Street	London SW1P 2AG
London SW1E 6SW	071-276 2509 Fax 071-222 4707

Spanish Desk: 071-215 5611
Western Europe: 071-215 5336

Welsh Office Industry Department, Cardiff.
(0222) 825111 Fax (0222) 823088
Scottish Export Office of the Industry Department for Scotland, Glasgow.
(041) 242 5495 Fax (041) 242 5404
Industrial Development Board Export Development Branch, Belfast.
(0232) 233233 Fax (0232) 231328

Practical assistance can also be obtained from the LCCI (London Chamber of Commerce and Industry) 69 Cannon Street, London, EC4N 5AB tel.: 071 248 4444

MINI PHRASEBOOK

GREETING PEOPLE

Hola *hello*
buenos días *good morning*
buenas tardes *good afternoon*
buenas noches *good night*
adiós *goodbye*
Vale *OK*
de nada *Not at all/You're welcome*
lo siento *I'm sorry*
¿cómo? *Pardon?*

INTRODUCING YOURSELF

Soy [your name] de [name of the company you work for]
¿Cuál es su nombre? *What's your name?*
encantado/encantada *Pleased to meet you*
¿Cómo se escribe su nombre/apellido? *How do you spell your name/surname?*

INTRODUCING SOMEBODY ELSE

Le presento a [name of the person] *May I introduce…?*

JOB

¿Cuál es su ocupación? *What do you do for a living?/What's your job?*
Soy…[representante, director, etc]
Trabajo en [name of the company] *I work for…*

TAXI

al Hotel [name of the hotel] por favor *to the X Hotel*
a la estación de RENFE, por favor *to the railway station, please*
a la estación de autobuses, por favor *to the bus station, please*
al aeropuerto, por favor *to the airport, please*
¿Cuánto es? *How much is it?*
¿Me da un recibo, por favor? *Can I have a receipt, please?*

HOTEL ROOM

Tengo una habitación reservada *I have a room reserved*
¿Tiene una habitación? *Do you have a room available?*
  doble *double*; simple/individual *single*; con baño *with bathroom*; con ducha *with shower*; con lavabo *with washbasin*
  por una noche *for one night* por dos,tres noches *for two, three nights, etc*
  por una semana *for a week*
¿Cuánto cuesta por noche? *How much is it per night?*
¿Desayuno incluído? *Is breakfast included?*
¿A qué hora se sirve el desayuno? *At what time is breakfast served?*

ASKING IF SOMETHING IS AVAILABLE

¿Hay una habitación disponible? *Is there a room available?*
un despacho *an office*; una mesa *a table*; un stand *a trade fair stand*; una línea *a phone line*; una plaza en este avión/tren *a seat available on the plane/train*

BUYING A TICKET

¿Qué trenes hay de [name of place] a [name of place]? *What trains are there from …to …?*
Quisera un billete para el Talgo *I would like a ticket for the Talgo*
¿A qué hora sale el tren/el avión/el autobús? *At what time does the plane/train/bus leave?*
¿A qué hora llega? *At what time does it arrive?*

OVER THE PHONE

Dígame *May I help you?*
Quisiera hablar con [name] *I would like to speak to…*
¿De parte de quién? *Who's calling?*
Soy [name] de [company]
un momento *one moment,please*
está comunicando *it's engaged*

MAKING AN APPOINTMENT

Quisiera *I would like…*
…concertar una cita con [name of person] *make an appointment with…*
cambiar la cita *change the appointment*
aplazar *postpone*
adelantar *bring forward*
confirmar *to confirm*
reconfirmar *reconfirm*
cancelar *to cancel*

HIRING A CAR

Quisiera alquilar un coche *I would like to hire a car*
  turismo *private car*; de lujo *luxury car*; pequeño *small*; mediano *medium-sized*; grande *large*; con chófer *with chauffeur*; sin chófer *without chauffeur*
  para tres días *for three days*; para una semana *for a week*
¿Cuánto cuesta por día? *How much is it per day?*
kilometraje ilimitado *unlimited mileage*
Tengo el carnet de conducir internacional *I have an international driving licence*
¿Puedo dejar el coche en otra parte de España? *Can I leave the car in another part of Spain?*
Voy a dejar el coche en [name of a town or airport] *I am going to leave the car in/at…*

DIRECTIONS

Siga las señales de tráfico *Follow the road signs*
Siga todo recto por [name of the street] *Go straight on down …*
después de la glorieta *after the roundabout*
después del semáforo *after the traffic lights*

IS IT ALLOWED?

¿Se puede...? *Is it allowed?/Is it possible...?*
...enviar un fax *send a fax*; telefonear *to phone*; aparcar *to park*; fumar *to smoke*; almorzar *to have lunch*; viajar hoy *travel today*; viajar mañana *travel tomorrow*; cambiar dinero *change money*; cancelar esta cita *cancel this appointment*

EATING OUT

¿Quiere(n) tomar una copa/cenar/almorzar con nosotros?
Would you like to have a drink/lunch/dinner with us?
Sí, gracias/No, gracias *Yes, thank you/No, thank you*
¿Qué tapas hay? *What tapas are there?*

¿Qué van a tomar? *What are you going to have?*
¿Para beber? *What are you going to drink?*
¿Cuál es el menú del día? *What's the fixed menu?*
El menú, por favor *The menu, please*
¿Hay? *Is there/ are there/ do you have...?*
¿Qué nos recomienda? *What do you recommend?*
La cuenta, por favor *The bill, please*

DESCRIBING THE COMPANY

La compañía se llama … *The name of the company is...*
La compañía fue fundada en … *The company was founded in …*
Tenemos 600 empleados/ 5 sucursales *We have 600 employees/5 branches*
Fabricamos *We manufacture*
Compramos/vendemos/importamos/exportamos *We buy, sell, import, export*
¿Qué porcentage de su producción exportan? *What proportion of your output do you export?*
¿Tienen un catálogo? *Have you got a catalogue?*

ANSWERS

1 PREPARATIVOS

P 6 Director: Jesús Bahíllo, President: Adrián Piera/ In England

P 7 Porcelanas Denia S.A./Elvira Sánchez

P 9 1*a* buenos días **b** buenas tardes **c** buenas noches
d buenas tardes **3** Buenas tardes. Soy (your name) de (company name). Quisiera hablar con la señora Elvira Sánchez.

4 🎧
Pablo ¿Sí?
Raúl ¡Hola!
Pablo ¡Hombre!
Raúl Buenos días
Pablo ¿Qué tal?
Raúl ¿Cómo estás Pablo? ¿Qué tal?
Pablo Muy bien ¿y tú?
Raúl Muy bien. Estupendamente.

a ¡Hola! Buenos días ¿Qué tal?

P 10 *Track 5* ¿Me lo puede repetir?
Track 6 ¿Cuál es su nombre, por favor?/¿Cómo se llama usted?/ ¿Su nombre, por favor?

P 11 1*a* Mi nombre es.../Me llamo.../Soy...

P 12 **4** 1b 2f 3e 4a 5d 6c

P12 *a* Maite García's colleague is Aurelio Cuadrado/ Sr Martínez's partner is Sr Pérez Cuenca/Sra Sánchez introduces La Directora de Márketing de Arte Iberia

P13 1*a* Mi nombre es... Sra García, le presento al Sr Pastor.
b Buenos días Sr Muñoz; le presento al Sr Cañedo. *c* Buenos días Sr Cañedo, soy... *d* Mi nombre es...quisiera hablar con...

2 🎧
Antonio Linares Sevillano Soy Antonio Linares Sevillano, Director de Organización y Desarrollo de Recursos Humanos del Grupo Iberia.

a Antonio Linares Sevillano *b* Sr Linares Sevillano or Sr Linares *c* Grupo Iberia

3 🎧
David Horta Segarra Mi nombre es David Horta Segarra ... soy Concejal de Industria, Comercio y Turismo del Ayuntamiento de Vigo, una ciudad situada en Galicia, España.

a Councillor *b* Industry, Commerce and Tourism

P 14 Estudios Madrid / Representante;
Reme Sánchez Bocanegra/Ana Sánchez Bocanegra/Fátima Sánchez Bocanegra
Reme and Fátima have more or less the same job.

P 15 1*a* Soy Pablo Suárez. Soy Gerente de Márketing de Porcelanas Denia S.A.. Le presento a mi socio, la señora Carmen Tenorio. *b* Soy Ana López Martínez. Soy Contable de Arte Iberia. Le presento a mi socio el Señor José Gómez Ruiz.

2*a* ¿Cuál es su nombre? *b* ¿Cuál es su ocupación? *c* ¿Qué cargo tiene en la compañía? *d* ¿Qué tipo de compañía es?

P 16 🎧
Alfredo Pastor Bueno, soy Alfredo. Alfredo Pastor. Estás en Bidón 5. Es una agencia especializada en turismo alternativo, turismo verde, turismo ecológico y turismo de aventura.

a Alfredo Pastor *b* alternative tourism; green tourism; ecological tourism; adventure tourism.

6 a5 b2 c4 d1 e3 f6

P 17 **Intergift**: *a* designer and manufacturer *b* custom jewellery, glasses, hair accessories, handkerchieves, headscarves, bags, belts, buttons *c* designer and manufacturer of custom jewellery *d* Ramón Faus Santaeularia S.A.

2 LLEGADA

P 20 Hilton Hotel

P 21 1*a* *Taxista* Buenas tardes.
Usted A la Plaza de España, por favor.
Taxista Muy bien.
Usted ¿Cuánto es, por favor?
Taxista Son 1.450 pesetas.
Usted ¿Me podría dar una factura, por favor?

2 A la Cámara de Comercio e Industria, por favor./¿Me podría dar una factura, por favor?/Al aeropuerto, por favor.

P 22 for one night; *a* True *b* False

P 24 **2** Son las tres de la tarde. Son las cuatro de la tarde. Es la una/son las once y media de la noche. Son las ocho y veinte de la mañana. Son las veintiuna (cero-cero). Son las cuatro menos cuarto de la tarde. Son las doce y cinco. Son las catorce veinticinco. Son las seis y cuarto de la mañana. Son las seis menos veinte de la tarde. Son las doce menos diez de la mañana. Son las nueve y diez de la noche.

3a firma **b** deja **c** rellena **d** llama

4a fill in a form **b** sign something

5a el almuerzo **b** el desayuno **c** la cena

P 25 Ms Taylor's problem: the hotel doesn't have anything reserved in her name. The receptionist offers to contact another hotel to find alternative accommodation.

P 26 1a Soy **b** estamos **c** ¿estás? **d** es **e** es **f** son **g** tiene **h/i** tengo

2 a single room for three nights.

P 27 3 una habitación individual/con ducha/por una noche/con desayuno
una habitación doble/con baño/sin desayuno/por tres noches.

4 🎧

Pilar   Buenos días.
Recepcionista   Buenos días, señora.
Pilar   Mi nombre es Pilar Alvarez y tengo una habitación reservada en este hotel.
Recepcionista   A ver un momentito que lo voy a comprobar... no tenemos nada reservado a este nombre, ¿eh?
Pilar   ¡Uy!...pues me extraña muchísimo porque mi secretaria ha enviado un fax ...¿podría comprobarlo, por favor?
Recepcionista   Sí...pues no hemos recibido ningún fax a este nombre, ¿no puede estar para otro día la reserva?
Pilar   No, no. Reservamos para los 25, 26 y 27 de marzo.
Recepcionista   Pues...lo siento mucho pero debe haber una confusión, aquí no tenemos nada a ese nombre.
Pilar   Bueno, pues, ¿tienen ustedes habitación libre?
Recepcionista   A ver, lo voy a comprobar...Pues lo siento pero estamos completos para esta noche.
Pilar   ¡Qué problema! ¿y qué puedo hacer yo ahora?
Recepcionista   Si quiere, puedo buscar un hotel por aquí cercano...

4a 25, 26 and 27 March **b** they will have to find alternative accommodation

5a ¿tiene una habitación disponible? **b** una habitación individual para dos noches.

P 28 Pilar wants to go to Vigo. The Talgo leaves Chamartín station at 13.30.
The clerk gives Pilar the prices for first and second class tickets on the Talgo.

The discount on Días Azules is 12%. Pilar chooses to catch the Talgo from Madrid to Vigo. She is travelling on a Sunday. Pilar does not smoke. Pilar is paying by credit card.

P 30 2

Oficial   Buenos días.
Usted   Quisiera comprar un billete para Bilbao.
Oficial   ¿Ida o ida y vuelta?.
Usted   Ida y vuelta.
Oficial   ¿Para qué día sería el viaje?
Usted   Para el viernes.
Oficial   ¿En primera o en segunda?
Usted   En primera clase. ¿Cuánto cuesta el billete, por favor?
Oficial   Son 9.560 pesetas. ¿Paga con tarjeta de crédito o en efectivo?
Usted   Quisiera pagar en efectivo.

3 No, Intergift exhibe desde el 17 al 21 de enero y desde el 19 al 23 de septiembre./ No, Fitur exhibe desde el 29 de enero hasta el 2 de febrero.

P 31 4 🎧

Boy 1 El ocho
Boy 2 El uno
Boy 3 81
Female speaker: Han obtenido premio de 10.000 pesetas todos los billetes terminados en 81. Las once siguientes extracciones de tres cifras cada una, corresponden a los premios de 25.000 pesetas.
Boy 1 El uno
Boy 2 El siete
Boy 3 El nueve
Boy 4 El 179
Female speaker: Han obtenido premio de 25.000 pesetas todos los billetes terminados en 179.

The first prize announced is ten thousand pesetas. The second prize announced is twenty five thousand pesetas.

5a quisiera un billete. **b** ¿Hay?; ¿Tiene?

3 CITAS

P 34 *Track 1* It's afternoon. Sr Sivil is not available.
Track 2 ¿De parte de quién? No cuelgue por favor.

P 35 First of all, Sr Pérez isn't in his office; later he is in a meeting./ Say in Spanish: llamaré más tarde; ¿Cuándo puedo llamarle?

P 36 1 a2/4 b5 c1 d3

2a ¿Está de vacaciones? No, no está de vacaciones. **b** ¿Está en reunión? No, no está en reunión. **c** ¿Está en viaje de negocios?

No, no está en viaje de negocios

3a llamaré el martes **b** llamaré el miércoles **c** llamaré esta tarde **d** llamaré mañana por la mañana

4a Mi nombre es.../Soy... **b** (spell your surname)

5 ¿Cuándo puedo llamarle?; El Sr García está ocupado; Quisiera dejar un recado; Le llamaré mañana por la tarde.

P 37

Pilar   Le doy mi número de teléfono entonces el cuatro, cincuenta y nueve, setenta y cinco, treinta y dos. Este teléfono es de Madrid.
Recepcionista   Pues un momentito que le voy a dar mi tarjeta.
Phone number: 459 7532

8

Jaime Malgarejo Hola, buenos días.
Secretaria   Buenos días.
Jaime Malgarejo Soy Jaime Malgarejo, de la empresa Treserra. Tengo entrevista con Josep Rojas y Susana Paz.
Secretaria   Tendrá que esperarse un momentito, por favor, que están reunidos. Si se quiere sentar.
Jaime Malgarejo Muy bien, gracias.
They are in a meeting, but he won't have to wait long.

9 Un momento, por favor/No cuelgue

P 38 el departamento de marketing/el departamento de exportación

Answerphone message: Mi nombre es.../Soy...(job title) de (company name) de (country where you're based). Estoy en el Hotel Savoy. Mi número de teléfono es treinta y siete - sesenta y dos - dieciocho - ochenta y nueve.

P 39 1a Nuestra cocinera es española **b** La secretaria es inglesa y el secretario es español **c** Nuestras diseñadoras son francesas **d** Soy (your nationality) **e** La directora es italiana

P 40 3 Los productos europeos Los mercados internacionales Las Ferias Industriales Las compañías británicas Los apellidos españoles Las empresas modernas Sus socios Tus oficinas Vuestras recepcionistas Nuestros apoderados.

4a mi secretario, su recepcionista y nuestros empleados
b nuestro cocinero, nuestros camareros y nuestras camareras
c mis diseñadoras y sus diseñadores

5 ventas/exportación

P 41 Ben Smith wants to see Sr Farías Grisán this week. The secretary says this week is impossible. They arrange the meeting for the following week on Tuesday morning. The appointment is changed to Wednesday.

p. 42

Begoña Dígame.
Paloma Begoña.
Begoña Hola.
Paloma Hola, buenos días, soy Paloma.
Begoña Hola Paloma, buenos días.
Paloma Mira, Begoña, quería ver si puedes comentar por favor al señor Guiveralde que la reunión que estaba prevista para mañana a las diez de la mañana, a ver si podría ser en vez a las cuatro de la tarde.
Begoña Vale.
Paloma Aquí en el despacho del señor Ballvé, ¿de acuerdo?
Begoña Supongo que no tendrá ningún problema, de acuerdo.
Paloma Muchas gracias.
Begoña A ti, a ti.
Paloma Adiós, hasta ahora.

a morning **b** yes **c** 10 am **d** Señor Ballvé

2 a Quisiera/Necesito adelantar la fecha de la cita
b Quisiera/Necesito aplazar la fecha de la cita **c** Quisiera/Necesito cancelar la cita **d** Quisiera/Necesito confirmar la cita

3

Secretary Hola buenas tardes.
Assistant Hola buenas tardes. ¿Es la empresa Tixa?
Secretary Correcto.
Assistant Mire, quisiera hablar con el señor Sivil, por favor.
Secretary Bueno, lo siento muchísimo, pero no está, y ya no va a volver en todo el día. Yo soy la secretaria, si quiere hablar conmigo.
Assistant Mire, si quiere tomar nota; yo llamo del banco de Sabadell. Lo llamo referente al tema de la ronda de consultas de Estados Unidos.
Secretary Sí, lo conozco.
Assistant Creo que hablé con usted la última vez, y era para concertar una entrevista. Lo único que quedamos que la llamaría para reconfirmarla. Entonces era para confirmar la entrevista del próximo día quince.
Secretary Sí, día quince.
Assistant A las doce del mediodía.
Secretary A las doce del mediodía.
Assistant En nuestra sede central de Barcelona.
Secretary Muy bien en la sede central de Barcelona, ¿que está en qué calle por favor?
Assistant Eso está en Paseo de Gracia, número treinta y seis.
Secretary ¿Algún piso, alguna persona en particular...?
Assistant No, no, es planta, sí, puede llamar por la, por Silvia Garriga.
Secretary Silvia. Muy bien, pues allí estaremos el día quince... Muchas gracias.
Assistant Vale, a ustedes, adiós.

a verdad (true)   *b* mentira (false)

P 43 **4a** ¿Perdón?/¿Cómo?/¿Me lo puede repetir?   *b* ¿Qué quiere decir?/¿Cómo se escribe?   *c* ¿Puede hablar más lentamente, por favor?

5 🎧

Les habla el contestador automático de la firma Comercial Suiza. En este momento no podemos atenderle. Rogamos deje el nombre y el número de teléfono después de la señal. Nos pondremos en contacto con usted lo antes posible. Gracias.

a Soy... de (company name) de (location of the company headquarters). Mi número de teléfono es... Mi número de fax es... Quisiera confirmar la cita con la señora Maite García para el viernes.   *b* Quisiera concertar una cita con el señor Martínez el miércoles a las dos de la tarde.

P 44 **6** el pasaporte de Jane Carter; la agenda de Ben Smith; el despacho de José Pérez Robles.

🎧 Parla espanyol? El senyor Carreras, sisplau.

4   DESPLAZAMIENTOS

P 48 *Track 1* Yes   *Track 2* No.

P 51 *a* Hotel Príncipe   *b* Centro comercial   *c* Gran Hotel Real   *d* ¿Dónde está la parada de taxis?   *e* ¿Dónde está el Museo de Bellas Artes?   *f* ¿Dónde está el cine?   *g* bastante cerca   *h* bastante lejos   *i* parada de taxis   *j* farmacia   *k* Centro Comercial
🎧

Pilar   Perdone, ¿me puede indicar si hay una oficina de correos cerca?
Passer-by   Pues sí, mire ...no tiene nada más que seguir por aquí adelante y la primera calle que tiene usted a la derecha ...son dos manzanas, pues en cuanto llegue a...a la segunda esquina gire usted a la izquierda y a mitad de la calle ...pues allí tiene la oficina de correos.
Pilar   Muchísimas gracias.
Passer-by   De nada.

first right, second street to the left, walk half a block to get to the Post office

3 ¿Hay un banco cerca de aquí/por aquí?   ¿Hay una farmacia cerca de aquí/por aquí?   ¿Hay un restaurante por aquí/cerca de aquí?   ¿Hay un bar por aquí/cerca de aquí?

P 52 **4** a1 b5 c3 d4 e2

5a El Museo Naval está en el Paseo del Prado entre la Calle Juan de Mena y la Calle de Montalbán.   *b* Para ir a Alicante coja el Talgo de las 13.30 en la estación de Atocha.   *c* La oficina de la compañía está en la Calle de Cervantes a quince minutos andando.
6a ¿Dónde está la estación del metro?   *b* ¿Dónde está la parada de taxis?   *c* ¿Dónde está la estación del ferrocarril?   *d* ¿Está cerca la Calle de Cervantes?

P 53 Wednesday at 10 a.m. /Sra Berenguer/Gran Vía de las Cortes Catalanas between Pau Claris Street and Lauria Street, third floor, office No 302/Yes.

P 54 Route: follow the traffic signs to Gran Vía; continue straight on towards Plaza Tetuán; straight ahead at the roundabout at the junction of Gran Vía and Paseo de Gracia, the first street to the left is Pau Claris Street; there is a car park on the right hand side, on the corner of Pau Claris and Calle de la Diputación.

P 55 (see Unit 3 Track 9 for tapescript) **1a** el día quince a las doce del mediodía   *b* Banco de Sabadell; sede central de Barcelona   *c* Paseo de Gracia, número treinta y seis.

2 Coja usted la primera a la izquierda, siga todo recto por la calle del Consejo de Ciento, en Paseo de Gracia gire a la derecha, siga todo recto hacia el norte; y después del Metro Aragón, el hotel está a mano izquierda.

3a Yo voy a llegar tarde   *b* Mi cliente va a cancelar la cita *or* Mi cliente va a dejar un recado   *c* Los socios van a firmar un contrato   *d* La secretaria va a cancelar la cita *or* Mi secretaria va a dejar un recado   *e* Tú vas a alquilar un coche   *f* Marisa y yo vamos a ir a Torrevieja   *g* Vosotros vais a reservar una habitación

4a del/ de/ a/ de/ de/ en   *b* al/ de/ a/ de   *c* al/ de/ en   *d* en/ en

P 56 **5** a3 b9 c7 d8 e2 f6 g4 h1 i5

6a Sí, se puede   *b* No, no se puede   *c* Sí, se puede

7 Se puede coger /Coja el tren a la estación Kensington (Olympia); Se puede coger/Coja el metro a Earl's Court y luego a Kensington (Olympia); Se puede coger/Coja el autobús número... ; Para el coche hay un aparcamiento en Kings Mall, Hammersmith.

8 El lunes voy a viajar a Madrid. Voy a salir de Heathrow a las nueve de la mañana. Voy a llegar a Barajas a las doce y veinte. Voy a telefonear a Porcelanas Denia S.A. y voy a confirmar la cita para el miércoles. Voy a alquilar un coche. El viernes voy a viajar en coche a Valencia, a la feria. Voy a aplazar la cita con Modern Kitchens Ltd.

P 57 Pilar hires a small car, for a week. The clerk asks to see her driving licence and passport. The charge is 6.200 pesetas.

There is no extra charge for mileage.
Pilar wants to know if she can drop the car off in another
Spanish town. (Answer: Yes, she can.)

P 58 🎧
Pilar Entonces, ¿qué horas tengo que evitar?
Clerk Bueno, pues tienes que evitar las 9 de la...8...entre 8 y 9
de la mañana y entre 1 y 4 del mediodía. Luego, la salida del
trabajo por la tarde a las 6...7 de la tarde.

The rush hour in Madrid is between eight and nine in the
morning, one and four in the early afternoon and six and seven
in the late afternoon.

P 59 **1a** 8.000 ptas. **b** second class **c** Madrid-Valencia
d yes **e** when buying your ticket and when the inspector asks
to see your ticket

2a Yes **b** Sunday **c** No

5 ¡A COMER!

P 62 Pilar Alvarez is going to have a portion of Spanish
omelette and a dry sherry. Louise Taylor is going to have
potato salad in garlic mayonnaise and a glass of vermouth.

P 63 The waitress forgets to mention Spanish omelette. Ben
Smith is going to have Spanish omelette and mixed salad; Elvira
Sánchez is going to have garlic soup and fried fish.

P 64 **1a** ¿Me pone una ración de jamón serrano? **b** ¿Me
pone una ración de gambas/de calamares? **c** ¿Me pone una
ración de tortilla española? **d** ¿Me pone una ración de
chorizo/de champiñones?

3 🎧
Comensal 1 Pues depende de lo que haya, a ver, ¿qué nos
recomienda?
Camerero Las croquetas es lo típico de aquí, unos espetitos de
sardinas, unas almejitas salteadas, unas gambitas, unas cigalitas,
unos langostinos.
Comensal 2 ¿Qué pescado grande tenéis?
Camerero Pues mire usted, le puedo poner un dorado para la
espalda, a la plancha, aliñadito con ajo, perejil y aceite, o si
quiere un rodaballo, lenguado...
Comensal ¿Es de segundo?
Camerero Es de segundo.
Comensal 1 ¿Y de primero? Yo empezaba con unas cigalitas ...

a What do you recommend? **b** dorado; turbot; sole
c almejas (clams), gambas (prawns), cigalas (type of prawn),
langostinos (crayfish)

5a *José* Para mí el bistec. *Camarero* ¿Cómo lo quiere? *José* Lo
quiero a la plancha. **b** *Julia* Para mí las gambas. *Camarero*
¿Cómo las quiere? *Julia* Las quiero al ajillo.

P 65 Hake with garlic in parsley sauce. Medium.

P 67 **1a** *Customer* ¿Qué pescado hay?/¿Qué me recomienda?
Waiter Merluza a la sidra. (hake in cider sauce) **b** *Customer*
No quiero paella. ¿Qué me recomienda? *Waiter* Hay tortilla
de habas. **c** *Customer* ¿Hay potaje?/ ¿Qué me recomienda?
Waiter Hay cocido extremeño. **d** *Customer* No quiero
gazpacho. ¿Qué me recomienda? *Waiter* Hay sopa de
pescado/Hay olla cortijera de Córdoba.

P 68 Louise Taylor has a meeting. They are going to eat at
the restaurante Cádiz at nine o'clock. *¿Verdad o mentira?*
mentira; mentira

P 69 Towards the end of the meal, Ben Smith asks for the bill
to be added to his hotel bill.

1a ¿Quieren tomar una copa con nosotros? **b** ¿Quieren cenar
con nosotros?

2 *Customer* Quisiera reservar una mesa , por favor.
Waiter	¿Para qué día?
Customer	Para el próximo martes/ sábado.
Waiter	¿Para cuántas/cinco personas?
Customer	Para cuatro personas, por favor.
Waiter	¿Para qué hora?
Customer	Para las nueve/nueve y media.
Waiter	¿A nombre de quién?
Customer	(your name)
Waiter	¿Habitación número?
Customer	Ciento sesenta y siete/Doscientos tres.

3 🎧
Sr Plácido Arango Primero tenemos un horario muy amplio,
abrimos desde muy temprano por la mañana desde las nueve de
la mañana hasta las tres de la madrugada los siete días de la
semana. Creo que en Madrid por ejemplo por 1300 Ptas, 1385
para ser exactos, que es nuestro menú del día en VIPS que
incluye un primero, un segundo plato, un postre, café y tu
bebida, creo que por ese tipo de dinero y en ese ambiente y con
esa limpieza con aire acondicionado, no tenemos mucha
competencia.

a From 9am to 3 am. **b** First course, second course, dessert,
coffee and your choice of drink. **c** A good atmosphere,
cleanliness, air conditioning

P 70 *¿Verdad o mentira?* verdad; mentira; mentira

P 71 Louise Taylor is having rice Zamora style and vegetables.

167

Mr Smith's favourite dish is paella. On Monday Ben Smith is going to Frankfurt.

P 73 *a* calamares en su tinta; estofado de perdiz al aroma de jerez; osso-buco a la jardinera; lomos de salmón al vino blanco; pimientos de piquillo rellenos de bacalao; cazuela de pollo a la campesina *b* natural; no preservatives or colouring; individual portions *c* vacuum processed; chilled *d* microwave; steamed

6   DESPLAZAMIENTOS

P 76 The company was founded in 1958. It has been on the industrial estate for 31 years. It has two branches in Spain.

P 77 The office building is not large but it is comfortable and modern. *¿Verdad o mentira?* mentira; verdad; mentira. On the second floor are more offices, a large staff cafeteria and the central filing.
What's on the left hand side of the factory floor? The warehouse; the packing area and the offices of the supervisors and designers.

P 78 **1** Soy (name; job title); la compañía fue fundada en (year); tenemos (x) sucursales y (x) empleados.

Fíjense cómo se van clasificando por peso... según el peso. Bueno vamos a pasar directamente a ver la zona de deshuesado. Por aquí, por aquí. Vamos entrando por favor...¡cuidado! Bueno, vamos a ver también la empaquetadora.

P 79 **3** a3 b1 c5 d2 e4

4 Voy a llegar a España el martes 1° de junio; voy a ir al hotel; el hotel se llama...; vamos a alquilar un coche; vamos a viajar a un pequeño industrial cerca de Torrevieja; vamos a llegar a las once de la mañana a una pequeña fábrica de zapatos.

Bienvenidos. Soy Ramón López Dols y esta es la jefa de personal, la señora Josefa López Nadal. La firma se llama Zapatos y Accesorios S.A. La fábrica está aquí en las afueras de Torrevieja desde hace 29 años. La empresa fue fundada en 1961. Tenemos 35 empleados y un salón de ventas en la ciudad de Alicante. Esta es la fábrica, aquí está la cadena de producción y allí a la derecha está la zona de embalaje. Tenemos otro edificio pequeño al fondo. Allí está el almacén.

a Fact sheet: Ramón López Dols; Josefa López Nadal; Zapatos y Accesorios S.A.; outskirts of Torrevieja; 29 years; 1961; 35 employees; Alicante *b* production line/ packing area/ warehouse They have another smaller factory building.

P 80 *Fact sheet*: Modas Florencia S.A.; ropa para damas; algodón, lana y seda; porcentaje del mercado: bueno; volumen de ventas: varios millones de pesetas; planes: introducir productos en otros mercados.
¿Verdad o mentira? verdad; mentira; mentira; verdad.

P 81

Trabajamos veinticuatro horas... tres turnos de ocho horas. Producimos a la hora ocho toneladas y media, ¿eh?. Campofrío tiene una cuota del mercado de cincuenta por ciento aproximadamente.
There are three shifts of eight hours. The produce eight and a half tons per hour. The have about 50% of the market share.

3a ¿Cuándo fue fundada la compañía? *b* ¿Tienen sucursales? *c* ¿Usan fibras artificiales/usan poliéster? *d* ¿Dónde venden sus productos?

P 82 **4a** director regional *b* presidente *c* apoderada

5a Queremos trabajar en España y nos gustaría tener una sucursal en Madrid. *b* Nos gustaría vender nuestros productos en este país y también queremos introducir nuestros productos en Francia, Alemania e Italia.

P 85 **1** a4 b6 c1 d3 e2 f5

2 Se marca el número de teléfono; se dice el nombre; se propone el día y la hora para la reunión; se apunta en el diario.

P 86

Sr Ricardo Bocanegra ¿Un día típico? Pues llego a la oficina generalmente a las 9.30 de la mañana; entonces suelo dar cita de hora en hora. Después, resuelvo los asuntos que surgen y por las tardes, por las tardes recibo en mi despacho a mis empleados o hermanos, según, y resuelvo los problemas que surgen. Y cuando ya termino la jornada de cara al público a partir de las siete de la tarde, ya me quedo solo en mi despacho y generalmente me dedico a escribir, a estudiar, a preparar conferencias cuando me invitan a dar alguna conferencia, y sobre todo pues a estudiar y a escribir que creo que es muy importante.

He discusses cases in the afternoon and prepares lectures in the evenings.

4a Su despacho es pequeñísimo. *b* Esta firma vende un producto interesantísimo. *c* El polígono industrial es grandísimo. *d* Tienen un piso carísimo en Madrid.

5 Primero se llega entre las ocho y media y las nueve menos cuarto; se abren las cartas; luego se toma una taza de café; después se dan citas; se hacen reuniones y finalmente se toma el almuerzo.

168

P 87 *a* The key to the success of Chupa Chups is to look for perfection and use only natural ingredients. *b* (open answers) *c* *Fact sheet*: Chupa Chups; Javier Bernat; 1950s; advantages: very close family, dynamic, take decisions quickly; lollipops; 1500 million units a year.

7 CIFRAS Y PORCENTAJES

P 90 Chupa Chups have seven factories, three in Spain, two in France, one in St Petersburg, one in China. Chupa Chups produce 1500 million units a year.

P 91 Answer in Spanish: Chupa Chups exporta el noventa por ciento de su producción.
Track 2 : 10.000 million pesetas in sales revenue;*¿Verdad o mentira?* mentira.

P 92 **1** Libros de cocina. El precio de catálogo es un poco más alto que el precio de venta al público; Porcelanas: Las exportaciones de Porcelanas Marbella son mucho más altas que las exportaciones de Porcelanas Málaga; Restaurante: El precio del menú del día del Restaurante Galdós es mucho más bajo que el precio del menú del día del Restaurante Verbena; Tapices: La facturación de Tapices de Castilla S.A. es un poco más baja que la facturación de Alfombras Roselló S.A.

2a overheads 875; materials 695; labour 390; Total 1960 = pérdida **b** 1658 Profits; Materials (this year) 626; Total 1591 = ganancia

P 94
3 🎧
La bolsa alemana bajó primero 16 puntos y ganó luego 32. El resultado final del índice Dax indica una subida del 1,9%; 28,76 puntos. El Bono alemán ganó 2 puntos en su cotización. En Tokio el índice Nikkei bajó 200 yenes, un 1,32%. En Wall Street, el Dow Jones bajó en los primeros minutos pero luego subió. A media sesión este indicador bajó 1,8 puntos.

a Dax index rose by 1.9%/28.76 points; 200 yen.

4 ¿Qué porcentaje de su producción exportan?
Track 4 Campofrío has some 90.000 outlets in Spain. Sr Pedro Ballvé mentions France, Germany and England as having a more developed distribution system. Campofrío's present export figures are about 25 million dollars.

P 95 **1a** Esta compañía exporta el 50% a Francia, el 25% al Japón y el 15% a los Estados Unidos./ La compañía exporta la mayor parte de su producción a Francia.
b La compañía exporta al Japón 5% más que hace cinco años./ La compañía exporta a los Estados Unidos 5% menos que hace cinco años. /La compañía exporta a Francia 25% menos que hace cinco años.

P 96 **2a** verdad *b* mentira *c* verdad *d* El 39% de los expositores son mayoristas/ El 61% de los expositores son fabricantes *e* Hay pequeñas empresas españolas que tienen un mínimo de 29 empleados *f* Solamente un 3% de empresas pequeñas tiene participación de capital extranjero.

3 *Director de Márketing* ¿Cuáles son los productos de la compañía?
You Chaquetas y camisetas.
Director ¿Qué materias primas usan?
You La compañía usa solamente fibras naturales como lana y algodón.
Director ¿Dónde compran las materias primas?
You La compañía compra las materias primas en varios países de la Mancomunidad.
Director ¿A qué países exporta Roxy Textiles Ltd?
You La compañía exporta a doce países, cinco en la CE: los países del Benelux, Italia y Alemania.
Director ¿Qué producción exportan a la CEE?
You 23%.
Director ¿Qué productos nuevos van a introducir?
You (por ejemplo) faldas, pantalones, chaquetas, etc.

P 97 Growth in total assets: 1.778.402 million pesetas. Percentage growth in net results: 18,96%; After-tax profits: 14,31%

P 98 **1a** El total correspondiente a 1992 es 15.500 y el total correspondiente a 1993 es 15.500.
b En 1993 se registra un aumento de existencias de 650.
c El total general de 1993 es igual que el total general de 1992./El total general de 1993 no es ni más alto ni más bajo que el total general de 1992.

P 99 **2a** Las tres cuentas principales de un negocio son la cuenta de pérdidas y ganancias, el balance y el presupuesto del cash flow.
b Los tres registros de un negocio son: el libro de caja, el registro de ventas y el registro de compras.

3a verdad *b* mentira *c* mentira

P 101 *a* verdad *b* verdad *c* mentira

8 AL CONTADO

P 104 Approximately one thousand gift ideas. 70 pesetas and 59 pesetas respectively.

P 105 *¿Verdad o mentira?* mentira; verdad.

There is a minimum order of 40.000 pesetas; delivery is immediate.

1 🔊

Raúl Mira de Julio González nos quedan 2000.

Pablo Muy bien. ¿En cuánto tiempo estaría disponible todo el stock?

Raúl Yo creo que en dos semanas tengo el stock definitivo.

Pablo No hay problema.

Raúl Pues, yo estoy hablando aproximadamente de más o menos 700 del Henry Moore.

Pablo Bueno, más o menos 700 ejemplares.

Raúl Vamos a ver. Podemos hablar, mira el todo Dalí, que su precio de catálogo está ahora mismo en 10.000 pesetas; el Julio González, que ahora mismo está en 9.000 pesetas venta al público, y que aun lo seguimos vendiendo; y el Henry Moore, que vale 11.000 pesetas, yo te puedo hacer para el Julio González, que tengo más ejemplares, que tengo 2.000, te puedo hacer un 70% de descuento, para el Julio González, que hay 2.000 ejemplares. Y para los otros dos, te puedo hacer un 75% de descuento, que los considero un poco más duros de venta y te ofrezco cinco puntos más de ventaja ¿no? Yo no sé si esto empieza a entrar dentro de tus números.

a The catalogue price of the books on Dalí is 10,000 pesetas; Henry Moore 11,000 pesetas; Julio González 9,000 pesetas.

b Raúl has got 2,000 copies of the book on Julio González and he is prepared to offer the buyer 70% discount.

2 a3 b5 c2 d1 e4

P 106 3 *Sales Manager* Aquí tiene el catálogo de regalos de empresa.

You Gracias. Me gustarían las agendas.

Sales Manager Estas agendas son de primerísima calidad.

You ¿Cuál es el precio por unidad?

Sales Manager Estas cuestan 7.000 pesetas cada una. Por pedidos de 100 agendas le puedo hacer un descuento del 9%.

You ¿Hay un descuento adicional por pago al contado?

Sales Manager Sí. Hay un 5% de descuento adicional por pago al contado, con entrega inmediata.

4a 30% **b** Optica Roma **c** 700 pesetas **d** Rola **e** Rola

P 107 *¿Verdad o mentira?* mentira; mentira; verdad

P 109 1 1c 2a 3b

2 Asunto; el envío; agenda, camisetas, llaveros; le saluda

P 110 3a

Señores   Date, Address

Asunto: Petición de información.

Les agradeceremos el envío de la siguiente información: lista de precios, tamaños y colores, descuentos por pago al contado y plazo de entrega de los siguientes complementos decorativos: bolsas publicitarias, cintas de fantasía, papel de regalo y pegatinas. En espera de sus gratas noticias, les saluda atentamente. (signature).

b

Señores   Date, Address

Asunto: Pedido

Les agradeceremos el envío de los siguientes productos: (quantity) cuadros marineros, número de catálogo ... Por favor enviar a la siguiente dirección...(delivery address). En espera de sus gratas noticias, les saluda atentamente. (signature).

Track 4 Two reasons why the books could be sold easily: quality and price. If Pablo gets the discount he wants he will buy all the books and Raúl will have no further storage problems.

P III *Track 5* The first speaker says their prices include F.A.S. (free alongside ship) port of Barcelona; the discount mentioned is 20%; the terms described by the second speaker are bankers draft on presentation of the invoice; the bill of exchange is due after 45 days.

P 113 1a atractivos...estos libros sobre Dalí (or your choice of book title); **b** competitivos....vuestros precios/los precios de (company name); **c** alto...el precio de los llaveros/(or your choice of product); **d** buena...la calidad de los productos de (name of the company)

2a agotado/a; **b** saldos; **c** días laborables; **d** la temporada baja

3 *First letter.* Please find enclosed freight note and duplicate invoice. The goods will be sent by fast goods train. *Second letter.* Please find enclosed freight note Transportes Altamirano S.L. and invoice.

P 114 4 El pago inicial es el 40% del precio; diez mensualidades a pagar por letra de cambio al 12% anual. Pago inicial 200.000 pesetas; mensualidades 30.000 pesetas cada una; interés anual 9.000 pesetas; mensualidades más interés 30.900 pesetas cada una.

P 115 España exporta la mayor cantidad de artículos de regalo a Estados Unidos, Francia, Alemania, Italia y Portugal./ 7.845.132 miles de pesetas son las cifras de ventas al exterior de ropa de cama, mesa y tocador./ Los productos que han experimentado un aumento en sus exportaciones son: los objetos de escritorio (25,40 por 100), los objetos de vidrio (19,39 por 100) y la ropa de cama y mesa (2,3 por 100).

P 118 Product: English tableware/crockery/china; company: Churchill; reasons for exhibiting: sell to wholesalers; meet retailers; raise the profile of the company.

P 119 The average Spanish customer reacts favourably to foreign products. The exhibitor is pleased with the location of the stand.

P 120 **1a** Fabricamos y vendemos loza inglesa. **b** Queremos exponer en Madrid y Valencia el año próximo. **c** Estamos contentos con el stand.

2 Four good reasons for speaking Spanish at the fair: establish contact with many non English-speaking visitors; publicise the name of the company; talk to many wholesalers without having to travel all over Spain; create a list of interested customers.

3a Vendemos muebles. **b** La compañía se llama Furni. **c** Nuestros clientes son mayoristas. **d** Tenemos un catálogo. **e** El precio de un sofá es de cien mil pesetas.

4 *Visitante* ¿Qué producto venden ustedes?
You La compañía vende loza/Vendemos loza.
Visitante ¿Cómo se llama la compañía?
You (your choice of name) de Staffordshire, Inglaterra.
Visitante ¿A quiénes venden ustedes?
You Vendemos a detallistas/minoristas y mayoristas.
Visitante ¿Son fabricantes?
You Sí.
Visitante ¿Venden ustedes por correo? ¿Tienen catálogo?
You Tenemos catálogo pero no vendemos por correo en España; solamente en Inglaterra y Alemania.
Visitante Me gustan mucho estos productos. ¿Tiene usted una lista de precios a mano?
You Sí. Los precios son muy razonables/competitivos.
Visitante Me gustaría recibir un catálogo.
You Con mucho gusto. Me dice su nombre, su dirección y su teléfono por favor.

5
Martin Doro O.K....mi colega...Señor Willmoth.
Russell Willmoth ¡Hola!, encantado.
Martin Doro Sí. ¿Estás en Barcelona?
Customer Sí. Sí. Sí.
Martin Doro Bien. Esta señora es de un catálogo que...
Russell Willmoth Y ¿qué clase de artículos se venden en...el catálogo?
Customer Se va...a vender de todo.
Russell Willmoth Ah...
Customer Yo estoy seleccionando un poco vajillas de todos los niveles, cristalerías de todos los niveles...
Russell Willmoth De acuerdo.

Customer Estoy conectando mucho con gente que tiene cosas portuguesas.
Russell Willmoth Claro.
Customer ...porque me ofrecen muy buenos precios.
Russell Willmoth Muy bien. Pues creo que nos pondremos en contacto más adelante. Para este número tengo todo comprado.
Martin Doro Ya. ¿Cuándo compra la próxima vez?
Customer Pues...hacia marzo o por ahí...Quizá en la feria de enero. En la feria de enero podéis estar aquí ¿no?
Martin Doro Sí.

a She is selecting articles for a catalogue. **b** a bit of everything. **c** crockery and crystal **d** because the prices are good **e** January or March

6a ¿Son fabricantes? **b** Me gustaría recibir un catálogo.

P 122 The fair is like a shop window; it is a meeting place for all the key people in the field.

El Señor Prieto es el Director Adjunto del Grupo de Empresas Alvarez./ El grupo comercial se dedica a la fabricación y venta de artículos de porcelana y loza./ El Sr Prieto dice que la feria es importante para el producto porque es un escaparate y porque es un centro de reuniones de los profesionales de la compra y de la venta del producto cerámico.

P 123 **1a** Ahora estoy representando a una compañía colombiana. **b** Ahora estoy haciendo poco deporte. **c** Ahora estamos cogiendo ideas de otros clientes. **d** Ahora estamos fabricando loza de uso doméstico.

Gala Sánchez Hola. Soy Gala Sánchez y representamos el stand de 'Elizabeth Lord' en el pabellón de Regalos Fama, bueno, 'Intergift' en este caso, en setiembre. Y... bueno pues estamos aquí...nos hemos instalado en el pabellón N 4, justo en...una esquina bastante buena, por donde pasa mucha gente, porque es la que comunica un pabellón con otro. Nosotros somos distribuidores de una agencia, bueno, de una serie de productos ingleses aquí en España. Estamos intentando ver...cómo...qué reacción tienen los españoles ante estos productos y es bastante aceptable.

a Elizabeth Lord. **b** Intergift, room 4. **c** yes

Explain in English: We are distributors./ It's quite satisfactory.

4
Elizabeth Lord Sí...Me llamo Elizabeth Lord y vivo en Inglaterra...y vi que había mucha oportunidad de hacer comercio en España. Soy medio española y hablo español; soy bilingüe. Entonces empecé...a....exportar cosas inglesas...y...ya llevo seis, seis meses. Y desde luego hay mucho futuro aquí en España. La gente, como han, han habido muchas restricciones económicas y las fronteras han estade cerradas, claro es

171

totalmente nuevo y quieren gastar, y comprar, y les gusta comprar cosas para la casa que es...una cosa nueva aquí.

P 124 Elizabeth Lord exports English products to Spain. She says that the Spanish are enjoying a new feeling of freedom and want to spend money on new products, especially things for the home.

5a Cheques are not/hardly ever used here (in Spain).

P 125 According to Russell Willmoth what's different about exhibiting in Spain is that the exhibitor cannot choose the location for the stand.
Se puede regatear means 'one can bargain'. *Se han portado muy bien conmigo* means 'they have been very good to me'.
Gala Sánchez thinks that her stand is attractive both because of the way it is set up and because of the product on display.

P 126 Rafael Prieto's stand has a bar. *a* mentira *b* verdad *c* mentira

P 127 1a hemos estado *b* hemos montado *c* hemos vendido *d* hemos representado

Visitante Hola, buenos días, señorita, por favor, ¿me puede indicar el stand de Collie?
Azafata Sí, es stand de Collie; ¿ve, ve esta columna a la izquierda del stand? Entonces, en esa misma columna, al fondo, allí está Collie.
Visitante Vale, y ¿hay algún servicio de teléfono?
Azafata Sí, el servicio público de teléfonos está a mano izquierda, al fondo.
Visitante ¿Y para mandar algún fax a mi despacho, a mi oficina?
Azafata Ah, eso tendrá que preguntar a las oficinas. Las oficinas están, mire usted, a mano derecha; sigue usted, entonces encontrará una puerta. Entonces encontrará unas escaleras. Suba usted las escaleras y allí está la oficina.
Visitante ¿Y tenéis algún listado, algún catálogo de los expositores de este certámen?
Azafata Sí, desde luego. Tenemos aquí el catálogo con toda la relación de los expositores, las marcas, las actividades y las direcciones.
Visitante Muy bien. Muchas gracias.
Azafata ¿Le sirve?
Visitante Sí, sí, muchas gracias ¿eh?
Azafata De nada.

a Behind the column on the left. *b* The public telephone is at the back of the room on the left-hand side. *c* The fax machine is in an office on the first floor. *d* The catalogue contains a list of exhibitors, brand names, activities and addresses.

P 129 3a Sí, hay una parada de autobuses en el acceso sur; está a la izquierda. *b* IFEMA tiene doce cafeterías self service. *c* El multiestanco está en el pabellón 5. *d* El pabellón 2 está lejos del acceso norte. *e* En el pabellón 3 hay servicio de teléfono y fax. *f* En el pabellón 6 se puede alquilar un coche. *g* El servicio médico está en el pabellón 1. *h* La oficina de la Cámara de Comercio e Industria de Madrid está en el pabellón 4.
i IFEMA tiene ocho pabellones con cinco restaurantes, doce cafeterías, una oficina de correos, bancos, servicio de teléfonos y fax y servicio de alquiler de coches. Iberia y la Cámara de Comercio e Industria de Madrid tienen oficinas en IFEMA. Hay también un auditorio moderno.
j Barajas airport, Chamartín station, Hotels: Barajas, Alameda, Meliá Castilla, Eurobuilding, Tryp Plaza, Husa Princesa, Miguel Angel, Tryp Fenix.
k 0900-2000 every 30 minutes.
l Autobús línea 827; Metro Arturo Soria, Metro Canillejas.
La Sala de Prensa: a First floor *b* Telephone, fax, computer terminals, database, TV, individual desks, telephone booths, boardroom *c* Fototeca

10 HABLEMOS DE NEGOCIOS

P 132
Sr Maltes' responsibilities are: management, marketing and administration.

P 133 *Track 1* Cabrea de Mar is a town. Collie S.A. manufactures knitwear./ La compañía tiene cincuenta empleados. La compañía tiene una facturación de 800 millones de pesetas./ Collie distribute their products through agents. They do not export their products.
Track 2 Seventeen years. The company knows the Spanish consumer.

P 134 Contrapunto understands the habits, language and lifestyle of the average Spanish consumer.

1 a4 b2 c3 d1

P 135 2a Porcelanas Santa Clara S.A. fabrica artículos de porcelana y loza. *b* Campofrío S.A. vende productos comestibles. *c* Contrapunto ofrece un servicio de publicidad.

3 La compañía está situada en (town). Está cerca de (major town). Está a ...km de Londres. Fabricamos (product). Tenemos (number) empleados. Es una compañía británica. El capital es (100)% británico. Tenemos una facturación anual de...millones de libras esterlinas. Vendemos nuestros productos en el Reino Unido y exportamos un pequeño porcentaje a....

5a Pienso que el producto es atractivo./ Creo que hay un mercado para este producto./ Pienso que la publicidad es importante para vender el producto.
b Lo siento, pero pienso que el producto es demasiado caro./ Lo siento, pero pienso que hay un problema de distribución.

P 136 The different kinds of promotional activity carried out by Banco de Sabadell are: listas/promociones a través de Bancos/misiones comerciales/ferias/promotores comerciales.
A sales promoter visits a company, finds out more about the product and carries out a promotional campaign lasting several months.
Banco de Sabadell buys space at a fair to be shared and paid for by several exhibitors.

P 137 Banco de Sabadell produces one single catalogue featuring products from four or five different manufactures who then share the production expenses.

🎧(4)

Entrevistador ¿Es importante hacer publicidad para un producto nuevo en España?
Miguel Muñoz Bueno,...la publicidad es siempre importante. Es decir, la publicidad no hace maravillas pero la publicidad ayuda a vender como elemento del marketing y entonces, es decir, el...producto es bueno, la publicidad responde. La publicidad siempre necesita el soporte de un producto bueno.
Sr Miguel Muñoz says that publicity helps to sell a product.

P 138 🎧(5)
Pablo Moreno Normalmente tenemos contacto con editores, con proveedores. En el extranjero, tenemos proveedores en Estados Unidos, en Inglaterra, Países Bajos, entonces normalmente contactamos en ferias internacionales, en Frankfurt principalmente, y también vienen a visitarnos aquí a Madrid y ofrecer sus productos.
Entrevistador ¿Cuál es el, digamos el cliente que tiene Vd en mente cuando compra?
Pablo Moreno El cliente es normalmente un ciudadano medio. Joven, y medianamente culto. Habitualmente tenemos promociones. Entonces buscamos siempre poder ofrecer los

mejores precios, con una buena financiación, y libros de máxima actualidad o de máximo interés.
Temáticas como pueden ser arte, diseño, cine, publicidad, todo este tipo de cosas.

a International trade fairs/visits to Madrid by representatives **b** young, averagely educated **c** books about art, design, cinema, publicity.

4a Hacemos publicidad, listas de direcciones, promoción por teléfono, ferias industriales.

5a Pensamos que las ferias son una buena idea. **b** Creemos que el producto es apropiado para el mercado europeo. **c** Creemos que nuestros precios son competitivos.

P 139 This cocktail cabinet fits into any space. The Bank representative thinks the cabinet should be shown in their open showroom in the U.S.A. The Bank proposes to send a mailing list to contact 150 key interior designers with a catalogue and an invitation to the showroom.

P 141 **1a** Estoy de acuerdo. **b** Estoy de acuerdo. **c** No estoy de acuerdo. **d** No estoy de acuerdo. **e** No estoy de acuerdo.

2 El showroom ofrece un contacto más personal y la gente está interesada en el producto./ La desventaja de la feria es que el contacto es impersonal; la ventaja es que se puede ver más gente que en el showroom.

4 *Juego de té*: **a** Es ligero. **b** Es atractivo. **c** El diseño es bueno. **d** Es resistente al microondas. **e** No es demasiado caro./ *Teléfono*: **a** Es pesado. **b** El diseño no es muy bueno. **c** Es mucho más caro que el antiguo modelo.

5a Ofrecemos; preferimos/proponemos; ofrecemos; preferimos/proponemos.

P 142 **6a** Lo siento, no estamos de acuerdo. Pensamos que el descuento del 6% no es suficiente. **b** Lo siento, no estamos de acuerdo. Pensamos que el plazo de entrega de dos meses no es adecuado. **c** Lo siento, no estamos de acuerdo. Pensamos que el pago de un depósito es necesario.

GLOSSARY

This glossary includes most of the words that appear in this book. Certain less common words have been omitted.

The meanings given to words fit their use in this book. In some cases set phrases containing a particular word have been added to the main entry, eg:

por *for*, **por ciento**; **por cierto**; **por ejemplo**; **por favor**; **por lo tanto**; **[al] por mayor**; **[al] por menor**.

Nouns are listed in their singular form. The gender of nouns is indicated by the addition of the corresponding definite article: eg **el**, **la**, **los, las**.

In a few cases the indefinite article has been added when its use gives the noun a different meaning: eg **la franquicia** *exception*; but **una franquicia** *a franchise*. The plural has not been indicated on each noun listed but a reminder of how the plural of nouns is formed has been included at the top of the glossary. A few nouns have been listed in the plural because that is how they are used most of the time in everyday speech: eg **los acreedores** *creditors*; or because the particular item mentioned comes in pairs: eg **los audífonos** *hearing aid*.

Adjectives are listed in their masculine singular form. When the feminine form has a different ending it is shown as follows: eg **abierto/a.**

Verbs have been listed in the infinitive form: eg **abastecer** *to supply*. Regular verbs are followed by **[r]**; irregular verbs are followed by **[irr]**; reflexive verbs are followed by **[ref]** and radical changing irregular verbs are followed by **[irr A]**, **[irr B]** and **[irr C]**. The letter A, B or C in each case indicates the category they fall into (see the Grammar section for full conjugation of these verbs).

[r] regular verb
[irr] irregular verb
[ref] reflexive verb
[irr A/B/C] radical changing irregular verb category A, B or C.
Plural of nouns: vowel ending = add **s**; consonant ending = ad **es**.

A

el abanico *range/fan*
abastecer [irr] *to supply*
abierto/a *open*
el acceso *entrance*
los accesorios *accessories*
el accidente *accident*
la acción *action*
las acciones *shares*
los accionistas *shareholders*
el aceite *oil*
la aceituna *olive*
la aceptación *acceptance*
aceptar [r] *to accept*
el acero *steel*
los acreedores *creditors*
el acta *minutes (of a meeting)*
la actividad *activity*
activo/a *active*
los activos *assets*
el acuerdo *agreement*
el acuse de recibo *acknowledgement*
adelantar [r] *to bring forward*
además *besides/also*
adiós *goodbye*
adjunto/a *enclosed*
la administración *administration/government*
la aduana *customs*
el aeropuerto *airport*
la agencia *agency*
la agenda *diary*
el/la agente *agent*
agotado/a *sold out/exhausted*
el agua *water*
ahora *now*
ahora mismo *right now*
ahorrar [r] *to save (money/energy)*

los ahorros *savings*
el ajo *garlic*
al *to the*
al contado *in cash*
al detalle *retail*
al menos *at least*
al por mayor *wholesale*
precio al consumidor *retail price*
algo *anything/something*
el algodón *cotton*
algunos/as *some*
el almacén *warehouse*
el almacenaje *storage*
almacenar [r] *to store*
el ambiente *atmosphere*
almorzar [irr C] *to have lunch*
el almuerzo *lunch*
alquilar [r] *to rent/let/hire*
el alquiler *rent*
alrededor *around*
alto/a *tall*
la altura *height*
el aluminio *aluminium*
allí *there*
el/la amigo/a *friend*
analizar [irr] *analyse*
ancho/a *wide*
la anchura *width*
andando *walking/on foot*
andar [irr] *to walk*
anterior *previous*
antes *before/soon*
anual *annual*
el año *year*
el aparcamiento *parking/car park*
aparcar [irr] *to park*
el apellido *surname*
aplazar [irr] *to postpone*
el/la apoderado/a *authorised signatory*
apropiado/a *appropriate*

aprovechar [r] *to take advantage of*

aproximado/a *approximate*
aproximadamente *approximately*

apuntar [r] *to make a note of*

aquí *here*
aquí mismo *right here*
aquí tiene *here you are*

el archivo *filing cabinet/archive*
arriba *up/above*

el arroz *rice*

el arte *art*

el artículo *article/item*

el ascensor *lift*

los aseos *toilets*

el asesoramiento *advice/consultancy*

asesorar [r] *to give advice*

asistir [r] *to attend*

atender [irr] *to look after*

el atún *tuna*

los audífonos *hearing aid*

aumentar [r] *to increase*

el aumento *increase/rise*
aunque *although*

el autobús *bus*
automático/a *automatic*

la avenida *avenue*
ayudar [r] *to help*

el ayuntamiento *town hall*

el azúcar *sugar*
azul *blue*

B

bajar [r] *to drop/ go down*
bajo/a *low/short*
bajo control *under control*

el balance *balance sheet*

el banco *bank*

el baño *bathroom*

la base *base*

la base de datos *database*
bastante *quite a lot*

beber [r] *to drink*

los beneficios *profits*
bien *fine/OK*

los bienes *assets*

el billete *ticket/bank note*

el billón *billion*
blanco/a *white*
blando/a *soft*

la blusa *blouse*

el bolígrafo *ballpoint pen*

la bolsa *plastic bag*

la Bolsa *the Stock Exchange*

el bono *bond*

la botella *bottle*
brevemente *briefly*

el bricolage *DIY*
bruto *gross*
bueno/a *good*
buenos días *good morning*
buscar [irr] *to look for*

C

caber [irr] *to fit*
cada *each*
cada uno/a *each one*

la cadena *chain*

el café *coffee/café*

la caja *petty cash*
la caja de ahorros *Savings Bank*

el/la cajero/a *cashier*

el cajero automático *cash machine*

los calamares *squid*

la calculadora *calculator*
calcular [r] *to calculate/to figure out*

la calidad *quality*

la calle *street*

la cama *bed*

la cámara *chamber*

la cámara de comercio *Chamber of Commerce*

el/la camarero/a *waiter/waitress*

cambiar [r] *to change*

el cambio *change/ the exchange rate*

la camiseta *T-shirt*

cancelar [r] *to cancel*

la capacidad *capacity*

el capital *capital*

la capital *the capital of a country*

caro/a *expensive*

la carretera *road*

la carta *letter/menu*

la casa *house/home*

casi *almost*

casi nunca *hardly ever/ seldom*

el catálogo *catalogue*

la cena *dinner*

cenar [r] *to have dinner*

el centro comercial *shopping centre*

la cerámica *ceramics*

cerca de *close to*

cerrado *closed*

cerrar [irr A] *to close*

la cerveza *beer*

las cifras *figures*

la cinta transportadora *conveyor belt*

la cita *appointment/meeting*

la ciudad *city/town*

clasificar [irr] *to classify*

el/la cliente *customer*

la cobranza *collection*

cobrar [r] *to charge*

el cobro *charge*

el cobro revertido *C.O.D.*

el coche *car*

la cocina *cookery/kitchen*

el/la cocinero/a *cook*

coger [irr] *to take/catch*

coja Vd. *take/catch*

el/la colega *colleague*

colaborar [r] *to cooperate*

el color *colour*

la columna *column*

el comedor *dining room/restaurant*

comenzar [irr A] *to begin*

comer [r] *to eat*

comercial *commercial*

comercializar [irr] *to market*

el/la comerciante *dealer/ merchant*

el comercio *business/commerce*

la comida *lunch*

el comienzo *beginning*

la comisión *commission*

¿Cómo? *how?/Pardon?*

como *like*

cómodo/a *comfortable*

la compañía *company*

la comparación *comparison*

competir [r] *to compete*

los competidores *competitors*

el comprador *buyer*

comprar [r] *to buy*

la(s) compra(s) *purchases/ purchasing*

comprobar [irr] *to check/ verify*

comunicar [irr] *to communicate*

comunicando *engaged (on the phone)*

la comunidad *community*

con *with*

concentrar [r] *to concentrate*

concertar [irr A] *to make an appointment with*

el/la concesionario/a *agent/ dealer*

las condiciones *terms*

conducir [irr] *to drive*

confeccionar [r] *to make clothes*

la conferencia *conference, lecture*
  la conferencia telefónica *phone call*
  confirmar [r] *to confirm*
el conjunto *group*
  conocer [irr] *to know something*
  conocido/a *well-known*
el conocimiento *knowledge*
  conseguir [irr B] *to obtain*
la consigna *left-luggage locker*
la consignación *consignment*
el consorcio *consortium*
  constituir [irr] *to constitute*
  construir [irr] *to build*
el consumidor *consumer*
  consumir [r] *to consume*
el/la contable *accountant*
la contabilidad *accountancy*
el contacto *contact*
  contar [irr C] *to count*
al contado *cash*
  contento/a *happy*
el contestador automático *answering machine*
  contestar [r] *to answer*
  contratar [r] *to hire (somebody)*
el contrato *contract*
las contribuciones *contributions/rates*
(me) conviene *it suits (me)*
  conveniente *convenient*
la cooperativa *cooperative*
  Correos *post office*
  correspondiente *corresponding*
la cosa *thing*
el coste/costo *cost*
la costumbre *habit*
la cotización *quotation/price*
  creado/a *created*
  crear [r] *to create*

el crecimiento *growth*
el crédito *credit*
el cristal *crystal*
el cuadro *picture*
  ¿cuál? *which?/what?*
  cualquier *any whatsoever*
  ¿cuándo? *when?*
  ¿cuánto? *how much?*
  ¿cuántas/os? *how many?*
  ¿cuánto tiempo? *how long?*
  cuarto *quarter*
no cuelgue *Hold on, please (on the phone)*
la cuenta *account*
  ¡cuidado! *Be careful!*
  culto/a *educated*
la cuota *market share*

CH

el champiñón *mushroom*
la chaqueta *jacket*
el cheque *cheque*
el chorizo *spicy sausage*
el churro *clay sausage for pottery making*

D

  dar [irr] *to give*
los datos *data/personal particulars*
  de *of/from*
  decir [irr] *to tell*
el/la decorador/a *interior designer*
  dedicar [irr] *to dedicate*
los defectos *defects*
  dejar [r] *to leave something behind*
  deletrear [r] *to spell*
la demanda *demand*
  la oferta y la demanda *supply and demand*
  demasiado *too*
las demostraciones *demonstrations*

dentro de *inside/within*

el departamento *department*

depende *it depends*

depender [r] *to depend*

el/la dependiente/a *sales assistant*

los deportes *sports*

la depreciación *depreciation*

derecha *right*

desafortunadamente *unfortunately*

el desarrollo *development*

el desayuno *breakfast*

desayunar [r] *to have breakfast*

el descuento *discount*

desde *from/since*

los desembolsos *expenses*

despacio *slow*

el despacho *office*

el/los desplazamiento[s] *journey/move*

después *after*

la desventaja *disadvantage*

el detalle *detail*

al detalle *retail*

el/la detallista *retailer*

la deuda *debt*

el día *day*

diario/a *daily*

el diario *diary*

la diferencia *difference*

difícil *difficult*

dígame *Can I help you?*

el dinero *money*

la dirección *address*

el directivo *company official*

el/la director/a *director*

el/la diseñador/a *designer*

el diseño *design*

la disminución *decrease*

disponible *available*

la distancia *distance*

distinguido/a *distinguished*

distinto/a *different*

la distribución *distribution*

el/la distribuidor/a *distributor*

distribuir [irr] *to distribute*

la diversificación *diversification*

los dividendos *dividends*

dividir [r] *to divide*

la divisa *currency*

la docena *dozen*

el domicilio *home address*

a domicilio *door-to-door*

la dotación *endowment*

la ducha *shower*

duplicado *duplicate*

por duplicado *in duplicate*

la duración *duration*

durante *during*

E

ecológico/a *ecological*

la economía *economy*

económico *economic*

el edificio *building*

el/la editor/a *editor and publisher*

la editorial *publishing house*

efectivamente *effectively*

el efectivo *cash*

la eficiencia *efficiency*

el ejercicio *exercise*

el ejercicio anterior *last tax year*

el ejemplar *copy (of book or magazine)*

elegir [irr] *to choose*

el embalaje *packing*

la empaquetadora *packaging machine*

empezar [irr A] *to begin*

el/la empleado/a *employee*

la empresa *company/enterprise*

la empresa familiar *family business*

en *in*

179

encaminado/a *directed*

encantado/a *pleased to meet you*

encontrar [irr C] *to find*

el encuentro *meeting*

enfrente de *in front of*

la ensalada *salad*

enseñar [r] *to show*

entender [irr A] *to understand*

entero/a *whole*

entonces *then*

la entrada *entrance*

entre *between*

la entrega *delivery*

la entrevista *interview/meeting*

enviar [irr] *to send*

el envío *shipment/delivery of goods*

el equipo *team/equipment*

la(s) escalera(s) *stairs*

escoger [irr] *to choose/select*

escribir [irr] *to write*

el escaparate *shop window/display*

eso/a *that*

el espacio *space/room*

español/a *Spanish*

especializado/a *specialised*

el espejo *mirror*

la esponja *sponge*

la esquina *corner*

establecer [irr] *to establish/ to set up*

la estación *station*

el estanco *tobacconist's*

estar [irr] *to be*

este/a *this*

el estilo *style*

estudiar [r] *to study*

la estrategia *strategy*

los eurobonos *Eurobonds*

europeo/a *European*

evitar [r] *to avoid*

exactamente *exactly*

exclusivamente *exclusively*

las existencias *stocks*

el éxito *success*

la explotación *exploitation*

exponer [irr] *to exhibit*

la exportación *export*

exportar [r] *to export*

la exposición *exhibition*

el/la expositor/a *exhibitor*

extender [irr A] *to extend*

exterior *exterior*

el/la extranjero/a *foreigner*

el extranjero *abroad*

F

la fábrica *factory*

el/la fabricante *manufacturer*

fabricar [irr] *to manufacture*

la factura *invoice/receipt*

la facturación *sales revenue*

la falda *skirt*

el fallo *fault*

la farmacia *chemist's*

el favor *favour*

la fecha *date*

la feria *trade fair*

los ferrocarriles *railway*

las fibras *fibres*

fijo/a *fixed*

la financiación *financing*

financiero/a *financial*

el fino *dry sherry*

la firma *firm/signature*

firmar [r] *to sign*

el fisco *Inland Revenue*

físico/a *physical*

el flete *freight*

el flujo de dinero *cash flow*

el folleto *brochure*

fomentar [r] *to encourage*

los fondos *funds*

la forma *way/shape*

la formación *training*
formar [r] *to give shape*
el formulario *form*
la fotocopia *photocopy*
la franquicia *exception*
    una franquicia *franchise*
frito/a *fried*
la fruta *fruit*
fuera de *out/outside*
fuerte *strong*
fumar [r] *to smoke*
el/la fumador/a *smoker*
    fumador *smoking*
    no fumador *non smoking*
fundado/a *founded*
fundador/a *founder*
fundar [r] *to found/to establish (a company)*

G

las gafas *glasses*
    las gafas de sol *sunglasses*
la gama *range*
    la gama de productos *product range*
la gamba *prawn*
la ganancia *profit*
ganar [r] *to gain*
la garantía *guarantee/security*
garantizado/a *guaranteed*
la gasolinera *petrol station*
gastar [r] *to spend*
los gastos *expenses*
la generación *generation*
el género *material/merchandise*
la gente *people*
el/la gerente *manager*
la gestión *management*
la gestoría *agency (undertaking business with government departments)*
    girar [r] *to turn/to draw [a draft or bill]*

gire Vd. *turn*
el giro bancario *bankers draft*
la glorieta *roundabout*
el gobierno *government*
grato/a *pleasant*
gratuito/a *free of charge*
(me) gusta *(I) like*
    gusto *pleasure/taste*
    mucho gusto *pleased to meet you*

H

la habitación *room*
los hábitos *habits*
hablar [r] *to talk*
hacer [irr] *to do/to make*
Hacienda *Ministry of Finance/Treasury*
hasta *until*
    hasta luego *I'll see you later*
hay *there is/there are*
hecho/a *made*
    hecho/a en España *made in Spain*
    hecho/a a mano *hand-made*
la higiene *hygiene*
el hogar *home*
la hoja *sheet/form*
el hombre *man*
los honorarios profesionales *professional fees*
la hora *time*
    la hora punta *rush hour*
    las horas extraordinarias *overtime*
el horario *timetable*
el hospital *hospital*
el hotel *hotel*
hoy *today*
    hoy en día *nowadays*
la huelga *strike*

I

(de) ida y vuelta   *return*
la idea   *idea*
la iglesia   *church*
ilimitado/a   *unlimited*
la imagen   *image*
la importación   *import*
el/la importador/a   *importer*
importante   *important*
importar [r]   *to import*
el importe   *price/amount/cost*
imposible   *impossible*
los impuestos   *tax*
incluir [irr]   *to include*
el inconveniente
   disadvantage/inconvenience
la indemnización
   compensation
la indicación   *indication*
indicar [irr]   *to indicate*
índice   *index*
individual   *individual/single*
la industria   *industry*
ineficiente   *inefficient*
la inflación   *inflation*
información   *information*
informar [r]   *to inform*
el informe   *report*
la infraestructura   *infrastructure*
los ingresos   *income*
iniciar [r]   *to initiate*
inmediato/a   *immediate*
instalar [r]   *to install*
integrar [r]   *to integrate*
el interés   *interest*
interesado/a   *interested*
el intermediario   *middleman*
internacional   *international*
introducir [irr]   *to introduce*
invertir [irr A]   *to invest*
la inversión   *investment*
la investigación   *research*
investigar [irr]   *to research*
el invierno   *winter*

la invitación   *invitation*
ir [irr]   *to go*
[el] IVA   *VAT*
izquierda   *left*

J

el jamón   *ham*
el jefe/ la jefa   *head/chief/boss*
joven   *young*
jugar [irr C]   *to play(games/
   sports)*
el juicio   *judgement*
a mi juicio   *in my opinion*
junto/a (s)   *together*

K

el kilo   *kilo*
el kilómetro   *kilometre*

L

el lado   *side*
   al lado de   *next to*
la lana   *wool*
el lanzamiento   *launch*
lanzar [irr]   *to launch*
largo/a   *long*
el lavavajillas   *dishwasher*
la leche   *milk*
lejos   *far*
el lenguaje   *language*
lentamente   *slowly*
las lentillas   *contact lenses*
la letra de cambio   *bill of
   exchange*
libre   *free*
el libro   *book*
limitado/a   *limited*
el límite   *limit*
la limpieza   *cleanliness*
la línea   *line*
   línea de conducta
   guidelines
la lista   *list*
   la lista de precios   *price list*

el litro *litre*
el local *premises*
la localidad *town/area*
la loza *china*
luego *then, later*
el lugar *place*

LL

llamar [r] *to call*
llamarse [ref] *to be called*
el llavero *keyring*
la llegada *arrival*
llegar [irr] *to arrive*
llevar [r] *to carry*

M

la madera *wood*
la Mancomunidad *the Commonwealth*
mandar [r] *to send*
la mano de obra *workforce*
mantener [irr] *to maintain*
el mantenimiento *maintenance*
la mañana *morning*
  por la mañana *in the morning*
mañana *tomorrow*
el mapa *map*
la máquina *machine*
la marca *brand/make/hallmark*
marcar [irr] *to mark/brand*
el márketing *marketing*
más *more*
  más tarde *later*
las materias primas *raw materials*
los materiales *materials*
la (placa de) matrícula *number plate*
mayor *main/larger/older*
la mayoría *majority*
el/la mayorista *wholesaler*
me *me/to me*

¿Me da? *Would you give me?*
¿Me dice? *Would you tell me?*
Me dedico a *My job is*
Me llamo *My name is*
mediano/a *medium-sized*
las medidas *measurements*
medianoche *midnight*
medir [irr] *to measure*
mediodía *midday*
menos *less*
las mensualidades *monthly payments*
mentira *false*
  es mentira *it's not true*
el mercado *market*
  el Mercado Común *Common Market*
  el mercado interior *home market*
las mercancías *goods*
el mes *month*
la mesa *table*
el metal *metal*
metálico *cash*
el metro *metre*
el Metro *Metro/Underground*
  el metro cuadrado *square metre*
mezclar [r] *to mix*
el microondas *microwave*
mientras *while/meanwhile*
mi *my*
mil *a thousand*
  miles de *thousands of*
el millón *million*
el mínimo *the minimum*
el minorista *retailer*
la misión *mission*
mismo/a *same*
mientras *in the meantime*
la mitad *a half of*
mixto/a *mixed*

183

el modelo *model*
moderno/a *modern*
el momento *moment*
la moneda *coin/currency*
  la moneda de oro *gold coin*
  la moneda extranjera *foreign currency*
el monopolio *monopoly*
montar [r] *to set up*
  montar un negocio *to set up a business*
  montar un stand *to set up a stand*
moverse [irr C] *to move*
muchísima/o *very many*
mucho/a *much*
  mucho gusto *pleased to meet you*
  muchas gracias *thank you*
el mueble *piece of furniture*
la muestra *sample*
la mujer *woman*
multiplicar *to multiply*
el mundo *world*
mundial *worldwide*
el museo *museum*
muy bien *very well*

N

nacer [irr] *to be born*
nacional *national*
la nacionalidad *nationality*
nada *nothing*
  de nada *Not at all/You're welcome*
necesitar [r] *to need*
  necesito *I need*
negociar [r] *to negotiate/trade in*
el negocio *business*
neto *net*
el nivel *level*

no *no*
la noche *night*
el nombre *name*
las normas *standards/norms*
nuevo/a *new*
el número *number*

O

o *or*
o sea *that is to say/in other words*
los objetivos *objectives*
el objeto *object*
  los objetos de valor *valuables*
  los objetos perdidos *lost property*
las obligaciones *debentures/liabilities/debts*
observar [r] *to observe*
obtener [irr] *to obtain*
la ocupación *job*
ocupado/a *busy*
los ocupantes *occupants/passengers*
la oferta *offer*
la oficina *office*
ofrecer [irr] *to offer*
el orden *order*
el ordenador *computer/WP*
el oro *gold*
el otoño *autumn*
otro/a *other/another*

P

el pabellón *pavilion*
pagadero/a *payable*
pagar [irr] *to pay*
el pagaré *IOU*
el pago *payment*
el país *country*
los pantalones *trousers*

la pantalla *screen*
el papel *paper*
  papel de regalo *gift wrapping paper*
  papelería *stationery*
  para *for*
la parada *(bus) stop*
la parte *part*
  la parte del león *the lion's share*
la participación *investment*
  participar [r] *to participate*
la partida *consignment*
el pasaporte *passport*
  pasado/a *past*
  el año pasado *last year*
  pasar [r] *to pass*
la patata *potato*
  patrocinador/a *sponsor*
el pedido *order [for merchandise]*
  el pedido mínimo *minimum order*
  el pedido suelto *individual order*
  la hoja de pedido *order form*
  pedir [irr B] *to ask for*
las pegatinas *stickers*
  ¡peligro! *danger!*
  pensar [irr A] *to think*
la pensión *pension/guest house*
  pensión completa *full board*
  pequeño/a *small*
la pérdida *loss*
  perfecto/a *perfect*
el período *period*
el permiso *permit*
  permitir [r] *to allow*
  pero *but*
la persona *person*
el personal *personnel. staff*
el pescado *fish*

peso *weight*
la pieza *piece, item*
  la pieza de recambio *spare part*
el piso *floor/flat*
el plano *street map*
la planta *plant/factory*
  la planta baja *ground floor*
la plantilla *staff*
  plástico/a *plastic*
el platillo *saucer*
el plato *plate/dish*
la plaza *square/seat (on a plane or train)*
el plazo *period/time limit/ delivery date*
un poco *little*
  poder [irr] *to be able to*
la policía *police*
el poliéster *polyester*
el polígono industrial *industrial estate*
la política *politics/policy*
  la política de la empresa *company policy*
  la póliza de seguros *insurance policy*
el pollo *chicken*
  poner [irr] *to put*
  por *for*
  por ciento *per cent*
  por cierto *by the way/ certainly*
  por ejemplo *for example*
  por favor *please*
  por lo tanto *therefore*
  al por mayor *wholesale*
  al por menor *retail*
  ¿por qué? *why*
  porque *because*
  por supuesto *of course*
la porcelana *porcelain*
  porcentaje *percentage*
  posible *possible*

posteriormente *subsequently/later*

el postre *dessert*

potencial *potential*

el precio *price*

preferir [irr A] *to prefer*

el proveedor *supplier*

preguntar [r] *to ask a question*

preparar [r] *to prepare*

la prensa *press*

prensar [r] *to press*

preparar [r] *to prepare*

presentar [r] *to introduce*

le presento *May I introduce?*

el/la presidente *president*

el préstamo *loan*

el presupuesto *budget/estimate/tender*

la prima *premium/bonus*

la primavera *spring*

primero/a *first*

principalmente *principally*

el problema *problem*

la producción *production*

producir [irr] *to produce*

la productividad *productivity*

el producto *product*

el promedio *average*

prometedor/a *promising*

la promoción *promotion*

la promoción por correo *direct mail*

la promoción por teléfono *direct marketing by telephone*

la promoción de ventas *sales promotion*

el/la promotor/a *promoter*

promover [irr] *to promote*

proponer [irr] *to propose/to put forward*

la propuesta *proposal*

pronto *soon*

lo más pronto posible *as soon as possible*

el proteccionismo *protectionism*

próximo/a *next*

la publicidad *publicity*

publicitario/a *promotional*

el pueblo *small town*

la puerta *door*

el puerto *port*

pues *well...*

el punto *point/knitting*

el punto de vista *point of view*

el punto de encuentro *meeting point*

las PYMES [Pequeñas y Medianas Empresas] *small and medium-sized companies*

Q

¿qué? *what?*

que *which/that*

querer [irr A] *to want*

el queso *cheese*

la quiebra *bankruptcy*

¿quién(es)? *who?*

quisiera *I'd like*

quizá(s) *perhaps*

R

la ración *portion*

la reacción *reaction*

las rebajas *marked down goods*

el recado *message*

la recepción *reception/receipt*

el/la recepcionista *receptionist*

el recibo *receipt*

reciclar [r] *to recycle*

la reclamación *claim, complaint*

formular una reclamación *to lodge a complaint*

recoger [irr] *to pick up*

recomendar [irr] *to recommend*

recto/a *straight*

los recursos *resources*

la red *network*

el reembolso *reimbursement*

contra reembolso *cash on delivery/COD*

la reestructuración *restructuring*

reforzar [irr] *to reinforce*

el regalo *gift*

regional *regional*

registrar [r] *to register*

el registro *register*

las relaciones públicas *public relations*

el reloj *clock/watch*

rellenar [r] *to fill in*

el rendimiento *output*

la renovación *renewal*

la renta *income/profit*

la rentabilidad *profitability*

las reparaciones *repairs*

el/la representante *representative*

representar [r] *to represent*

la reputación *reputation*

reservado/a *booked*

reservar [r] *to reserve*

resolver [irr] *solve*

responder [r] *to respond*

la responsabilidad *responsibility*

la restricción *restriction*

el resto *the rest*

el resultado *result*

revisar [r] *to check*

la reunión *meeting*

rígido/a *hard*

el rincón *corner*

la ropa *clothes/garments*

S

sacar [irr] *to take out*

la sala *room*

el salario *salary*

el saldo *bargain/balance*

salir [irr] *to depart/leave*

el/la secretario/a *secretary*

el sector *sector*

la seda *silk*

la sede *headquarters*

seguir [irr B] *to follow*

segundo/a *second*

la seguridad *security*

seguro/a *sure*

el seguro *insurance*

seleccionar [r] *to select*

la selección *selection*

el semáforo *traffic lights*

la semana *week*

la señal *signal*

las señas *address*

el señor *Mr/sir/gentleman*

la señora *Mrs/madam/lady*

la señorita *Miss*

ser [irr] *to be*

la serie *series*

el servicio *service*

el servicio post-venta *after-sales service*

los servicios *toilets*

servir [irr] *to serve*

si *if*

sí *yes*

siguiente *following*

sin *without*

sin duda *without any doubt*

sin embargo *however*

el sitio *place*

la situación *location/situation*

situado/a *located*

sobre *on/about*

la sociedad anónima *public limited company*

el/la socio/a *business partner*

solicitar [r]   *to ask for/to order*

su   *your [formal], his, her, its, their*

la subasta   *auction*

la subida   *rise*

subir [r]   *to go up*

la sucursal   *branch*

el sueldo   *salary*

suelto/a   *loose*

sufrir [r]   *to suffer*

el supermercado   *supermarket*

el/la supervisor/a   *supervisor*

T

las tablas   *charts*

el talón   *stub/voucher*

el tamaño   *size*

también   *also*

tan ... como   *as ... as*

tarde   *late*

la tarde   *afternoon*

la tarifa   *fare /rate*

la tarjeta   *card (any type)*

la tarjeta de crédito   *credit card*

la tasa   *rate*

la tasa de inflación   *rate of inflation*

el/la taxista   *taxi driver*

la taza   *cup*

técnico/a   *technical*

telefonear [r]   *to telephone*

el teléfono   *telephone*

la temporada   *season*

temporal   *temporary*

tener [irr]   *to have*

tener contacto con   *to be in touch with*

tengo que   *I have to*

tercero/a   *third*

textil   *textile*

el tiempo   *time/weather*

la tienda   *shop*

típico/a   *typical*

el tipo   *type*

tirar [r]   *throw away*

todavía   *still/yet*

todo/a   *every*

todos/as   *all*

tomar [r]   *to take/to have (food or drink)*

el tomate   *tomato*

la tortilla   *omelette*

el total   *total*

trabajar [r]   *to work*

el trabajo   *work/job*

el tráfico   *traffic*

el traje   *dress/suit*

los trámites   *procedure*

la transacción   *transaction*

la transferencia   *bank transfer*

el transporte   *transport*

a través   *through*

el tren   *train*

el turismo   *tourism/private car*

el turno   *shift/turn*

es su turno   *it's your turn*

U

un/una   *a/an/one*

un momento, por favor   *one moment please*

un poco   *a little*

un poco de todo   *a bit of everything*

unido/a   *close/united*

la unidad   *unit*

uniforme   *standard*

unir [r]   *to unite/to join together*

urgente   *urgent*

usar [r]   *to use/to utilize*
utilizar [irr]   *to utilize/to use*

V

las vacaciones   *holidays*
la vajilla   *crockery*
valer [irr]   *to cost/to amount to*
vale   *OK*
vamos   *we go/let's go*
varios/as   *several*
el vencimiento   *maturity/expiry date*
el/la vendedor/a   *seller*
vender [r]   *to sell*
venir [irr]   *to come*
la(s) venta(s)   *sales*
venta a plazos   *hire purchase*
precio de venta   *sale price*
la ventaja   *advantage*
ver [irr]   *to see*

el verano   *summer*
verde   *green*
viajar [r]   *to travel*
el viaje   *journey*
la vida   *life*
el vidrio   *glass*
el vigilante jurado   *security guard*
el vino   *wine*
el/la visitante   *visitor*
visitar [r]   *to visit*
vivir [r]   *to live*
el volumen de ventas   *turnover*
el vuelo   *flight*

Y

y   *and*
ya   *already*
el yen   *yen*

Z

la zona   *area/zone*

ACKNOWLEDGMENTS

The authors and publishers wish to thank the following for their
assistance and for permission to reproduce copyright material:
Mr F.A. Beresford, Banco Exterior de España, London; Hotel Ciutat
Vic; Gran Hotel Rey don Jaime, Castelldefels; IFEMA – Feria de
Madrid; Rent Services S.L., Palafrugell; RENFE; Campofrío; Chupa
Chups; Optica Roma; Rola Opticos; Banco de Sabadell.

Every effort has been made to trace all copyright holders but the
publishers will be pleased to make the necessary arrangements at the
earliest opportunity if there are any omissions.

Photograph credits: A.G.E./ Images *64, 69, 90 (top)*; John Birdsall *10,
22, 48 (bottom), 62*; Anthony Blake *63*; Chupa Chups SA *86, 90*;
Churchill China plc *119*; Terry Doyle *76, 79, 80, 104, 111, 127, 132,
138*; Fototeca IFEMA *118, 126, 127*; Grupo de Empresas Alvarez *83,
84*; Image Bank *6 (top)*; Impact *30*; Picture Bank *48 (top)*; Roberto
Quintero *83*; RENFE *28*; P J Sainsbury *91*; Select *44, 52*; Telefonica
38; Telegraph Colour Library *20, 58*; Colette Thomson *6 (bottom), 13
(bottom), 16, 25, 121, 122, 124*

BBC Language books and cassettes

Phrase books
Arabic • French • German • Greek • Italian • Portuguese
Spanish • Turkish

When in ... series
France • Germany • Italy • Spain

Passport to ... series
France • Germany & Austria • Italy • Spain

Get by in ... series
Arabic • Chinese • French • German • Greek • Hindi Urdu • Italian •
Japanese • Portuguese • Russian • Spanish • Turkish

Get by in Business ... series
French • German

... Means Business series
French • German • Spanish

Major Language Courses
1st, 2nd, or 3rd stage study
French • German • Italian • Spanish • Gaelic • Greek • Hindi Urdu •
Japanese • Latin American Spanish • Portuguese • Russian

For a free catalogue and further information write to:
BBC Books
Language Enquiry Service
Room A3116
Woodlands
80 Wood Lane
London W12 0TT